Gertrude Lefferts Vanderbilt

The Social History of Flatbush

And manners and customs of the Dutch settlers in Kings County. Vol. 1

Gertrude Lefferts Vanderbilt

The Social History of Flatbush
And manners and customs of the Dutch settlers in Kings County. Vol. 1

ISBN/EAN: 9783337309480

Printed in Europe, USA, Canada, Australia, Japan

Cover: Foto ©ninafisch / pixelio.de

More available books at **www.hansebooks.com**

THE

SOCIAL HISTORY

OF

FLATBUSH,

AND

*MANNERS AND CUSTOMS OF THE DUTCH
SETTLERS IN KINGS COUNTY.*

BY

GERTRUDE LEFFERTS VANDERBILT.

"To Holland they felt a deep, unalterable, hereditary attachment.
Nor have the vicissitudes of time extinguished that sentiment in their
descendants. Two centuries have scarcely weakened the veneration
which citizens of New York of Dutch lineage proudly cherish toward the
fatherland of their ancestors."
—*History of the State of New York. J. Romeyn Brodhead.*

NEW YORK:
D. APPLETON AND COMPANY,
1, 3, AND 5 BOND STREET.
1881.

TO

THE DESCENDANTS

OF THE

DUTCH SETTLERS IN KINGS COUNTY

THESE PAGES ARE

𝕯𝖊𝖉𝖎𝖈𝖆𝖙𝖊𝖉.

PREFACE.

The Rev. Thomas M. Strong, D. D., for nearly
forty years beloved pastor of the Reformed Church,
Flatbush, collected, as far as practicable, facts pertaining to the early settlement of the town.

These facts were in the first instance brought
before the public in the form of lectures delivered
before the Flatbush Literary Association.

Subsequently, at the request of his friends, these
lectures were collected in a volume, entitled "The
History of the Town of Flatbush," and published
in 1842.

Since the publication of this interesting volume,
there have been great changes in this little town.
The day is probably not far distant when it will
become a part of the adjoining city of Brooklyn; then
all traces of its village life and its individuality as a
Dutch settlement will be lost.

In all love and respect for the memory of Dr.
Strong, I have taken up the pen which he laid down,

not so much in continuation of his subject as to give it from a different standpoint. As a woman, I have inclined to the social side of life, and have endeavored to record the changes which time has made among the people in their homes and at the fireside.

I have undertaken this as a pleasant task, bringing to the work at least so much of fitness for it as may be caused by familiarity with those changes, and a knowledge of the traditions, customs, and manners of the Dutch.

At an early period all the families in this county were united through marriage and intermarriage, thus forming one large family circle. I have assumed with greater confidence the preparation of this work because, as I do not address the great world beyond, I may, for that reason, escape unfriendly criticism; these simple annals being only intended for this family circle of the descendants of the Dutch settlers, who alone can find an interest in the record.

GERTRUDE L. VANDERBILT.

Flatbush, 1880. .

CONTENTS.

CHAPTER		PAGE
I.	INTRODUCTORY	9
II.	EARLY SETTLEMENT OF KINGS COUNTY .	11
III.	CHARACTERISTICS OF THE HOLLAND SETTLERS .	17
IV.	GRADUAL CHANGE FROM DUTCH TO ENGLISH,	24
V.	NAME OF THE VILLAGE OF FLATBUSH . .	31
VI.	DUTCH NAMES	38
VII.	USE OF THE DUTCH LANGUAGE . . .	50
VIII.	EXTERIOR OF DUTCH HOUSES, . .	58
IX.	INTERIOR OF DUTCH HOUSES . . .	66
X.	FURNITURE	79
XI.	PREPARATION OF WINTER STORES . .	102
XII.	COOKING UTENSILS	111
XIII.	SILVER AND CHINA	115
XIV.	MUSICAL INSTRUMENTS AND PICTURES .	121
XV.	DRESS	127
XVI.	WEDDINGS	149
XVII.	FUNERALS	152
XVIII.	THE GRAVEYARD OF THE REFORMED DUTCH CHURCH	158
XIX.	HEALTHFULNESS OF FLATBUSH, AND MORALITY OF THE INHABITANTS	169
XX.	FARMS AND THEIR OWNERS . . .	175
XXI.	DOMESTIC SERVICE	249
XXII.	AGRICULTURE	269

8 *CONTENTS.*

CHAPTER   PAGE

XXIII. FRUITS AND VEGETABLES . . . 277
XXIV. GARDENS, WILD FLOWERS, AND WOODS . 284
XXV. VILLAGE ROADS 299
XXVI. CHURCHES IN FLATBUSH . . . 305
XXVII. RELIGIOUS SOCIETIES 319
XXVIII. WAR OF THE REVOLUTION—1776 . . 322
XXIX. WORK FOR THE SOLDIERS . . . 327
XXX. TOWN-HALL 328
APPENDIX 330

SOCIAL HISTORY OF FLATBUSH.

CHAPTER I.

INTRODUCTORY.

OUR Dutch ancestors were slow to accept innovations. It is probable that before the beginning of this century their manners and habits had remained for generations the same. Such is no longer the case. We need only go back a few years to find customs which have now ceased to exist. Neither Flatbush, nor any of the towns on Long Island settled by the Dutch from the Netherlands, differ for that reason from other towns and villages in the State.

Nearly every trace of Dutch descent has been swept away ; there only remain the reminiscences and traditions, while the old family names mark the localities still, as the projecting peaks mark the submerged rock.

All that relates to home and kindred has its interest, especially when we know that the home is soon to be broken up and the ties of kindred sundered. In this we find our excuse for calling together the family circle of Dutch settlers in Kings County, to talk with them of changes which have taken place in social life, and to review customs and habits which are almost forgotten.

It seems presumptuous to dignify with the name of history this fragmentary account of old and familiar things ; perhaps we might offer it as the "landscape of the age" in which the actors of Dr. Strong's History lived. As such it may help us to understand some things which time is every day rendering more indistinct.

Dr. Stiles, in his history of Brooklyn, apologizes for giving comparatively unimportant minutiæ, with the plea that it is "for those who are to come after us, and to whom these matters may be to a considerable extent unattainable except through our pages." He continues : " ' Posterity,' it has been said, ' delights in details,' and to many of our readers themselves, if they should live to a good old age, years will bring a truer appreciation of the value of these little points, which are now unheeded in the rush and bustle of the active present."

We may plead in the same words for the many apparently unimportant things which we have related ; they may be so familiar now as to be almost unworthy the record, but they will grow in importance as the years pass on.

As one gathers a leaf or presses a flower from a spot which is full of pleasant memories, so we gather these leaves, and present them as memorials of the pleasant garden spot of which, in time, there will be little left save these mementoes which we here offer.

CHAPTER II.

EARLY SETTLEMENT OF KINGS COUNTY.

COMPARATIVELY few of the towns and cities of the United States have a history which extends far into the past. They are of to-day ; they glory in their rapid and vigorous growth. Last year there was the stillness of the unbroken forest ; this year is heard the pioneer's axe ; next year you may find a thriving and populous town.

Such is not the case with the villages of Kings County. Their place is among the earliest of American settlements. The uncouth ships, which in slow and perilous voyages brought our ancestors from the Netherlands, sailed at a time just after the second William of Orange had died, when De Witt was made Grand Pensionary of Holland, Oliver Cromwell held rule in England, and Louis XIV reigned in France.

As long ago as that, our ancestors left their homes in Amsterdam and Rotterdam, in Utrecht and Dordrecht, in Leyden and Delft, and embarked in the ships that sailed from the ports of North Holland for the, as yet, unsettled shores of the New World.

They came of a race of soldiers and sailors ; they had fought against their Spanish oppressors, and had obtained the freedom they desired. They had wrestled with the tides of the strong North Sea, and they had conquered their land from its dominion. The sailors among their people were found in every port and on every coast.

But these men came to the new world neither as soldiers nor sailors, not even as traders ; agricultural pursuit was their aim. They were attracted toward the new territory beyond the sea by the descriptions of the rich soil and the abundant harvests that repaid the culture of the unappropriated lands. They were not driven out by oppression, as were the Puritans ; for there was no country in the world that was so liberal as to religious opinions at that period, and so tolerant, as was Holland. They came, a hardy, energetic race, at the freedom of their own choice, in the strength of an independent manliness, to earn an honest living by their own industry. They brought their families with them and all their household effects ; for they looked forward to making the New World a permanent home for themselves and their children.

Following the route taken by Hendrick Hudson, they steered toward the island called Manhattan, where already the home government had offered inducements for them to settle, and from which friends had written beckoning letters. For a while they may have lingered among their countrymen there, but, casting their eyes southward toward the wooded heights beyond the swift-running river that divided Manhattan from the island called by the natives Seawanhacka, influenced by their agricultural proclivities, they sought a richer soil than New Amsterdam afforded.

And now the little towns began to spring up in the wilderness.

In 1636 there were a few settlers along the shore line, and in time, as a house here and there appeared, their settlement got to be known as Breuckelen. In the same year Ex-Governor Van Twiller had a tobacco farm on the opposite shore ; and the houses that gathered in its vicinity, and the farms that gradually were brought under cultivation, became another town called Amersfoort, after the birthplace of the good patriot Oldenbarneveldt. Greatly must we regret the descriptive propensities that forced the original names of Amersfoort and Medwoud into Flatlands and Flatbush.

In 1643 the English held a patent from the Dutch, under allegiance to the States-General, and Governor Kieft calls their seaside home s'Gravensande (the Count's Beach), and Lady Moody introduced some English names and English blood into the settlement ; but the good Baxters and Hubbards and Stilwells intermarried with the Dutch after her ladyship went away, and s'Gravensande became as thoroughly Dutch as any of us.

In 1654 some families from Holland, still following the coast line, took up their abode in another little settlement, in which they also commemorated their love for the fatherland by calling it New Utrecht. It was not until 1660, or later, that they obtained a patent, and the little town began to grow.

Midway between Amersfoort and Breuckelen in 1651 there lay a tract of land which gladdened the heart of the Hollander, because, with its level surface, it also gave promise of rich soil ; a small portion southward was even a level flat without trees. They soon found, however, that the densely wooded was the richer land. Here the farmers began their work of forming homes in the primeval forest by cutting down the great trees of hickory and white oak and black oak. Perhaps it was in memory of the hard labor that the heavy timber cost them that they gave the name of *Midwood* to that little clearing. It lay on an inclined plane, elevated some fifty feet above the level of the ocean, toward which it gently sloped southward.

Thus it was that, looking here and there, and bargaining for patents or formal grants, and perhaps getting a little angry now and then, and having their plucky nature tried to the utmost by disputes between various claimants, and as to the limits of various boundaries, they finally came, each one, into possession of a certain allotment of land, and here and there grew family homes, and under the names of Breuckelen, Medwoud, Amersfoort, Utrecht, and s'Gravensande appeared the five Dutch towns of Kings County.

Silas Wood, in his "Sketch of the First Settlement of Long Island," says that "the western part, if not the whole of it, was in a great measure bare of timber."

This may possibly be true of some portions of the island, but it was not true of Flatbush. Dr. Strong says that the "lands in and about Flatlands were level and free from woods"; but, in speaking of Flatbush, he says, "it comprised a tract of woodland bounded on the north by hills, on the south by Flatlands, and extending east and west in one continual forest." Elsewhere he says : "At time of purchase it was heavily covered with timber."

In the orders and proclamations of the Governor to the different towns at various times there is inferential proof that Dr. Strong is correct, for in 1656 the inhabitants of Flatbush were ordered to inclose their village with palisadoes, within the inclosure of which they retired for mutual protection during the night ; the first church was also fenced in with strong palisadoes.

A law was passed commanding the inhabitants of New Utrecht to cut down the belt of trees around their settlement, which formed a hiding-place for lurking savages. Also in 1646 the people of the town of s'Gravensande, by a vote of the first town meeting, ordered "every inhabitant to make poles of fence to inclose a common field of corn." In like manner, they voted in 1648 to make a common pasture for their calves. As these palisadoes were probably young trees, it would have been difficult to enforce these laws if the island had been so wholly destitute of timber.

In the Journal of the Labadists, translated by Hon. H. C. Murphy, they refer, in 1679, to the woods seen on approaching the land at the Narrows.

They distinctly mention passing through woods on their first visit to Breuckelen, and when they enjoy the hospitality of the settlers at Gowanus they make marked reference to the free use of fire-wood, which could scarcely have been the case unless the woodland had been not only abundant, but very accessible. They say : "We found a good fire, half way up the chimney, of clear oak and hickory, of which they make not the least scruple of burning profusely."

Hence we judge that the axe rather than the plow first gave employment to the settlers. To those who in the Netherlands had toiled hard to reclaim their land from the ocean, this must have been unaccustomed, but it could not have seemed like hopeless or discouraging work. They were now to cultivate a wilderness that had never been plowed or planted before, but these men brought to the task the energy they had gained in their labor among the dikes and dunes of Holland, and, because they came of a stalwart race, they were not afraid of work.

The west end of this island was described by Hendrick Hudson's men as being "full of great tall oaks, and the lands were as pleasant with grass and flowers and .goodly trees as they had ever seen, and very sweet smells came therefrom."

Surely the land "so pleasant with grass and flowers and goodly trees" has been true to the promise it gave to its discoverers, and has, for these two hundred years, borne rich harvests.

Under their careful cultivation, the beautiful garden and farming land of Kings County has supported many generations ; their industry has given it as a legacy to us, and we surely owe them the slight tribute which may be included in a recognition of their toil.

CHAPTER III.

It has been the fashion to laugh at the Dutch settlers. They have been held up to ridicule, and their manners and customs have been considered an excellent subject for a jest. But a caricature is not a true picture ; it would be folly to consider that intended as a likeness which was acknowledged to be an exaggerated representation.

It has been said by a great historian that "the English courtiers sneered at the honest Dutchmen of the Netherlands, whose virtues were a reproach to them and their king, and whose national prosperity caused them intense jealousy." That was in the distant past, but lingering echoes of these sneers long followed the Hollander ; perhaps they were heard the more distinctly for the silence that followed, neither the Dutchmen in the Old World nor their descendants at a later period in the New pausing amid their industries to listen and retort.

Honesty, industry, economy, prudence, self-reliance, truthfulness, patience, and forbearance were characteristics of these people ; but, as some one has wisely said, "these are not flashy virtues, they are not even attractive to thoughtless youth, and they are despised thoroughly by reckless adventurers. Nevertheless, they are the virtues which make good and happy homes, a stable government, and a prosperous community." Such were the characteristics of these men, and upon these as a foundation they laid the corner-stone of their home in the New World.

"The New Englanders," says a popular writer, "have had full justice done to their colonial and their subsequent enterprising achievements in building up the new republic of America. . . . With the people of Holland it is different, and until recently comparatively little has been known in this country of their national heroic history and character."

When Motley, the great historian of the Dutch republic, placed before the world the national history of our ancestors, he laid us, in common with all others of Dutch descent, under infinite obligations to the culture of New England that produced the historian so entirely worthy of this theme. We find it now easier to prove that these original settlers of our Dutch towns were not the boors which they are sometimes called, because it has been shown to the world that, in the country from which they came, "political and religious freedom was most highly prized, popular education nearly universal, and regard for law and order was most profound; where the rewards of industry were widely shared, the necessities of life most abundantly secured, and the blessings of civilization were equally diffused."

We have every reason to believe that the Dutch desired to perpetuate the political and religious freedom to which they had been accustomed; for, says Brodhead, speaking of the colony, "Up to this time (1688) New York had always been differently governed from any other British American colony. She had never been a chartered or a corporate government under Dutch or English authority. Her eclectic people never wished to be ruled by incorporated oligarchies like those of New England. What they desired, and what for a season they enjoyed, was a ' Charter of Liberties,' securing to every inhabitant a share in local legislation, freedom of conscience, and equality of all modes of Christianity. While a Dutch province, New York, with the comprehensive liberality of her fatherland, had invited strangers of every race and creed to nestle among her own early colonists."

When Governor Stuyvesant undertook to drive the Quakers from the colony, he was reprimanded by a letter from the Dutch West India Company in 1663, in which it is asserted that "the consciences of men ought to be free and unshackled." Furman says that this is the only instance in which the Dutch colonial government attempted to exile a man for his religious principles. It is said that in after-years the old Dutch Governor admitted his mistake, and offered as his excuse that he thought it was intended to make political use of the liberty sought.

The Dutch Government refused to recognize witchcraft or to inflict the death penalty upon those who were suspected by others; in this respect they were surely in advance of an age which gave the fullest credence to this superstition, and persecuted unto death the poor victims who might be suspected.

The Rev. George W. Bethune, D. D., said, in speaking of Holland : " The world, especially this country, owes Holland a large debt of gratitude for the earliest lessons of modern freedom, the foremost lessons of religious toleration, and the finest exhibition of the influence which general education and simple religious habits have upon the character and happiness of a people."

Another writer on colonial times, speaking of the Dutch settlers, says : "If there be any who, in looking back to the period and persons we are sketching, feel a sort of compassion for their supposed inferior chances and lower development, we advise them to spare their benevolence and apply it where it would be more truly needed. The comparison of merit between the inhabitants here during the last century, or of the years previous, with the present time and all its vaunted educational and fashionable advantages, is not a whit in favor of our own day in all the important respects that make manly and womanly excellence."

We may question the educational advantages of that period if the writer has reference to those derived from books and study, schools and colleges ; but there are other sources for the development of character, and these may have had greater power and efficiency in producing a sturdy manhood then than many of the molding influences to which young men and women in this age are subjected.

As to the religious training, its results upon character may have been as efficient as that of to-day. It was certainly all that the age could give. The fruit of October may have been advanced by the May sunshine proportionately with the more perceptible mellowing of the August heat.

The Dutch were a religious people. They prized highly the services of the sanctuary, and established their churches with their first settlement. In New York as early as 1626 they assembled together for worship, and for forty years theirs was the only church in that settlement. At the recent quarter-millennial anniversary of the Collegiate Church, the dates upon the walls, interwoven with flowers, were 1628–1878.

Even before the new colony was supplied with a minister, his duties were undertaken by men known as "Krank-besoeckers," or "Ziekentroosters," i. e., consolers of the sick, whose duty it was also to read the Scriptures to the people on Sunday.

As to the estimation in which they held learning, Brodhead says : "Neither the perils of war, nor the busy pursuit of gain, nor the excitement of political strife, ever caused the Dutch to neglect the duty of educating their offspring to enjoy that freedom for which their fathers had fought. Schools were everywhere provided, at the public expense, with good schoolmasters to instruct the children of all classes in the usual branches of education."

A church was built in Flatbush as early as 1654, and we have the records of schoolmasters from 1659 ; but there was a school even before this date. This early attention to the education of the children is what we might expect of settlers from a country which, says Charles Sumner, " is placed in the very front rank as the land which first established common schools, and threw the doors of its universities open to all." " And," says another historian, speaking of this time, " it is not too much to say that they [the inhabitants of the Netherlands] were far in advance of all other nations in every element of civilization, whether material, intellectual, artistic, moral, or religious."

Says T. W. Field, writing of Brooklyn and its vicinity : " In every town of the New Netherlands which was settled under the Dutch Government a school was established, which was taught by a competent teacher under a license of the Government, which paid him a small salary in addition to his other emoluments. . . . After the conquest by the English in 1664 the teachers received no salary from the Government, which did little to encourage education. . . . The liberality of the paternal Dutch Government was thus strongly contrasted with the stinginess of the English authorities, who never dreamed of such extravagance as paying salaries to teachers."

T. G. Bergen says that this liberality was not that of the paternal Dutch Government, but of the Dutch Church.

Furman says, in reference to this, that Governor Stuyvesant recommended a suitable person for the schoolmaster in Breuckelen, because they regarded it as being so important, not only "to establish schools, but to secure the service of proper men to conduct them," and therefore they would select no one unless "the Governor was satisfied of his competency." Furman adds, speaking of schools among the Dutch, "With them it was a cardinal principle to diffuse the means of education as widely as possible."

The prestige of the Latin School of Dordrecht was such that, in 1635, it was considered the best in north-western Europe.

The advantages for obtaining an education in the Netherlands were so general that the most of those who came from there to settle here could read and write. They brought not only their great Dutch Bibles and Psalm-books with them, but many a little parchment-covered volume, in heavy black-letter, with here and there quaint pictures on its pages, that still remain to attest their love of reading, notwithstanding the necessity for their constant, plodding labor. They not only established Dutch schools at an early date, but they encouraged the study of English, when a knowledge of that language gave greater advantages to their children. In the old, worn Dutch dictionaries that lie on our upper shelves we find the proof that even the older people endeavored to improve themselves in English by the study of the "Groot Woordenboek," the great word-book, as the dictionary was aptly called : the "Groot Woordenboek der Engelsche en Nederduytsche Taalen ; nevens eene spraakkonst derzelver."

The children were thoroughly drilled in lessons upon the Bible, so that from their youth up they might be a God-fearing as well as a moral community. They were also thoroughly indoctrinated in the articles of their faith by the study of the catechism.

We find in the inventory of an estate of an old land-owner, born 1684, that among his other properties he had in his house eleven Dutch catechisms. Under the discipline of such training as this grew up the children of successive generations in the homes of our Dutch ancestors, and, if they were not morally sound and hardy, there must have been great waste of precept and example.

CHAPTER IV.

AROUND these early settlers on Manhattan and on Long Island stretched an unknown continent in unbroken wilderness, save as here and there along the coast glimmered the lights of some small and widely separated settlements like their own. But it was not by these, nor yet by themselves, that their destiny was shaped. It was the cabinet intrigues of the Old World that gave them Dutch rulers or made them the subjects of an English king. The political broils, the international feuds and jealousies, or the open wars of Europe, were the pebbles thrown into the stream that in ever-widening circles reached and agitated the little towns that lay close to the shores.

The effect of change from Dutch customs, manners, and form of government to English was so slow as to be in process of growth almost imperceptible. At first the settlers built their houses of brick imported from Holland, and in many other ways, from force of habit, attempted the useless task of trying to make their new homes conform to those which they had left.

What is said in Bryant's "Popular History of the United States" about New York, in its period of transition under the early English governors, was equally true of the little towns and villages around that city, settled at the same period and by the same people : " Its customs long remained those which its first settlers had brought with them out of the Dutch fatherland. Its architecture, most of its local names, and even its more common speech, were Dutch. Its domestic and social life was regulated by the customs of Holland. If it was simple and somewhat heavy, it was at the same time healthy, virtuous, and full of kindliness and hospitality. If the stout burghers moved slowly, thought only of the practical side of things, and went to bed at nine o'clock, they also worked steadily, governed their households wisely, and persecuted nobody. If they introduced for a brief period into their new home the law they brought from Holland of the great burgher-right and the lesser burgher-right, those who received the former were worthy of the dignity, and those who were confined to the latter valued their citizenship and educated their children none the less carefully."

Says one, sketching this period : " The settlement of Kings County and Manhattan Island was essentially Dutch, not only in its social, but in its political customs and institutions. . . . From 1620 to the close of the century Long Island was solely Dutch, and when afterward the English took possession there was no social or domestic change."

It is probable that the energies of these pioneers were taxed to the utmost to obtain the comforts to which the civilization of the Netherlands had accustomed the Hollander ; for rude and meager as their surroundings were, compared to the luxurious abundance in the reach of every industrious householder of this age, yet they were far in advance of those of the same social status in many other countries of Europe.

2

On this account they had the less time to waste upon the political changes, which had, after all, little perceptible effect upon their liberty and prosperity. Their language, their schools, their religious privileges were not interfered with. It was expressly stipulated that the Dutch, in capitulating to the English in 1664, should enjoy "liberty of their conscience in divine worship and church discipline." Also that they should "enjoy their own customs concerning their inheritance." The Dutch are essentially a law-abiding people, and as their English rulers secured to them all which their own home government had granted, they were willing to recognize their power and acknowledge their sovereignty. As open rebellion or unwilling submission would have done very little to change matters, we must admit that peaceful acquiescence was the wiser policy.

Says Dr. Morgan Dix, speaking of this period in the history of the Dutch settlers : " New Amsterdam was taken ; it became New York ; and the Church of England was planted where the Classis of Amsterdam had been the supreme and only ecclesiastical authority. But observe how scrupulously the rights of your forefathers were respected. There is nothing like it in history ; never did conquerors treat the conquered with such deference and consideration. As far as possible the old customs were preserved ; private rights, contracts, inheritances were scrupulously regarded ; and, as for the Reformed Dutch Church, it seems almost to have been treated as a sacred thing. It was more than protected ; it was actually established by law by an English governor under English auspices. This was, perhaps, no more than a fair return for the good deeds done by your people. When your turn came to be under the yoke, it was said to you in substance : 'You shall still be free ; not one of your old customs shall be changed until you change them yourselves ; by us you shall not be meddled with ; keep your places of worship, your flocks, and all you have, in peace.' And so to their old church of St. Nicholas inside the fort did your people continue to wend their way in absolute security, though English sentries were at the gates ; and within the walls over which the standard of England waved did the good Dutch dominie speak his mind as freely as ever to his spiritual children ; nor was it until they had finished their devotions and withdrawn that the English chaplain ventured within the same house of worship to read his Office from the Book of Common Prayer. I see in this what does credit to humanity—kind consideration, mutual respect, and on both sides a study of the things that make for peace." Speaking of this, Brodhead says that the Reformed Church was virtually "established" in New York by its English rulers. The same generosity was extended to the Dutch on Long Island, and with similar results.

Under the English laws a constable and overseers were added to the town officers ; it was one of their duties "frequently to admonish the inhabitants to instruct their children and servants in matters of religion and the laws of the country." This could not have been considered an unusual thing for those who were so eminently law-abiding, and who were accustomed to the same admonitions from their own rulers.

Thus it happened that gradually, and almost unconsciously, they glided along the smooth current which, from that day to this, has been changing them from Dutch to English.

Looking back to their daily life, we find that they had many things to contend against which must have given them more uneasiness than this change, which was attended with so little inconvenience to themselves.

The cutting down of the forest and making their clearings was very different work from the agriculture to which they had been trained upon the polders, the rescued lands, of Holland ; nor was a knowledge of the dikes and drainage of the Zuyder Zee available in the dry and sandy farms " op 't ijlant Nassau."

A still greater cause of anxiety, however, must have come to them from contact with the savages who at this period peopled the continent. The uneasiness of the pioneer settlers in Plymouth and Jamestown must also have been felt in a slight degree by the settlers on Long Island, for in 1656 an order was given to erect palisadoes, so as to protect the town against the Indians, who lurked in the forest with tomahawk and scalping-knife.

It may have been that the peaceful Dutchmen of Kings County did not provoke the aboriginal settler to retaliation ; for, says B. F. Thompson, in his history : "The Indians on Long Island were less troublesome to their white neighbors than the Indians north of the Sound, nor does it appear that any formidable conspiracy ever existed among them to destroy the settlers."

George William Curtis, who can not be regarded as one biased in favor of the Dutch, said, in an address recently delivered at Deerfield, Massachusetts, that "the Dutch settlers, who never broke faith with the aborigines, suffered from them comparatively little trouble."

The land in the Dutch towns of Kings County was not wrested from the native tribes, but amicably obtained by regular purchase from its owners, the Canarsee Indians, who, in 1609, were the first to welcome Hendrick Hudson to the shores of the New World.

Governor Stuyvesant, in 1647, prohibited the sale of strong drink to the Indians under a heavy penalty, together with the "responsibility for all the misdemeanors that might result from its use." He was also very peremptory in his charge that justice should be shown in all cases to the Indians.

"Both the English and the Dutch on Long Island respected the rights of the Indians, and no land was taken up by the several towns, or by individuals, until it had been fairly purchased of the chiefs of the tribes who claimed it," says another historian of Long Island.

There may have been less distrust on this account, for the inhabitants of Midwood did not keep even the vigilant guard which the law required ; and when, in 1675, the English held their court of sessions over this district, called by them the "West Riding of Yorkshire," and which included the five Dutch towns, we read that Midwood was much censured for having neglected to keep up the fortifications as safety demanded to insure protection against the savages.

In 1658 Flatbush was the county market-town. Here, also, was the seat of justice for the county ; here the courts were held ; here the sheriff lived, and the county clerk. Here also the schoolmaster dwelt, and the minister who preached at stated times in the five Dutch towns, and who from respect to his office was considered a most influential member of the settlement.

The change in regard to the civil importance of

Flatbush has been recorded in Dr. Strong's history.   In these pages we only propose to refer to the public records when they reflect light upon the home life of the people.

In regard to language, manners, and customs, the change has been in accordance with the progress of the age, as the people have been called to keep step in that advancing line of onward march in civilization in which the Anglo-Saxon race has led the world.

CHAPTER V.

AT its settlement in 1651 Flatbush was variously called Midwout, Midwoud, and Medwoud ; it is difficult to say why or when the change was made to Flatbush. Various opinions have been offered as to the meaning of the name.

In a paper read before the Historical Society of the State of New York, December 31, 1816, there is a conjecture offered to the effect that, as Breuckelen and Amersfoort were, from their proximity to the water, earliest settled, and a space intermediate and about equidistant between them remained as woodland, it was therefore designated by the Dutch words " woud " or "bos," signifying woods, thereby becoming, " med woud," or middle woods. Or, as it was a plain—" vlachte," in order to distinguish it from the wooded heights—" Gebergte "—between this plain and Brooklyn, it was called the " Vlachte bos," or the wooded plain.

Teunis G. Bergen says that Medwoud and Oostwoud, now Flatbush and New Lots, were both named after villages in North Holland. There are others who give the name a different derivation, and say that it does not come from " woud," a forest, but from " woon " or "woonen," to dwell, having reference to the people who lived in the middle district between the two settlements of Breuckelen and Amersfoort.

In the town records of 1681, New Lots is called Oostwoud, and Flatbush, Medwoud.

At a convention, held at Hempstead in 1665, Long Island and Staten Island were erected into a shire, and divided into districts called Ridings ;* Flatbush was in the West Riding of Yorkshire. It has been said that the name of Medwoud was changed at that convention. If so, the change was not generally accepted, for it was called Medwoud after that on many public occasions, and in many public documents.

All these names, Medwoud, Midwoud, Midwout, and Vlachte Bos, appear upon the old town records ; and in all the public writings they seem to be used interchangeably, as we shall see.

On an old grant, signed by Governor Stuyvesant, bearing date 1661, and still in possession of the family to whom the land was given, the name of the town appears as Midwout. The first provincial seal of the New Netherlands is upon this grant : a shield bearing a beaver, proper, surmounted by a count's coronet, and encircled by the legend "Sigillum Novi Belgii." In another old Dutch writing of the same character, bearing date 1677, Flatbush is called Vlackebos. In a dispute as to the boundaries between Flatbush and Brooklyn, which occurred in 1678, our people call Flatbush "onse Dorp Midwout." In a dispute as to the boundaries between Flatbush and Flatlands, which took place

---

* In 1683 the province was divided into counties, and the "ridings" were abolished.

in 1688, the two towns are spoken of respectively as Midwout and Amersfoort.

In other papers relating to the boundaries of the Dutch towns, bearing date 1677, our people "von het bos," say, " Wij, gemeente von Midwoud," i. e., we, the commonalty, or community, of Midwoud. In other disputes relative to boundaries, bearing date 1666, the town is called Flackebos. In an old Dutch deed, among the town papers relating to taxes, dated 1676, the place is called Flackebos. In 1677, in an old paper written in in English, as few among the town records are, the settlement is called "Flatbush, alias Midlewood"; and subsequently through the paper it is called Midlewood.

In a paper among the old town records signed by Pieter De la Noy, and bearing date 1680, the village is called " Het Dorp Midwout." In another old paper, dated 1681, found among the town records, being a receipt for certain books transferred to the town by Joseph Hegeman, the date is given from Midwout.

In April, 1693, the Colonial Legislature passed an act changing the name of Long Island to Nassau Island, but the act did not affect the old name or make it permanent, although sometimes in the old writings Flatbush is spoken of as " op 't ijlant Nassau." The Indian names of this island were Paumanacke, Mattouwack, and Seawanhacka,* each of which names is variously spelled.

---

* Seawan-hacky means the "island of shells." Seawan was the name of their money, made from the shells which are abundant on the southern coast; the wampum, or the white, was made from the periwinkle; the black was made from the quahaug. B. F. Thompson says, speaking of its value : " Three beads of black and six of white were equivalent to an English penny or a Dutch stiver."

In a bill among some old family papers we read :

" I Bekome ontfangen te hebbe von R. Hegeman de somme von vyf pondt, etc.

"JACOBUS BEEKMAN.

"FLACKEBOS, *Den* 20 *Ag't*, A. D. 1717."

In an old will, written in 1715, in English, we find the modern name appears :

" In ye first yʳ reign of our Sovereign Lord, George of Great Brittain, France, and Ireland, King, Defender of ye faith, etc., etc., and in ye year of our Lord Christ one thousand seven hundred and fifteen, ———, of Flatbush, in Kings County, on ye Island of Nassau, in ye Province of New York," etc. An old agreement, of more value than the above, we find dated, " Midwout, Oct. 1, 1718." In 1732 we still find the name of Midwoud :

" Midwoud, Den 21 Augustes, A. D. 1732.   Ontfangen de somme dertigh gulden, etc.

(Signed)   " PIETER STRYCKER."

Another old paper, dated " Anno dom 1745," speaks of the signer as being a resident of " Flatbush in King's County, on Nassau Island, in the Province of New York." A more intelligible, because not faded, writing, bearing date " Anno dom 1748," calls Flatbush Flackebos. In a will bearing date 1759 the town is called Flatbush and the island Nassau.

We have copied from old writings these different ways of naming the village, not because the particular sources of information are in themselves of any value, but because they show how long, and upon what various occasions, the names seem to be used interchangeably and somewhat at random. Through all these years the name might be written Midwout, Midwoud, Medwoud, Flackebos, Vlactebos, until it became Flatbush ; either name being at the option of the writer.

Thus for a century the names in their variations came down the stream of time together, side by side. We do not know upon what petty obstruction in the channel foundered at last the sweet rural name of Midwood, but some of the early years in the last century proved the bar over which it did not pass. It has been gradually lost sight of in the distance, and now we can only find it when we look back to the days when the village was shut in by the primeval forest, and the name so aptly described it as Midwood.*

Flatbush had at an early period names for its different sections. The north end was called "Steenraap" ; the center, "Dorp" ; the south end, "Rustenburgh."

The English of "steenraap" is stone-gathering, from steen, a stone ; raapen, to reap, implying that it was rough and stony, or a place where stones could be gathered. As the meaning of the word "raap" is a turnip, it may also mean, not a wild and rocky place, but where small stones, like turnips upon a cultivated

---

* It is curious to observe the changes in the Dutch names given by the Dutch settlers :

Hell Gate, supposed to be named from dangerous navigation, was formerly " Hellegat," after a river in Flanders. Breuckelen was named after a village in the province of Utrecht. Gravesend was not named by the English under Lady Moody, but was called s'Gravensande by Governor Kieft, after a seaport near the river Maas, signifying the Count's Sea-beach : graf or graven, counts ; sande, a sandy beach. Just as the Hague, at first a hunting-seat of the Counts of Holland, was called s'Graven Hague, or the Counts' hedge or woods.

field, lay thick upon the surface. This suggestion as
to the derivation of the word is given by Teunis G.
Bergen, whose close attention to Dutch names and their
derivations makes it worthy of attention. The soil in
the northern part of the town is rich, but the fields did
at one time present a surface covered with small stones,
such as might be described very properly by a word with
such a derivation.

This name may, for another reason, have been applied
to this portion of the town. There was at one time a
brick kiln, "steenbakkery," upon the farm owned by
Mr. John Lefferts. The name of steenbakkery was still
applied as late as 1876 to the large pond formed by the
digging out of clay for the bricks. The clayey soil
made it almost impossible to drain the pond, and it was
used by the school-boys in the town as a skating pond
in winter, and always was known by them as the
"steenbakkery." It was not until the hollow was filled
up to make a causeway for the railroad from Nostrand
Avenue to Flatbush Avenue that the pond began to disappear.

The land on the southern side of Kings County is
remarkably free from rocks ; beyond the central ridge
of the island there are none. There is said to be an
Indian tradition to the effect that Satan threw all the
rocks from Long Island across the Sound to Connecticut in a fit of anger ; if so, he certainly cleared this part
of the island very effectually.

The middle of the town was called "Dorp," a village
or country town ; that is, the village proper and the
business center. The south end of the town was known
as "Rustenburgh," or the resting-place. With what
peculiar fitness this name was given we can not say,

unless the calm restfulness and repose of the landscape was impressive. It may have been, as the earliest settlers had each a portion of the open and unwooded land while the forest was being cut down in Dorp and Steenraap, that they had their first homes in Rustenburgh ; thus this portion of the town may have been their temporary resting-place. But history in this instance, as is often the case in more important things, gives no answer to our questions.

The present name of the village is not an improvement upon that first given ; and it is much to be regretted that the pretty village should not have retained the title applied so aptly by the old settlers— Midwood. It was appropriate in all its significations, whether referring to the people who lived in the middle district, or the little town in the midst of woods.

Looking down upon it from the highest point in Prospect Park, it is so shut in by trees and shrubbery that we might say, almost as appropriately now as two hundred years ago, it is Midwood still.

CHAPTER VI.

UNTIL this century the Dutch names from the fatherland were still given by the descendants of the settlers to their children. Some of us can remember names which were once household words in every family, as being the names of parents and grandparents, but which now are never heard. We can trace them through the county in their English translations ; but the originals, like the old people who bore them, have died out.

We here furnish some of the names which are found constantly recurring in the old records of the town, to which we add the translations under which they now appear :

Aart (Arthur), Aries (Aaron), Arian (Adrian), Andries (Andrew), Bornt (Barent or Bernard), Christofflle (Christopher), Claes or Nicolaes (Nicholas), Dirk or Diederick (Richard), Guilliam (William), Hans, the nickname for Johannes (John), Joris (George), Jacobus (James), Lucas (Luke), Paulus (Paul). Pieter (Peter), Roelef (Ralph), Wouter (Walter), Wilhelmus (William), Yacob (Jacob), Jacques (James), Joost (George).

There are other names which were never changed by translation ; some of them are probably family names :

Wolfert, Gysbert, Volkert, Wynand, Lambert, Ger-
brandt, Rynier, Myndert, Baltus, Rutgert, Harmanus,
Ulpius, Jurian. Rembrandt was abbreviated to Rem,
and under that form it was a name frequently given.
There are other names which might have been translated, but are still continued in their original form, viz.:
Coert is probably Courtland ; Gerret is Gerhard or Ger-
rard ; Evert is Everard ; Laurens is Lawrence or Loren-
zo ; Teunis is Anthony.

The family name Denyse is from Denis, and is the
contraction of Dionysius. St. Denis is Dionysius the
Areopagite, converted by Paul's sermon on Mars Hill.

The family name Tiebout, at one time numerous in
Kings County, is, in its translation, Theobald.

The English rendering of some of these names seems
to us somewhat arbitrary. Cobus was a common nickname for Jacobus ; it would seem natural to have the
English translation of it, Jacob ; but we find that it has
been always translated into James. In the patent obtained from James, Duke of York, by Governor Sir
Edmond Andros, the Duke is called "Jacobus, Hertzog
von York and Albany." From this we judge that this
translation was the general one, and not a local rendering by the farmers.

The names of the women seem to have undergone
even a greater change than those of the men. The di-
minutive je, pronounced as we do ia, is attached to most
of the feminine names. In a dictionary published in
Amsterdam, 1749, there are some pages devoted to
"Naamen van Mannen en Vrouwen"—names of men
and women. In this the author gives a most uncompli-
mentary reason for the fact in the explanation that,
"since the Female Sex is lookt upon as inferior to the

Male, these diminutives are applied to women." As these diminutives were also expressive of endearment, in view of the strength of family ties among the Dutch, we find a stronger reason in the expression of affection by father and husband, rather than in attributing their use to an arrogation of superiority.

The following names of our grandmothers and great grandmothers appear upon the baptismal records of the past century :

Aaltje (Aletta or Alida), Annetje (Anne), Arriantie (Adrianna), Beletje (Bella), Dirkje or Dortie (Dorothea), Elsie (Alice), Evau (Eve), Femmetia (Phebe), Gertje (Gertrude), Grietje or Margarietje (Margaret), Engeltie (Ann), Helena (Helen), Jannetje (Jane), Lammetje (Lemmian), Lysbet (Elizabeth), Katrina or Trientje (Catharine), Morritje (Mary), Neeltje (Cornelia, sometimes Nelly), Pieterneltje (Petronella), Willimentje (Wilhelmine), Leentje (Magdalena), Scytia (Cynthia), Yda (Ida), Motje (Martha). Hieltie, also spelled Hilletie, is probably the abbreviation of Hildegonda, Tiesie (Letitia), Gashie (Garrita).

There are some names which are nearly obsolete, if not entirely so ; these are : Hildegonda, Geradina, Petronella, Wilhelmina, Lemmian, Alida, Garetta, Adrianna, Blandina. There are other names which have gradually fallen into disuse, such as Phebe, Cynthia, Dorothea, Catalina.

Family names were strictly adhered to, and the eldest son was given either that of his father or one or the other of his grandparents. Thus it happened that certain names were found descending from father to son through many generations ; there are names in this county always to be found in certain families. Some of these appear in the documentary history of this State at a very early period, and are repeated upon the town records through successive years to this present time. The Van Brunt family have never been without a Rutgert or Rulif; Wynant is the family name in the Bennett family; Coert and Lucas in the Vorhees family.

As early as 1700 the names of Domenicus and Cornelius appear among the Vandeveers; there is the record of Englebert Lott in 1666 : these names are not yet extinct.

Jacques has been a family name in the Cortelyou family since the first settlement of New Utrecht.

Gerret has been the family name in the Stryker family; Hendrick has been in the Suydam family since 1663, when the ancestor of that name came to this country; Adrian, Marten, and Gerret have been names in the Martense family for an equal length of time. Jan, and formerly Douwe, were names generally found in the Ditmas family.

The unusual name of Leffert occurs constantly in the family bearing that surname; wherever the family name of Lefferts is found, there may be seen its repetition, in the old family custom of calling one of the sons Leffert Lefferts.

This name also appears frequently in connection with other families : as early as 1700 it was used in the Waldron family; in 1720, in the Martense family; in 1768, in the Ryerson family; in 1776, in the Polhemus family; in 1783, in the Lloyd family; in 1789, in the Bergen family; in 1792, in the Gerretson family; in 1807, in the Schenck family. The above names were probably given through intermarriage, but, as Leffert Pieterse was the name of the ancestor of this family who

settled in Flatbush in 1661, it is probable that, originally, Leffert was a given and not a surname.

There are names on the assessment roll of 1676 which
still appear in Flatbush :

Jan Jansen van Ditmersen (ancestor of Ditmas
family), Pieter Loott (ancestor of Lott family), Leffert
Pieterse (ancestor of Lefferts family), Jan Streycker,
Hendrick Streycker, Aris Jansen Van de Bildt, Jacob
Janse Van de Bildt, Abraham Hegeman.

From a record of the heads of families in Flatbush
in 1687, we select the following names of those whose
descendants are still living in the town, many of them
bearing the same names as their ancestors :

Englebert Lott, Pieter Strycker, Pieter Lott, Joseph
Hegeman, Lefferd Pieterse (in the next generation,
called Peter Lefferts), Jan Van Ditmaertz (now spelled
Ditmas), Aris Vanderbilt, Jacob Vanderbilt, Marten
Adrianse (Marten de Boer, ancestor of the Martense
family), Jan Oake, Jacob Remsen, Pieter Williamson,
Jan Cornelissen Vander Veer, Gerret Janse Strijker.

In the year 1698 there were in the whole of Kings
County: men, 308 ; women, 332 ; children, 1,081.
There were also at this time 296 negroes in the
county.

From "a list of the inhabitants of the township of
Flatbush," in the year 1738, we give the following names,
still represented by families in the town :

Dominicus V. D. Veer, Peter Leffertz, Jan Van der
Bilt, Abraham Lott, John Vanderveer, Cornelis Sudam,
John Sudom, Adrian Hegeman, William Bennett, Hen-
drick Wickoff, John Lot, John Striker, Laurens Detmas,
John Detmas, Isaac Oakey, Dom. Antonidus, Rem Mar-
tense, Adrian Martense, Gerret Van Duyne.

There is great difficulty in tracing names of our Dutch ancestors, from the fact that on the earliest records the names were not fixed. Thus, Peter's son being named Jan, he wrote his name as Jan Petersen, but, he in turn calling his boy after his father, the boy's name in time came to be Peter Jansen. Also, the same name is spelled in so many different ways, by members of the same family not only, but by the same person, that it is at times difficult to identify it.

As an example of the first, we may refer to the ancestor of the Lefferts family, who appears upon the record of 1676 as Lefferd Peterse, and in the next generation it was changed again to Peter Lefferts, ever since remaining as Lefferts. The same change was made with the name of the Martense family.

In the old family Bible in the possession of the descendants is the record that "1659, July 29, es Adrian Reyerz getrout met Annetje Martense."

1660, Marten Adrianse (son of Adrian) was born, and his children were called Marten's sons, which name, at first as Martensen and afterward under the contraction of Martense, has continued to be the patronymic of the descendants of Marten Adrianse, son of Adrian Reyerze.

As to the spelling of names we find the following changes in the same family name :

Stryker, Striker, Strycher, Streycker, Strijcker, Streicker ; Martens, Martense, Maertense, Maerthense ; Loot, Loott, Lot, Lott ; Conover, Couwenhoven, Kouenhoven, Von Couwenhoven, Von Couwenhooven. Couvenhoven, Koowenoven ; Vanderbilt, Van Der Bilt, Vanderbildt, Van de Bildt ; Cortelyou, Corteljou, Cortelliau, Corteljouw ; Vorhees, Voris, Van Voorhuys, Von Voorhuijs; Wyckoff, Wijkoff, Wickhof, Wycoff; Lefferts, Loffert, Leffertt, Leffertze.

The birthplace has in many cases furnished the name of the family. The prefix Van, like the German Von, undoubtedly refers to the place whence the family came. In some cases it has become incorporated in the name, as : Vanderveer, Vanderbilt, Vandervoort ; in other cases it was more properly written with distinctive reference to its derivation, as : Van Deventer, Van Arsdalen, Van Dyck.

Mr. Teunis G. Bergen says that the name of Van Brunt is an exception, and that a family, and not a place, is referred to.

Barkeloo, Deventer, Wyck, Antwerp, Buren, and many other towns, in and near the Netherlands, have furnished names to the families who, leaving there, have settled in America. The name of Ditmas was derived from the place in Holland whence the family came ; for the early settler is recorded upon the assessment roll as Jan Van Ditmarsen.

In a list of those coming over in 1657, is Claes Pouwelson from Ditmarsum, and Jan Petersen from Ditmarsen, showing it to be the name of a place.

The letters "se" which, in many of the Dutch names were the final letters, are an abbreviation of "sen." Thus, Martense is the the son of Marten ; Lefferts was the son of Leffert ; Denyse was the son of Denis ; Janse was the son of Jan.

There are probably very few towns in this country, if any, in which the farms have been held in the same names so long as they have in Flatbush. Living in a land where everything seems in almost perpetual change, the old homesteads yet shelter the families by whom they were built, and the farms belong to the children of those by whom they were settled, while before the baptismal bowl in the old Dutch church the same names have been repeated from father to son for two hundred years.

We copy the following from a letter published in 1859 by Hon. II. C. Murphy, of Brooklyn. It was written during his stay in Holland, and is dated from the Hague : *

"In order to show what difficulties the peculiar systems adopted in this country [Holland], and continued by the settlers in our own, have thrown in the way of tracing genealogies, it is to be observed that the first of these in point of time was the patronymic, as it is called, by which a child took, besides his own baptismal name, that of his father with the addition of *Zoon* or *Sen*, meaning son. To illustrate this: if a child were baptised Hendrick and the baptismal name of his father were Jan, the child would be called Hendrick Jansen. IIis son, if baptised Tunis, would be called Tunis Hendricksen. The son of the latter might be Willem, and would have the name of Willem Tunissen. And so we might have the succeeding generations called successively Garret Willemsen, Marten Garretsen, Adrian Martensen, and so on through the whole of the calendar of Christian names; or, as more frequently happened, there would be repetition in the second, third, or fourth generation of the name of the first; and thus, as these names were common to the whole people, there were in every community different lineages of identically the same name. This custom, which had prevailed in Holland for centuries, was in full vogue at the time of

---

* We were not aware at the time of taking this letter from the newspaper in which it was published that it had been copied in Stiles's "History of Brooklyn." We shall not withhold the portions of it selected for use here, however, on that account, as it verifies much that we have said, and may interest those of our readers who have not seen it elsewhere.

the settlement of New Netherland. In writing this termination *sen*, it was frequently contracted into *se* or *z* or *s*. Thus the name of William Barentsen, who commanded in the first three arctic voyages of exploration, in 1594, 1595, and 1596, is given in the old accounts of those voyages Barentsen, Barentse, Barentz, Barents; sometimes in one way, sometimes another, indifferently. Or, to give an example nearer home, both of the patronymic custom and of the contraction of the name, the father of Gerritt Martense, the founder of a family of that name in Flatbush, was Martin Adriense, and his grandfather was Adræn Ryerse, who came from Amsterdam. The inconveniences of this practice, the confusion to which it led, and the difficulty of tracing families, led ultimately to its abandonment both in Holland and in our own country. In doing so, the patronymic which the person originating the change bore, was adopted as the surname. Most of the family names thus formed and existing among us may be said to be of American origin, as they were first fixed in America, though the same names were adopted by others in Holland. Hence we have the names of such families of Dutch descent among us as Jansen (*anglice* Johnson), Garretsen, Cornelisen, Williamsen or Williamson, Hendricksen or Hendrickson, Clasen, Simonsen or Simonson, Tysen (son of Mathias), Arendsen (son of Arend), Hansen, Lambertsen or Lambertson, Paulisen, Remsen, Ryersen, Martense, Adrian, Rutgers, Everts, Phillips, Lefferts, and others. To trace connection between these families and persons in this country, it is evident, would be impossible, for the reasons stated, without a regular record.

"Another mode of nomenclature intended to obviate the difficulty of an identity of names for the time being, but which rendered the confusion worse confounded for the future genealogist, was to add to the patronymic name the occupation or some other personal characteristic of the individual. Thus Laurens Jansen, the inventor of the art of printing, as the Dutch claim, had affixed to his name that of Coster, that is to say *sexton*, an office of which he was in possession of the emoluments. But the same addition was not transmitted to the son; and thus the son of

Hendrick Jansen Coster might be called Tunis Hendricksen Brouwer (brewer), and his grandson might be Willem Tunissen Bleecker (bleacher). Upon the abandonment of the old system of names this practice went with it; but it often happened that while one brother took the father's patronymic as a family name, another took that of his occupation or personal designation. Thus originated such families as Coster, Brower, Bleecker, Schoonmaker, Stryker, Schuyler, Cryger, Snediker, Hegeman, Hofman, Dykman, Bleekman, Wortman, and Tieman. Like the others, they are not ancient family names, and are not all to be traced to Holland as the place where they first became fixed. Some of them were adopted in our own country.

"A third practice, evidently designed, like that referred to, to obviate the confusions of the first, was to append the name of the place where the person resided—not often of a large city, but of a particular limited locality, and frequently of a particular farm or natural object. This custom is denoted in all those family names which have the prefix of *Van, Vander, Ver* (which is a contraction of *Vander*), and *Ten*, meaning, respectively, *of*, *of the*, and *at the*. From towns in Holland we have the families of Van Cleef, Van Wyck, Van Schaack, Van Bergen, and others; from Guelderland, those of Van Sinderen, Van Dyk, and Van Buren; from Utrecht, Van Winkel; from Friesland, Van Ness; from Zeeland, Van Duyne. Sometimes the *Van* has been dropped, as in the name of Boerum, of the province of Friesland; of Covert, of North Brabant; of Westervelt, of Drenthe; of Brevoort and Wessels in Guelderland. The prefixes *vander*, or *ver*, and *ten* were adopted where the name was derived from a particular spot, thus: Vanderveer (of the ferry), Vanderberg (of the hill), Vanderbilt (of the bildt, that is, certain elevations of ground in Guelderland and near Utrecht), Vanderbeck (of the brook), Vandervoort (of the ford), Vanderhoff (of the court), Verplanck (of the plank), Verhulst (of the holly), Verkerk (of the church), Ten Eyck (at the oak), Tenbroeck (at the marsh). Some were derived, as we have observed, from particular farms; thus, Van Couwenhoven (also written Van Cowdenhoven—cold farms). The founder of that family in America, Wolphert Gerrissen Van

Cowenhoven came from Amersfoort, in the province of Utrecht, and settled at what is now called Flatlands, in our county, but what was called by him New Amersfoort. Some names in the classification which I have attempted have undergone a slight change in their transfer to America. Barculo is from Borculo, a town in Guelderland; Van Anden is from Andel, in the province of Groningen; Snediker should be Snediger; Bouton, if of Dutch origin, should be Bouten (son of Boudwijn, or Baldwin), otherwise it is French. Van Cott was probably Van Cat, of South Holland. The Catti were the original inhabitants of the country, and hence the name. There is one family which has defied all my etymological research. It is evidently Dutch, but has most likely undergone some change, and that is the name of Van Brunt. There is no such name now existing in Holland. There are a few names derived from relative situation to a place; thus Voorhees is simply *before*, or in front of, *Hess*, a town in Guelderland, and Onderdonk is *below Donk*, which is in Brabant. There are a few names more arbitrary, such as Middagh (midday), Conrad (bold counsel), Hagedorn (hawthorn), Bogaert (orchard), Blauvelt (blue field), Rosevelt (rosefield), Stuyvesant (quicksand), Wyckoff (parish court), Hooghland (highland), Dorland (arid land), Opdyke (on the dike), Hasbrook (hares' marsh), and afford a more ready means of identification of relationship. The names of Brinkerhof and Schenck, the latter of which is very common here, may be either of Dutch or German origin. Martin Schenck was a somewhat celebrated general in the War of Independence.

"Ditmars is derived from the Danish, and Bethune is from a place in the Spanish Netherlands near Lille. Lott is a Dutch name, though it has an English sound. There is a person of that name from Guelderland residing in the Hague. Pieter Lots was one of the Schepens of Amersfoort in 1676, and I infer from the patronymic form of his name that Lott is a baptismal name, and is derived from Lodewyck or Lewis, and that Pieter Lots means Peter the son of Lodewyck, or Lot, as the former is often contracted. Some names are disguised in a Latin dress. The practice prevailed at the time of the emigration to our country of changing the names, of those who had gone through the university and received a degree, from plain Dutch into sonorous Roman. The names of all our early ministers were thus altered. Johannes or Jan Meckelenburg became Johannes Megapolensis; Evert Willemse Bogaert became Evarardus Bogardus; Jan Doris Polheem became Johannes Theodorus Polhemius. The last was the founder of the Polhemus family of Brooklyn. The records here show that he was a minister at Meppel, in the province of Drenthe, and in 1637 went as such to Brazil under the auspices of the West India Company, whence he went to Long Island. Samuel Dries, who, by the way, was an Englishman, but who graduated at Leyden, was named Samuel Drisius. It may, therefore, be set down as a general rule that the names of Dutch families ending in *us* have thus been Latinized.

" There were many persons who emigrated from Holland who were of Gallic extraction. When the bloody Duke of Alva came into the Spanish Netherlands, in 1567, clothed with despotic power over the provinces by the bigoted Philip II, more than a hundred thousand of the Protestants of the Gallic provinces fled to England under the protection of Queen Elizabeth, and to their brethren in Zeeland and Holland. They retained their language, that of the ancient Gauls, and were known in England as Walloons, and in Holland as Waalen, from the name of their provinces, called Gaulsche, or, as the word is pronounced, Waalsche provinces. The number of fugitives from religious persecution was increased by the flight of the Protestants of France at the same time, and was further augmented five years later by the memorable massacre of St. Bartholomew. When the West India Company was incorporated, many of these persons and their descendants sought further homes in New Netherland. Such were the founders of the families of Rapelye, Cortelyou, Dubois, Debevoise, Duryea, Crommelin, Conselyea, Montague. Fountain, and others."

3

CHAPTER VII.

Dr. Strong states in his history that the first school established in Flatbush was in 1659. Mr. T. G. Bergen places the date at one year earlier. There is also a difference of opinion as to the person who first filled the office of schoolmaster. Dr. Strong heads the list with the name of Adrian Hegeman ; Mr. Bergen says it was Rynier Bastiansen van Giesen who first accepted the position at an annual salary of two hundred florins. O'Callaghan says that in 1683 the schoolmaster in Flatbush was paid his salary in wheat, "wampum value."

The instruction given at that time was entirely in the Dutch language. Petrus Van Steenburgh, who was appointed schoolmaster in 1762, was the first who taught English ; he had pupils in both languages. Anthony Welp, his successor in 1773, was the last teacher who was required to teach Dutch. We have found two of the original school bills of these teachers ; it is not often that school bills are preserved for more than one hundred years. The handwriting of Master P. V. Steenburgh is very distinct, and abounds in flourishes, particularly in his signature.

EVERT HEGEMAN, Dr.

To P. V. STEENBERGH.
1773, *August* 5th.

To schooling from the 15th March to this day ... 9*s*. 5*d*.
For half a load of wood.................... ... 2　6
　　　　　　　　　　　　　　　　　　　　　　—————
　　　　　　　　　　　　　　　　　　　　　£0 11 11
　　　　Received the full contents:
　　　　　　　　　　　　　P. V. STEENBERGH.

The following, from Mr. Anthony Welp, is perfect as to its penmanship, which is as regular and legible as print ; but we find that Mr. Welp, who, in Article 2d of his agreement, engages to teach English spelling, is himself a little careless in that respect :

　　　　　　　　　　　FLATBUSH, *March ye* 24, 1774.
Mr. HEGEMAN,
　　　　　　To ANTHONY WELP, Det.,

To Teaching of Polly Sebree, 3 ms.,
　　The English spilling .... 4*s*.
　　To one load of wood...................... 6*s*.
　　　　　　　　　　　　　　　　　　　　—————
　　　　　　　　　　　　　　　　　　　£0 10 0
　　　　Received in full per me :
　　　　　　　　　　　　ANTHONY WELP.

The load of wood referred to in each bill is in accordance with the requisition in Article 3d, that "a load of firewood shall be bought for each scholar every nine months for the use of the school."

The price of tuition, according to the agreement Mr. Welp signed, amounted to the sum of four shillings for three months' instruction in low Dutch spelling, reading, and writing ; five shillings for the same in English ;

six shillings for instruction in ciphering. The position of schoolmaster was no sinecure in those days. Let us hope that he faithfully discharged his duty ; but if, in its multitudinous requirements, he sometimes proved delinquent, the most exacting must surely have forgiven him.

The children were to be instructed in the ordinary branches of a Dutch education, although we confess ignorance as to what may have been comprised therein. In addition, there was to be a thorough course of catechism ; and the schoolmaster was required, when these little ones were publicly catechised, to encourage them "to be friendly in appearance." We regret that the method for accomplishing this is not designated. He was to keep the church clean and ring the bell. Before the sermon he was to read a chapter out of the Bible, the ten commandments, the twelve articles of faith, and then take the lead in singing.

The afternoon duties were of a similar nature. When the minister preached in some other village he was required " to read twice before the congregation, from the book commonly used for that purpose, and also to read a sermon on the explanation of the catechism." He was to provide the bread and wine for the celebration of the Lord's Supper and the water for the administration of baptism. He was to invite to funerals, being paid extra if required to go to New York for that purpose ; he was to dig the grave and toll the bell. As at that time the practice of burying under the church was quite general, the schoolmaster was to see that the grave was seven feet deep, and he was required " to remove all the dirt out of the church."

The person who was capable of accomplishing all

this must have been a most energetic schoolmaster. Such a position at the present day would involve the use of multipled talents. He would relieve the minister of half the church service ; he would supply the place of choir, organist, and organ-blower ; he would fill the place of the principal of Erasmus Hall ; he would assume the responsibilities of all the Sunday-school teachers, and would perform the duties of the sexton. This was required of the schoolmaster a hundred years ago. But even these were not all his duties ; for, during the session of the court, he was employed for the service of "court messenger for the village of Midwout, to serve citations," etc., for which, however, he was "entitled to proper compensation," in addition to his ordinary pay.

In 1776, in order to oblige the children to learn English, they were compelled to converse in that language in school, and were punished if they spoke Dutch.

At home, however, where no compulsory measures were used, they naturally fell into the old familiar words, and their language there was still that of the fatherland. At the fireside, on the farm, in the street, they spoke Dutch ; the colored people in the kitchen, the master and mistress in the house, neighbor to neighbor and friend to friend, all conversed in Dutch. Business was transacted in that language, wills were written and agreements made in that familiar tongue ; and on the Sabbath-day they read from their Dutch Bibles, sang from their Dutch Psalm-books, and listened to sermons in Dutch from ministers who, as late as 1746, came from Holland. They had their store of old Dutch books, bound in parchment, and meant to last, as they faithfully have done. We have some of

them still on the upper shelves and in the old chests of
the capacious garrets. Many of them are illustrated
with quaint old plates.

There is "Batavische Arcadia," published by "Johannes van Ravesteyn, Boekverkooper en Ordinaris,
Druker defer stede 1662."

There are religious books by "Michiel de Groot,
Boekverkooper, Anno 1663."

Others are published by "Cornelis Jacobsz Naenaart,
Boekverkooper woonende op het Oude Kerkhof, in't
jaar 1675," and others published by "Jacobus Wolffers,
Boekverkooper in de Beursstraat 1724."

These were all purchased in Amsterdam ; some of
them doubtless were brought over by the early settlers
themselves, and others were subsequently sent for.

There are books on the knowledge or science ("wee-
tenschappen") of arithmetic, geometry, trigonometry,
and algebra, by Christian Wolff, published "Te Amsterdam by de Janssoons van Waesberge, 1738," and other
books, from the same publishers and by the same author,
on architecture (de Boukonst), on ·fortifications, and
hydraulics.

"Drie Parabolen ofte Gelykenissen," etc., is the
title of a large parchment-covered volume published in
Amsterdam in 1665 which is still in possession of a lady
in Flatbush, and which has descended to her through
several generations. It was probably brought from Holland when her ancestors first settled here.

It was not until 1792 that the afternoon services in
the congregations of Brooklyn, Flatbush, and New
Utrecht were in English.

As late as 1830, and even 1840, when elderly people
met together socially, it was quite common for them to

drop gradually into the use of the Dutch tongue, even
when the conversation had begun in English ; a little
confidential talk between old ladies was sure to be in
Dutch. So gradual was the change that the elderly
members of a family would often consult with each
other on any important matter in Dutch, and, turning
to their children, address them in English. This inter-
changeable use of the two languages may have been the
means of prolonging a knowledge of the Dutch, and of
having caused the young children to catch many a quaint
word and odd expression ; for the mother tongue of so
many generations could not pass away without leaving
some sign, or dropping some phrases into the memory of
the children who stood looking up, eager-eyed, as father
and mother talked together.

For a long time, in this mingling of two languages,
neither of them was grammatically spoken ; bad English and worse Dutch were the result, until finally the
Dutch was vanquished and the tongue of the Anglo-
Saxon was triumphant. But there were many words
which lingered and fell behind the ranks of the retreating army. Some of these were caught by the children,
others were imprisoned in the memory of those older,
so that, long after Dutch sentences were forgotten,
Dutch words and quaint expressions might be heard in
the family.

A child who was querulous was said to be "krankie,"
from "krank," weak, sick. One who complained without sufficient cause was said to be "kleynzeerig." A
thriftless person, one who could with difficulty earn a
livelihood, was called an "arm sukkelaar." One who
was sad and downhearted was spoken of as "bedroefd."
The word "begryp" was often used instead of the English

"comprehend," as being more forcible, and that which was comprehensive was, from the same verb "begrypen," called "begrypelyk." "In doods nood," was to be in danger of death. Easter was long known as Paasch, and Whitsuntide was Pingster. A child who was restlessly creeping on the floor was said to be "kriewelen." The tin dipper that hung at the well curb was a "blikke," from the Dutch word "blik," for tin.

We remember to have heard children call their grandmother "Grootje." Kelder was cellar; Opperzolder was garret; little cakes, Koekjes (the sound of j is that of i) ; Zoetekoek was a kind of sweet cake raised with yeast, which had sometimes currants and raisins in it. The wife of the minister was always called "Joffrouw." The word Sprookjes was used for stories which tended to the ghostly and marvelous.

Even many of the proverbs of this period are ours in their translations :

" De pot verwyt den ketel dat hy zwart is," alluding to the proverbial jealousy of pot and kettle.

"As you have brewed, so you must drink " : " Dat gy gebrouwen hebt moet gy zelf drinken," is the proverbial expression for bearing the evils we bring upon ourselves, and which has its counterpart in an English proverb, which says, "As you make the bed, so you sleep in it."

" The burned child dreads the fire," we say of the wisdom we gain from bitter experience, and the old Dutch people expressed it in the same figure : " Een gebrond kind schroomt het vuur."

" Die dat opstaan zyn plaats vergaat," was also a common saying.

These words and sentences have lingered in the memory of the generation that is not yet past. There are aged people still living in Flatbush who keep in mind the Dutch language, and a few of the old colored people remember some familiar words and expressions, but these all are only as the rustling leaves upon the dead oak, which will be swept away when the tree falls, if not loosened before that time, as the withering branch loses its power to hold them.

CHAPTER VIII.

INTRODUCTORY to what we have to say about Dutch homes and customs, we would here state that some of the changes recorded we give from personal recollection, others from memory of what was told by the old people at the fireside. The information gathered has been from varied, but, in every case, from reliable, sources. In sympathy with the antiquarian, it has been a pleasant task to search among relics of the past. We have found many a remnant from which to learn what were the colors of the garment when it was new ; we have collected the broken fragments to judge of the shape of the vessel when it was whole ; aged persons have opened to us the storehouse of their memory, from which we have gathered things forgotten by the world. We have ransacked old garrets, which have for generations held their treasures fast with human penuriousness, and we have loosened from their grasp many a babbling bit of furniture and many a garrulous old account-book. Old chests and old desks have offered us their treasures, and we have taken what each had to give. But, as we survey our booty, we greatly fear that the most we have gathered will prove, like a reliquary filled with bones of a saint, only valuable for the sake of those to whom they once belonged.

Stiles, in his " History of Brooklyn," says : " The farmhouses on Long Island were more generally constructed, in a rough but substantial manner, of stone, lighted by narrow windows containing two small panes of glass, and protected against the ' overloopen,' or escalading, of any savage foe, by strong, well-painted palisades. Snugness, economy, safety, were the characteristics of these country dwellings." This was in 1665 ; we do not propose to go so far back as that. There are no houses now remaining in Flatbush which were built before the eighteenth century. The house now owned by the heirs of the late John C. Bergen was standing during the War of the Revolution. If it was built by Dominie Freeman, as there is reason to suppose it was, then it must have been erected some time between 1714 and 1741. The house lately occupied by the family of Dr. Robinson, at the corner of Winthrop Street and Flatbush Avenue, was erected about 1740 or 1750 ; both of these are still standing and in tolerably good repair. About thirty years ago the old brick house of the Stryker family was pulled down ; the date marked upon that was 1696.

The style of these old houses on Long Island was different from any of those which are built in this age. The architect of to-day does not model his plans after these. The young couple just starting in life do not build after the pattern of the old homestead. And yet, at the time in which they were built, they were capacious and comfortable ; but they are not suited to the change in our mode of living. The low ceilings were necessary where the rooms were only heated by open wood fires ; the great cellars were indispensable where they were required for the storage of the whole winter's provisions ; the roomy garrets were a convenience when the great spinning-wheels were to be temporarily set aside. But we require different arrangements now.

The old houses were long and low, rarely more than a story and a half high. The roof was heavy ; sometimes it was broken by dormer windows, but oftener it sloped from the ridge-pole in unbroken descent, and extended so as to form a front piazza, while at the rear the slope in some of these houses extended so low that it reached to six or eight feet from the ground.

We have good authority for saying that the houses with an unbroken sweep from the ridge-pole to the eaves were those of earliest construction ; the roof was not built in a straight slant downward, after the style of a heavy Gothic roof, but curved slightly in the descent. The houses with a double pitch in the roof, both with and without dormer windows, were erected either just before the American Revolution or about the year 1800.

Extension rather than height was the aim in the construction of these old homesteads ; they were long, low, rambling houses, to which an addition might be made in any direction at the will of the owner, adding to its picturesqueness as well as to comfort.

This manner of building suggested the idea that land in those days was not very expensive ; the extension of the homestead was not skyward ; there was plenty of room upon the solid earth. These old Dutchmen believed in going about upon a plain without the tiresome climbing of long stairs, just as in the fatherland they were not accustomed to climb hills, but moved about on an unvarying level.

It is not probable that the houses of the early settlers had window-shutters ; at a later date all the houses, whether brick or wood, had wooden shutters opening outward and turning upon heavy iron hinges. These hinges, extending nearly across the shutter, were made the more conspicuous by being painted black.

For holding back these heavy shutters against the house when open, there was an awkward iron, somewhat in the shape of an elongated letter S, projecting some two inches beyond the house.

Some of the old houses had openings cut in the upper portion of the shutters, in the shape of a crescent, to admit the light in the early dawn.

Tin spouts to the gutters extended some two feet beyond the house at each corner. The water fell from these upon a flat stone below. At the rear of the house there were large casks frequently placed so as to catch the flow from these spouts ; especially was this the case after a drought, when the cisterns were nearly empty.

Previous to and about the year 1800, many houses had a projecting beam above, to which tackle might be fastened to hoist up any heavy article into the roomy garret. The grist from the mill was thus raised from the wagon, to be stored away. We have this information from elderly people in whose memory the custom still existed, and we can the more readily give credence to it as being very general, because this manner of raising heavy articles into the house is common at the present day in Holland.

The first houses of the old settlers which were built of brick usually had the date of their erection upon the front ; sometimes the figures were made of iron and fastened across the front, or they were built in with darker-colored brick. The modern fashion of two or four large panes of glass was then unknown, and six or nine panes filled each upper and lower half in the windows. The frames were broader and heavier that held these sashes, and the glass was by no means clear. It had seams and inequalities which tended to produce irregular outlines in objects seen through it.

The back of the fireplace was indicated by brick or stone-work on the exterior wall of the house, and the chimneys rose, broad, huge, and firm, from each gable-end.

The front door in these houses was always divided into an upper and lower half. The upper half was usually lighted by two round glasses, called bulls'-eyes. These served to light the halls in place of the sidelights introduced afterward. Round lights in the upper doors, such as these, are still used in Holland. The knockers on these were of brass or iron. Sometimes they were ponderous, and wrought with quaint device. The design most frequently seen was that of a lion's head holding a ring in its mouth. When the knocker was of iron, the door knob was of the same material, and so, also, when it was brass, the door knob was of brass.

The oldest fastening was a latch raised by the exterior knob; but, even when the usual style of lock and key was used, it was not inserted in the door as it now is, but fastened against it on the inner side.

When brass was the material used for the lock and the knocker, it was kept polished brightly with the assiduous care that the Dutch matron lavished upon every object in her domain which required manual labor.

The old houses in this village were built almost directly upon the street. Some of them, in order to have any inclosure in front, were fenced upon the sidewalk.

Being built when there was but little travel, and when settlers were few, they were naturally so placed as to bring them as near to their neighbors as the extent of their farms would allow.

The only old house which forms an exception to this rule is the one until recently occupied by Dr. Robinson, corner of Flatbush Avenue and Winthrop Street, and this was not built by the Dutch.

Probably at the early settlement of the town there were in the old houses built at that time two front doors, each opening from the "stoop" into the separate front rooms ; in such cases there was no hall. There have been, until a recent date, very old houses, almost going to decay, so arranged.

A southern exposure was almost a necessity in this peculiar style of Dutch architecture, because the unusual length of the house in proportion to its breadth made it desirable that it should be so placed as to receive the sunshine upon this long side. It was, therefore, quite customary to place the gable-end of the house to the street where that ran north and south, as is the case with the main street in Flatbush.

The long "front stoop" was an important feature in these Dutch houses. It was here the family gathered at the close of the day ; here the neighbors met together, and the men smoked their pipes and talked of colonial politics or, later, discussed the question as to who should be appointed to the Continental Congress. When the pipe needed replenishing, the little negro boy brought the brass chafing-dish filled with hickory coals.

In some houses a long seat ran the length of the "stoop" ; in others, there were seats at both ends.

The flat stone next to the stoop on the walk that led from the gate to the door was often a millstone, no longer required for its legitimate use. Upon this lay the mat, made of corn husks, crisp and bushy when new, and when flattened down by use consigned to some less conspicuous place.

It is probable that the addition of wings was the improvement of a comparatively modern era; the oldest houses were without these, and only when enlargement was necessary were wings added. A back kitchen at the rear formed the quarters for the colored people at the time when the slave population was large; this stood close to the house, but was detached from it. The material of which the Dutch houses were built was brick or wood; they were rarely built of stone; the most ancient were undoubtedly of brick. For some of these, the brick was brought from Holland, but there was at an early period a brick-kiln in Flatbush. The large pond on the southern side of what was once Mr. John Lefferts's farm, called the Steenbakkery, was formed by the digging out of the clay for bricks and pottery, as its name indicates.

Sometimes the lower portion of the house at the gable-end was of rough unhewn stone; or the lower story as far as the projection of the piazza was of stone and the remainder shingled, and at other times the front of the house was covered with a smooth stucco; but the majority of the earliest homesteads were built of brick, and these were in turn superseded by the frame houses of a succeeding generation, many of which still remain. The roofs were of shingles, and the sides the same. The "clapboards" in use at present were not then made. Although we can not definitely specify the exact year, we are safe in saying that it is only within the second quarter of this century that houses were boarded in Flatbush ; up to that time they were covered with shingles.

Thus stood those old Dutch houses, unpretentious, unostentatious, yet comfortable and roomy, just the picture that comes to mind when one thinks of an old-fashioned pleasant home ; just what is expressed by that phrase " the old homestead."

CHAPTER IX.

THE furniture which we are about to describe was not peculiar to Dutch houses. The articles in household use were probably the same as those in the homes of the Puritans, or in the houses of the English people of the same class in society. A certain degree of conformity to a particular style marks the household effects of each succeeding age ; this is varied and modified to suit the manner of living of the people by whom it is adopted. .

There were in the dwellings built in Flatbush during the last century certain characteristics common to them all. The ceilings were low, even when the rooms were large, and the rooms for this reason seem out of proportion. This may be accounted for in the fact that the only method of heating the apartments was by means of the large open fireplace ; the only mode of lighting them was by the dim yellow flame of tallow candles.

Our climate in winter is not mild and genial, so that draughts through the loose, rattling sashes and from the cracks and crannies in the heavy doors would have made it almost impossible to warm the rooms, had the ceilings been high in proportion to their size.

In many of the old houses the heavy hewn beams

which supported the upper story were projected across
the ceiling of the rooms upon the first floor ; these were
left the natural color of the wood. There are houses
still standing in Flatbush in which these cross beams
may be seen ; all such were built previous to the War of
the Revolution.

Wainscoting was the finish of the lower half of the
walls in many of the houses, but it was not general ; a
wooden molding, called a "chair board," often supplied
its place ; this extended around the room, about three
feet from the surbase.

In the old house, alluded to in Dr. Strong's history,
which stood at the southern extremity of the farm of
Mr. John Lefferts, and which was burned down by the
British in the battle of Flatbush, the surbase was made
of tiles, the same as those around the jambs of the chimney. We state this to show that the use of tiling as an
ornamental finish to the best apartments was more common than is generally supposed.

The old lady, in whose memory this room was most
tenderly held, thus described the method of cleansing
these tiles : they were first whitewashed ; this coating of
lime was allowed to become perfectly dry, and was then
rubbed off with a woolen cloth. Through this means,
not only did the tiles remain clean, but the interstices
were kept white.

The fireplace in houses of an early date occupied
nearly the entire side of the room, and was, as to importance as well as size, more conspicuous than the sham
chimney-piece which at present takes its place.

The delightful associations of the family gathering
have been felt even through less attractive surroundings,
so that the fireside has come to stand for the very home

itself. How strong, then, must have been the association of home and kindred with this broad, blazing chimney, around which all the family gathered through the long winter evening, the circle enlarged at times by neighbors and friends !

There were no libraries within their reach at that time from which they could procure a variety of books ; nor, had they such, were there good lights to attract the children to the reading-table ; the dark and unpaved roads did not tempt them to walk out, neither were there public amusements to divert them from the social gathering around the blazing fire. No wonder, then, that the prominent picture associated with the thought of home was the fireside.

The natural economy of the Dutchmen was not exercised in a direction that would curtail the comfort of their families, and the woodland, which formed a part of all the large farms, rendered the supply of fuel such as to be only limited by the wants of the household or the leisure to pile up the wood-yard.

We are not surprised that travelers visiting them should make allusion to their " fires of oak and hickory half way up the chimney."

Whittier, in " Snow-Bound," has given a description of the way in which the wood-fires were laid. The arrangement of the logs in the Long Island homestead was exactly the same as in his New England home :

> " The oaken log, green, huge, and thick,
> And on its top the stout back-stick :
> The knotty fore-stick laid apart,
> And filled between with curious art
> The ragged brush ; then, hovering near,
> We watched the first red blaze appear."

The hearth was brushed clean of ashes with a wing. Wings of ducks and geese, carefully prepared, served this purpose, and the ashes were never, in a neat household, allowed to be scattered over the hearth-stones.

The same use was made of wings in New England. Whittier alludes to this when he says :

> "Shut in from all the world without,
> We sat the clean-winged hearth about."

These old fireplaces were tiled in the best rooms ; the tiles were of chocolate-color, a reddish pink or pale blue, and generally represented Scripture scenes. At a later period cast-iron jambs were inserted, the fireplaces being smaller.

The kitchen andirons were large and of cast iron ; in the best rooms the shovel and tongs, fender, and andirons were of brass and kept brightly polished.

During the summer the bricks within the fireplace were painted with red-lead, to look fresh and tidy, and then a jar holding asparagus and other ornamental green branches took the place of the winter's log.

The mantel-pieces which were built in the beginning of this century were also of wood. They were sometimes over six feet high, and the shelf was very narrow. They were ornamented more or less with fluting and some fancy designs, but there was no fine wood-carving upon them. Marble mantel-pieces were in use in New York as early as 1772, for we find an advertisement in the "New York Gazette," as follows :

"TO BE SOLD.

"A negro man, an organ, two marble chimney-pieces and a marble slab for a hearth, and some sheets of gilt leather."

There were no "marble chimney-pieces" so early as that in Flatbush.

Anthracite coal was brought into use in Flatbush about 1830. The grates in which it was burned differed somewhat in construction from those subsequently used. The iron grate was hung between two brass columns, which were surmounted with large brass knobs. These columns were connected and stayed by a broad, curved band of brass below the grate. The grate-pan, which held the ashes, extended upon the hearth like a fender, and its outer curve was also of brass.

The huge, old-fashioned chimneys were not cleaned after the manner of the narrow flues which are now in use for the fires of hard coal, that, by means of furnace or grate, heat our modern rooms.

In earlier years little colored boys used to ascend the chimney from the open fireplace with scraper and brush. Poor little fellows! theirs was a hard life. It had, however, this alleviation, in the fact that they soon outgrew the possibility of its continuance, for only small children could creep up the chimney. When they reached the top, they were expected to thrust out their heads, like chimney swallows, and to sing their melancholy song from that height. This was the announcement that they had really reached the top before they began their descent. The song which they sang was the same by which they called the attention of housewives to their passing in the street ; it was a mournful song, and resembled the "yodeling" of the Swiss mountaineers if the sweep had a good voice. A man generally accompanied these little sweeps ; he it was who hired them and to whom the money for their work was to be paid ; but they were often very cruelly treated by their employers, and in this country, as well as in England, this manner of sweeping chimneys was finally forbidden by law.

There was, however, a more primitive method of cleansing chimneys, which was common in the country towns, but which from force of circumstances could not have been available in large cities.

A very rainy day, on which there was little or no wind, was taken advantage of as most suitable for the occasion. A huge bundle of straw tied on a pole was brought in from the barn, the fire in the fireplace was allowed to go out, and then this fagot of straw was lighted and held up the chimney. One man was stationed outside to watch if the rain extinguished every floating particle of straw or soot, for sometimes the flame reached beyond the chimney top ; the roaring was like distant thunder, and, when the pole was withdrawn, a shower of fiery flakes and smutty tips of burning straw followed, like a dull, red shower, in the fireplace. There have not been many chimneys swept in that way in this town for the last thirty years, and yet it was at one time the only method of getting the chimneys clean. While upon the subject of chimneys and fires, we must digress to say that, during the last century, and even during the early part of the present, in case of the destruction of a house or barn by fire, or in any accident which occasioned pecuniary trouble, the neighbors and friends always came forward to assist in making up the loss. There is on record, as early as 1675, the recommendation of Governor Andros to the people to assist by a day's work in repairing the loss, " through misfortune by fire," sustained by Jacques Corteleau.

It was also very common, when a building was to be

erected, for the farmers to be invited to assist in raising the frame. A branch of evergreen was placed upon the topmost point as a trophy of the completion of the work. Then a table was spread, and this was the occasion of feasting and merriment.

These pleasant, helpful acts certainly showed kind feeling between friends and neighbors, for there were no insurance offices and no fire alarms then ; they depended upon each other, and it was a dependence which did not fail.

WALLS.

Most of the houses at an early period were wainscoted ; above the wainscoting, they were plastered. Some of the walls in the houses built about 1800 were made with a smooth, clouded surface, as if to represent black-and-white marble.

The use of wall-paper in Flatbush probably dates from about 1830 ; but there is one house where, judging from the style of the paper, which is still in a state of good preservation, it must have been introduced before that date. This paper represents scenes in out-door life—chateaux surrounded by Lombardy poplars, gay ladies and gentlemen, evidently French, enjoying themselves upon a lawn, etc. The design is probably in imitation of tapestry hangings.

The ground-color of the papering at first used was darker than that which afterward came into fashion ; these deep shades were in turn cast aside for delicate tints of fawn-color, pearl, and a shade known as "ashes of roses."

A DUTCH GARRET.

Although the heavy Dutch roof contracted the height of the second-story chambers, it was generous in the space afforded to the garret, which usually extended in undivided length from end to end of the house.

Huge beams, hewn from the woods when the house was built, and which seem heavy enough to support a castle, hold up the broad roof, which here sloped down to the floor. There was an attractive mystery about the dim corners under these sloping eaves, for this was the receptacle for all the articles which had gradually come into disuse through the changes of fashion or the wear of time.

Here might be seen a corded bedstead with, perhaps, a dislocated leg, serving to support the feather-beds not needed in ordinary use, the huge pile being carefully covered with a faded but clean patchwork quilt. Here we may find long chests on ball feet ; the cradle and the crib outgrown by the children ; bags of feathers for future pillows ; the quilting-frame ; boxes of old newspapers or Congressional documents ; old hairy trunks, which look as if the animal that furnished the leather had been mangy ; old bandboxes, used at a time when the ladies' bonnets were huge in size ; furniture in all stages of dilapidation. All these things were placed in orderly rows along the roof between the beams, which, like watchful policemen, gave a rap on the head to the intruder who unwarily came too near the slope which they supported.

On each gable-end ran up two brick chimney-stacks, roughly mortared, joining at the upper end before they pierced the roof. The window within the peak thus formed not even the neatest housekeeper could always keep clear of the webs the busy spiders were ever hanging across the panes. Wasps were fond of this quiet retreat, although it was always a mystery how they got in ;

4

but there they were, buzzing angrily with extended wings against the glass, or sitting in motionless clusters along the molding.

It was in this roomy garret that the careful housewife had the week's washing hung in stormy weather ; the clothes-lines were stretched from side to side, and thus, when in winter the ground was covered with snow, it was a convenience to have the great basket of wet clothes carried up and hung out here, to freeze and dry undisturbed and out of the way ; for in those days the laundry was not a room apart, the washing and ironing being done in the kitchen.

The shingled roof which overarched the garret in all its length and breadth was discolored by time, and streaked and stained with the leakage occasioned by hard northeast storms ; there were tin pans and sea-shells, apparently placed at random over the floor in a purposeless way, but which were intended to catch the drip where the warped shingles admitted the rain.   In winter there were little drifts of snow here and there which had sifted through nail-holes and cracks.   A ladder resting upon the beams led from the floor to the scuttle in the roof.   The boards of the floor were not the smooth, white boards we use now for flooring ; they were dark and heavy, and looked as if they might have been sawn from the same trees that furnished the hewn beams supporting the rafters of the roof.

The great spinning-wheels, which have been unused for so many years, were also stowed away close to the eaves in these capacious garrets.   Near them remnants of flax hang on projecting wooden pegs, and hanks of thread are tucked between the beams and the time-stained shingles of the roof, as if the good old dames

proposed to come back soon and resume their spinning; but, meantime, the Fates who spin the thread of
human existence had taken the distaff, and Atropos had
cut their thread of life before they, our dear old grandmothers, could return to their spinning-wheels.

A DUTCH KITCHEN.

A Dutch kitchen ! what a comfortable-looking place
it was ! Not an underground apartment, with windows half darkened by area steps, but on the same
level with the rest of the house, and made pleasant
and cheerful by the combined influences of sunlight
and firelight.

There is no doubt that in early times the principal
kitchen was also the family sitting-room, and that a
smaller kitchen was at the rear of the large one for the
use of the servants, who at that time were slaves.

We know of several Dutch houses in which there
were these back kitchens ; they were probably attached
to every house of any pretension to style or belonging
to the more wealthy farmers.

The kitchen fireplace, with the oven attached, occupied nearly the entire space on one side of the room,
so wide was the opening of the chimney.

The back-log was the unsplit boll of a hickory-tree ;
it required the strength of two men to carry it in from
the wood-pile and place it back of the andirons. A front-
log, about one fourth as large as the back-log, was placed
next upon the andirons, and the interstices were filled
in with chips and corn-cobs.

There was a brilliant light when this wood was first
kindled ; the sparks went snapping and crackling up the
chimney ; the fire curled and spread, and broadened

upon its bed, until it went up in a sheet of flame that sent its glow across the kitchen.

After a while there was a rich bed of glowing hickory coals ; then the sap began to bubble out of the ends of the back-log and drip into the ashes, adding its monotonous undertone to the quiet singing of the tea-kettle.

At night the coals were covered with ashes ; for the fire in the kitchen, like the sacred fire on the altar of some of the heathen gods, was never allowed to go out.

The floors of these Dutch kitchens were kept sanded with white sea-sand ; this was scattered over the floor on one day, and on the next formed into various patterns with the broom. The boards of the floor, the tables, and the pails with brass hoops were assiduously scoured. Upon the walls were hung tin pans and pewter vessels of various sorts, while the kitchen " dresser " looked tasty and neat with its burden of blue or brown dishes, plates, bowls, and large pewter platters, each reflecting the firelight or throwing back the flashes from the bright tins on the opposite walls.

The huge kitchen fireplace was high as well as wide, and across the top was hung from side to side a blue or pink check valance, which was put on clean every Saturday afternoon. By the old people these were known as " schoorsteen valletje."

CELLARS IN OLD DUTCH HOUSES.

The kitchens of these old Dutch houses, as we have stated, were never in the basement ; that portion of the building was always adapted to the preservation of the provisions for winter use. Nothing was ever made or purchased by the old-time householders in small quantities at retail. Notwithstanding their habits of careful economy, they laid in a very bountiful winter store.

There was no convenient grocery just around the corner at that time ; no butcher making his daily rounds ; no stall where fresh vegetables could be purchased at a short notice, and, more than all, there were no canned fruits, vegetables, or meats.

The stores upon which the family depended for their winter use were carefully provided in the autumn, and the cellars of these old homesteads, broad as the house itself, were capacious enough and of a temperature fitted for the preservation of all the beef, pork, butter, fish, and vegetables which might be needed through the long, cold winters.

The cellars were carefully built, with a view to being cool in summer and warm in winter ; to accomplish this they were of rough, unhewn stone, with brick or earthen floors. To insure perfect cleanliness, the neat housewife had them thoroughly whitewashed semi-annually ; but, in spite of all her efforts, there was sometimes an unpleasant odor coming up from the great heaps of potatoes, turnips, and parsnips. This was especially the case toward spring, when the farmer set his men at work turning the potato heaps and pulling off the sprouts which the warmth of the cellar may have caused to grow. This sometimes was occasioned by the want of ventilation in the cellars, for it was customary in the autumn to close up the windows and gratings with salt hay, which was tightly packed against every opening, leaving only toward the southern exposure some entrance for a gleam of sunshine. A candle, or the open cellar-door, gave the visitor to these apartments the only means of picking his way there from December to March.

The furnaces with which we heat our dwellings would render such storage of winter provisions at the present time impossible, even were there not other reasons which make such a course unnecessary.

Here in these cellars might be seen huge hogsheads of salted beef, barrels of salted pork, hams in brine before they were smoked, firkins of salted shad and mackerel, firkins of home-made butter and lard, stone jars of pickles, and little kegs of pigs' feet in vinegar, called souse. Festoons of sausage hung in the cold-cellar pantry, "rolliches" and head-cheese were on the swinging shelf, which was constructed as a protection against the foraging mice.

In another portion of the cellar were bins for the potatoes, turnips, and parsnips. There were great heaps of apples for cooking or common use, barrels of apples of more choice varieties; barrels of vinegar, and of cider, and at the foundation of the kitchen chimney there was a receptacle for wood-ashes from the fireplaces above, to be used for ley in the making of soap.

These cellars were invariably entered from without by means of sloping doors over the steps. The doors were left open in dry and sunny weather, and fastened with a padlock at other times.

Thus the cellar in the Dutch homestead was the great storage-place for the provisions of nearly the entire year.

CHAPTER X.

WE know of no better way of giving the proximate value of housekeeping articles and furniture than to publish the list of prices paid for such when purchased.

We are enabled to do this by means of the possession of a bill of sale of the household effects of an old inhabitant of Flatbush, whose death occurred in 1767.

This faded document is an inventory of the articles sold at auction, probably held for the division of property among the heirs.

The following extracts show the cost of such articles more than one hundred years ago.

The family clock sold for £12. Laurence Ditmaerse bought "een kas" (a clothes press, or chest of drawers) for £8. Adraen Hegeman bought "een Brand-yzer, en een Tang, en een Aschchap" (a pair of andirons, a pair of tongs, and an ash shovel) for 15s. Jannetje Cornell bought "een deken" (a blanket) for 11s. 6d. "Een spiegel" (a looking-glass brought £2 5s. "Een zilver-gevest degen" (a silver-handled sword), £4 10s. "Een plaat," £2. A large looking-glass was purchased by Douwe Van Duyn for £3. A pewter platter was bought by Hendrick Suydam for 4s. 6d., and another for 7s. 6d. Adraen Hegeman bought for 15s. "Een knaap," a small stand such as was used for the evening candle. ("Zet de kaers op de knaap," to put the candle on the stand, was to begin the evening.) "Een tafel" a table, brought £1 12s. Whether this "tafel" was of deal, or of some more expensive wood, the inventory does not say. "Een bruyn tafel" (a dark table) brought 16s. "Drie dassjes en een suykeremmerjes," three small boxes and one small sugar pail or box, brought 3s. It was the custom to have a full, deep valance across the front of the kitchen chimney, as these open fireplaces were nearly as high as the ceiling; it is that which is meant by the following: "Een schoorsteen valletje" (a chimney valance), 5s.

This inventory and appraisement was made by two neighbors of the deceased, as they certify by their signatures:

"Opegenomen en geprecert by ons,
LEFFERT LEFFERTS.
LEFFERT MARTENSE."

At another auction sale of about the same period, in which the inventory is taken in English, which, however, scarcely renders it more intelligible, we find the following list of prices:

	£	s.	d.
Evert Hegeman, a psalm-book..............	0	0	6
Evert Hegeman, a psalm-book.............	0	2	5
Hendrick Suydam, Jr., a basket of books...	0	1	6
Samuel Garretsen, one frying-pan.........	0	4	0
Jan Suydam, an earthen dish..............	0	3	9
John Lefferts, half a dozen pewter plates...	0	9	9
Gulian Cornell, half a dozen pewter plates..	0	10	5
Peter Lott, knives and forks..............	0	1	7
Peter Vanderbilt, Jr., one looking-glass....	0	18	0
Douwe Van Duyne, one large looking-glass..	3	0	0

Then follow a great number of farming implements, for all of which the prices are stated, and the whole is certified as correct by Jer. Vanderbilt and Gerret Kouwenhoven.

In the year 1792 an appraisement of the property of Peter Lefferts, deceased, was made by John Van Der Bilt and Samuel Garretsen for division. We find the value of the articles thus given. We select a few from a long list :

	£	s.	d.
25 pewter plates, 1s. each....................	1	5	0
37 earthen plates.......................	0	10	0
9 pewter dishes, 4s. each................	1	16	0
8 earthen dishes, 2s. 6d. each............	1	0	0
2 waffle-irons, 6s. each.................	0	12	0
1 musket............................	0	16	0
1 saddle and bridle.................	3	0	0
10 keelers (wooden tubs used for milk).....	1	0	0
6 spinning-wheels, 12s. each.............	3	12	0
1 pair kitchen andirons.................	0	8	0
2 bookcases, 1s. 6d. each...............	0	3	0
1 bed, bedstead, and curtains............	10	0	0
1 dining-table.......................	0	16	0
1 looking-glass.......................	1	10	0
15 Windsor chairs, 6s. each..............	4	10	0
12 rush-bottom chairs, 2s. each...........	1	4	0
4 mahogany chairs, 8s. each.............	1	12	0
8 old chairs, 6d. each..................	0	4	0
1 mahogany dining-table................	4	0	0
1 writing-desk.......................	0	10	0
1 cupboard..........................	0	16	0
1 large chest........................	0	16	0
1 looking-glass......................	1	0	0
1 large Dutch cupboard................	4	0	0
1 bed, bedstead, and curtains...........	15	0	0
1 wild-cherry dining-table..............	1	0	0

	£	s.	d.
1 looking-glass	1	5	0
1 eight-day clock	14	0	0
1 looking-glass	5	0	0
1 desk and bookcase	20	0	0
1 mahogany tea-table	2	0	0
1 bed, bedstead, and curtains	10	0	0
1 Dutch Bible	2	0	0
1 English dictionary	1	0	0
1 parcel of books	7	0	0
6 sets of china cups and saucers	3	0	0
27 Delft plates	0	13	6
1 silver tankard	15	0	0
1 silver sugar-cup	14	0	0
1 silver milk-pot	4	0	0
13 silver table-spoons	13	0	0

CHAIRS.

The chairs which, a century ago, were used in the best rooms, were of hard dark wood. The seats of these were very broad, and were generally covered with a durable silk and worsted brocade. The backs were high and straight; the legs terminated in claw-feet clasping a ball. These chairs were of such good workmanship and good material that many of them may still be found in families in which, although in daily use, they have been preserved for more than a hundred years. Age has turned the wood of which they were made almost black, or of a dark walnut color.

There are kitchen chairs which have also survived a century of service; some of these may still be seen, being used as garden chairs, their durability, and the fact of their being entirely of wood, fitting them for such a purpose.

A low chair, with a seat of twisted osier, on which was tied a loose feather-filled cushion, covered with some gay material, was generally placed in the corner near a sunny window with a southern exposure. In front of this stood an array of favorite plants—roses, geraniums, or stock-gillies. On the back of these chairs hung the bag of knitting, the little red stocking, and the shining steel needles plainly visible, indicating that this was the favorite seat of the industrious mother of the family, and that this was the work she took up in her leisure moments—"between times," to express it idiomatically and forcibly, for, with these industrious people, time represented work; or a basket of patchwork held its place upon a low stool (bankje) beside the chair, also to be snatched up at odd intervals (ledige tyd).

In the corner of the fireplace stood the large arm-chair of father or grandfather : these were circular and broad-seated. They held their places in convenient contiguity to the narrow mantel-shelf on which lay crossed the long pipes, ready for use.

In the best bedroom was generally to be found a spacious stuffed chair, the back some five feet high, and padded throughout. This was for times of convalescence after sickness, or it may be that it was a pleasant retreat in which to take a midday nap ; the good mother rose at such an early hour she might be excused for this indulgence. These last-mentioned chairs, however, do not date farther back than the first years of this century.

WINDOW-CURTAINS AND BLINDS.

In the oldest houses, those of the first settlers, there were probably no blinds at the windows. The light was shaded by closing or bowing the outside wooden shutters. Succeeding generations used chintz curtains, and the remnants of these remain to offer hints, but not to furnish us with any assurance, as to whether they were hung in parlor or bedroom.

At no very distant period, green blinds, known as Venetian blinds, hanging inside of the window, served to soften the sunlight. They were formed of slats strung together with cords, and divided by a ladder of green worsted braid, depending from a green and gilt heading. They were opened at a greater or less angle by a green worsted cord and tassel at the left side, and were raised or lowered by a cord on the right side, which cord was wound round a gilt knob in the window-frame. This style of blind may still be found in England, but in this country they have fallen entirely into disuse, and with reason, for they were troublesome at best ; at the most inopportune times the strings would break, or the divisions of the braid ladder would become loosened, the broad swathe of light upon the carpet suddenly revealing their dilapidated condition.

As the ordinary outside blind took the place of the heavy wooden shutter, the convenient inside blinds have come into fashion ; these have displaced those formerly used.

CLOCKS.

The tall eight-day clock is to be found in all the families in this village. We are safe in saying that in every house in which live descendants of the Dutch settlers they can point to these old timepieces which once belonged to grandfather or great-grandfather, and which, old as they are, keep good time and need very little repair, although they have measured the hours of the past century.

In most of these clocks the face is of brass ; sometimes it is of porcelain ; but it is doubtful whether these fresh faces are the original ones. During the Revolutionary War the families who left the village took with them the works and left the case of the clock ; in consequence, there were many of the original cases broken or burned by the British.

Some of these clocks indicated the day of the month, as well as the hour of the day, and some showed the changes in the moon ; a few of them were musical, and played tunes at given hours. The mechanical arrangements for such performances have been worn out, however, and at present they make no higher pretension than do the cheap and common clocks which mark the hours with noisy ticking. The oldest clocks were ornamented at the top with brass balls. The most common devices for the embellishment of the face were the sun and moon rising above the horizon, or a representation of the antiquated Dutch galleon which swayed to and fro over the mimic waves with the movement of the pendulum.

We have the feeling that these old timepieces assume a peculiar dignity of their own, as they stand in such marked contrast to the fanciful French clock that ornaments the mantel-piece, or to the cheap and noisy bit of mechanism which flippantly hurries through the announcement that it has measured off another period of sixty minutes. There seems to be in the tall Dutch clock a realization of the importance of the hours, and a recognition of solemnity in the flight of time. It has marked so many changes that we almost invest it with a human sympathy for us mortals, whose short period of life it has so often measured. The key of the old clock has been handed down from generation to generation, as Time, the conqueror, has taken it from the fingers that were accustomed to wind up the weights, and has passed it on to a younger hand ; and when that, too, has fallen, nerveless and helpless, it has handed it on to the next; and there stands the old clock still, ticking, ticking—counting the moments of time while we pass into eternity.

DUTCH CUPBOARDS.

In an age when pantries were not considered a necessity in a well-planned house, the great cupboard supplied the convenience which we now find in the numerous closets designed by the architect in, and as part of, the house.

The dresser in the kitchen held the pewter and earthen platters in daily use ; the cupboard held the more expensive china and the silver.

It is probable that the word cupboard, however, came to be applied eventually to any large piece of furniture of the same shape, and that the table-linen and bed-linen were also kept in what were called cupboards, so that they were not used exclusively for dishes, but were filled with the family treasures, in whatever such consisted.

The old cupboards have been banished to the garret or consigned to the cellar ; only a few of them still remain with paneled doors and dark cherry-wood shelves, seeming to bid defiance to the ravages of time and to mock by their endurance the veneering of model furniture.

Those which have not been altered have very heavy overhanging moldings upon the top, and stand on huge ball feet. The inconvenience of moving such heavy pieces of furniture resulted in the cutting off of all unnecessary ornamentation, and thus many of these curious old articles of furniture have been remodeled into ordinary clothes-presses.

OLD CHESTS.

Long chests, also standing upon huge ball feet, were considered by our Dutch ancestors as a necessary and valuable bit of property to the householder. They were made of cherry or some dark, hard wood, and were about five or six feet long and two and a half feet wide. These were similar in size and shape to the elaborately carved coffers which one sees in the museums of the German and Italian cities, but, in the simple homes of our Dutch ancestors, they held no costly treasures of jewels and gold ; they were receptacles for the rolls of homespun linen, from which the bed-linen, table-linen, and toweling were cut. When the young wife was about to leave her father's house, it was from these stores that she received the linen for her new home, and, if some of it was not of her own spinning, it was because she was a bride too early in life to have assisted her mother and sisters at the spinning-wheel. There are some of these chests still remaining in the old houses ; they have been banished to the garret or to the linen closet ; but the housekeeper of to-day finds them as useful as they ever were, as they form a commodious receptacle for the curtains, the blankets, and whatever storage the changing seasons make necessary.

One of these old chests in the wide garret of the house of Mr. John Lefferts was found to have a false bottom. When the discovery was made, it contained a large amount of Continental currency. At the time it was so carefully secreted it was, of course, redeemable, but when found it was about as valuable as are now the bills of the Southern Confederacy.

It is probable that these chests are referred to in the old English story of the bride who playfully hid in the great chest in the lumber room, and was made prisoner by the spring-lock until, a century after, her bones were found and identified by her wedding finery.

CHESTS OF DRAWERS.

A style of bureau, made more recently than the chests and cupboards above described, consisted of inclosed shelves in the upper portion, a writing-desk with pigeon-holes and secret compartments in the central division, and drawers below. It was ornamented with plates of brass around the key-holes of the locks, and there were brass handles and plates upon the drawers. The brass mounting was kept brightly polished, which made this piece of furniture quite showy in appearance. The desk portion had frequently secret divisions and hidden drawers, to be opened by unseen springs, which revealed places for concealing valuable papers and money.

At a time in which there were no safe-deposit companies and no patent safes, the old parchment wills, bonds, and mortgages were generally kept within these secret compartments. While on the subject of writing-desks, it is in place to state that the writing paper was very different from the fine sheets which we can now procure at such a low price ; it was of a yellowish hue, not by any means smooth and clear. Envelopes were never used for letters ; the sheets were large enough to fold in such a way that the address could be written on the exterior of the last page. Pens were made of quills ;

these were sharpened every time they were used, the penknife being as necessary as the pen itself. Sand was sifted over the fresh ink, instead of using blotting-paper such as is now prepared for the purpose. Letters were sealed with red wafers or sealing-wax. If the family were in mourning, black wafers or black sealing-wax was used.

TOILET-TABLES.

Says one, writing for " Scribner's Magazine " on "New York fashions in 1814–1830 " : " Our toilet-tables I used to consider very pretty ; they were of half-moon shape, the top stuffed and covered with white, the frills, reaching to the floor, of transparent muslin over some bright color."

There were many of this kind also in the houses here ; some of them were covered with white dimity ; these were trimmed with ball fringe. Toilet-tables such as these were placed in small bedrooms under a hanging glass.

There were other styles of dressing-tables and bureaus, but they did not differ essentially from those made at the present day.

BEDSTEADS.

Until within the last fifty years it is not probable that there was in use any other style of bedstead than the high, four-post, rope-corded bedstead. What unwieldy things they were to manage in the semi-annual house-cleaning !

It required a man's strength to turn the machine that tightened the ropes in cording these beds when they were put together ; some one was stationed at each post to keep it upright, while a man—it might be pater-

familias himself—was exhausting his strength, and perhaps his stock of patience and good temper, in getting
the ropes sufficiently tight to suit the wife or mother
standing at one of the posts inspecting the work.

When the bedstead was duly corded and strung to
the tension required, then a straw bed, in a case of brown
home-made linen, was first placed over these cords, and
upon this were piled feather beds to the number of three
or four, and even more if this was the spare-room bedstead.

The sheets and pillow-cases were always of linen;
homespun open work or knit lace often ornamented
the end of the pillow-case; this was made the more
conspicuous by a strip of some bright color beneath it.
The blankets were home-made, and were woven from
the wool of the sheep sheared upon the farm. They
were not so soft and white as those which we may now
purchase, yet probably cost more for the spinning and
weaving. There were other coverings for beds besides
the blankets; these were made in the family, by dye-
ing the wool or flax and weaving the cloth in figures;
they were generally blue and white, as the dye was in-
digo, and, being used for upper coverings, went by the
name of " beddekleeden." The various intricate designs
of patchwork quilts occupied the spare moments of our
grandmothers, and were an expression of their love of
design and fancy work, just as worsted work or embroidery expresses a similar taste in their grandchildren.

It is a mistake, however, to think that these patchwork quilts, however neatly made or elaborately designed,
were considered for the last sixty years as the suitable
upper covering on the best bed. There was a heavy
white coverlet used for such a purpose, which bore some

resemblance to what is called now a Marseilles quilt; the figure upon it was more puffed out, being stuffed with cotton, and the coverlet itself was heavier than the modern material, which it somewhat resembled.

This white coverlet was used when white dimity curtains were upon the bedstead ; these were generally trimmed with ball fringe, and the hanging, festooning, and arranging of these curtains required a great amount of skill, patience, and labor. Another coverlet, much used, we might describe as a white cotton rep ; the figure was woven on the surface in little knots or knobs. The bedsteads, particularly those which were in the best bedroom, had the four posts richly carved ; these reached to the ceiling and were surmounted with a tester. Bedsteads similar to these are frequently seen in England, but now are rarely found here, they having been generally replaced by French bedsteads.

A material also much used for curtains and coverlets in the beginning of this century was of linen, printed in gay colors, with an India pattern of palm, trees and Oriental birds, with interlacing vines and foliage. When this was used as curtains, the coverlet was of the same piece. This material was expensive, but it was very durable, and no amount of washing, or even boiling, could make it fade.

We have seen a set of chocolate-colored curtains, which found great favor just after the close of the War of the Revolution, from the patriotic sentiments expressed thereon. They contained medallion heads of all the heroes of the war, while winged cherubs were blowing from their puffy cheeks substantial lines, supposed to be the breath of fame. Apparently in an ecstasy of cherubic delight, these little winged creatures

pointed to scrolls which contained couplets in praise of
the military heroes, whose staring eyes were not very
suggestive of repose or slumber.

These canopied bedsteads varied in shape ; some had
square tops reaching to the ceiling, with an upper valance
on three sides and long curtains at the posts. Others
were rounded over the top ; the posts, not being so tall,
were finished by an ornamental knob or ball ; the curtains were festooned below the canopy, which, springing from the posts, made an arch covered with chintz
like the curtains.

For young children a small bed called a "trundle
bed," in Dutch "een slaapbank op rollen," was frequently used. This was, as the name implies, a low bedstead upon rollers, which during the day was rolled
under the great high post bedstead and hidden by the
valance. At night this was rolled out at the side of the
mother, and was convenient for her watchful care over
the little ones ; for the Dutch mother never gave up
the care of her children to others, even in families where
the colored people in the kitchen were numerous enough
and willing to relieve her.

The cradles were not the pretty, satin-lined, rattan
baskets such as those in which the children of this generation are rocked. They were of heavy, solid mahogany,
with a mahogany roof, if we may so call it, which extended one third of the length above, to shield the light from
the eyes of the little sleeper. These cradles were handed
down from generation to generation ; some of them are
still in existence. With the cradle there has also survived an old Dutch lullaby. As it is a sort of tradi-
tional "Mother Goose" among our Dutch families, we
give it here, but we are not willing to vouch for the

spelling, as we have never seen the words printed ; probably it has never before been in print. We feel sure, however, that it is a familiar sound to the descendants of every Dutch family, and that grandpa and grandma have trotted many a little four-year-old upon their knees to the little song of

> "Trip a trop a tronjes,
> De varkens in de boonjes,
> De koejes in de klaver,
> De paarden in de haver,
> De eenjes in de waterplass,
> So groot myn kleine —— was."

A free translation of the above being that, to climb up to father's or mother's knee was for the child a little throne upon which he might be as happy as were the little pigs among the beans, the cows among the clover, the horses among the oats, and the ducks splashing in the water.

At the last line the singer is supposed to toss up the child as high as he could reach, giving the real name in the blank left above in saying, "So great my little —— was."

As a nursery rhyme it is certainly more rational than "Old Mother Hubbard," "The Cat's in the Fiddle," "Little Jack Horner," or the rest of the Mother Goose melodies with which the English babies of the same age were tossed up by mother or nurse.

We find upon inquiry that this little cradle song was everywhere in use in the Dutch settlements, from Albany to Long Island. It is familiar, and is recognized as the nursery song in the Dutch towns along the Hudson, so that, upon application, it has been sent to us from different sources, with only the slight variation occasioned by the loss of one line in the Long Island version. Following

"De eenjes in de waterplass,"

should be

"De kalf es in de long gras."

This is the only theft that time has succeeded in making for, perhaps, two hundred years, for we can give no date to the bit of rhyme; there is nothing in the words which makes it improbable that it came with the children from the fatherland.

Sometimes, instead of the child's name in the last line, it was altered thus :

"So groot myn kleine poppetje was."

That is, so tall is my little puppet, doll, or baby, as it may be translated—a term of endearment.

There is another little rhyme which we may also take as a sample of Dutch " Mother Goose." As it has been preserved in the memory of the Dutch people in Albany during these two centuries, we give it another toss onward to the coming years by placing it, probably for the first time, in print :

"Duur zat een aapje op een stokje
Achter myn moeder's keuken deur;
Hy had een gaatje in syn rokje,
Duur stok dat schelmje syn kopje deur."

The translation of this is : "A little monkey sat on a bench behind the kitchen door ; he has a hole in his jacket, and through that the little rogue (schelmje) sticks his head."

Under the faint disguise of "een aapje" we see little Hans himself, mischievously bent upon increasing the size of the hole in his jacket, while the reproof, rather insinuated than expressed, implied that the child surely would not care to be like a little monkey!

As we have wandered from cradles to cradle-songs, we will so far continue the subject as to copy from the "History of New York," by Mary L. Booth, a Christmas address of the children to Santa Claus, said to be repeated on Christmas-Day; but it was not so widely known as "Trip a trop a tronjes":

"St. Nicholaas, goed heilig man,
Trekt uw' besten tabbard aan
En reis daamee naar Amsterdam,
    Von Amsterdam naar Spanje,
    Waar appellen von Oranje,
En appellen von Granaten,
Rollen door de straaten,
    St. Nicholaas, myn goeden vriend
    Ek heb uwe altyd wel gediend
As gy my nu wat wilt geben
Zal ik uwe dienen als myn leven."

We would here remark in parentheses that we think the writer from whose pages we have transcribed the above scarcely appreciates the stern Calvinism of the Dutch, when, in another chapter, we read that "at nine o'clock they commended themselves to the protection of the good St. Nicholas and went to bed." The old worthies, brought up on the doctrines of the Heidelberg Catechism and the Synod of Dordrecht, would scarcely have appreciated the jest, so abhorrent to them was anything like prayers to the saints.

WARMING-PANS.

At a time when there were no furnaces nor stoves, and the cold was only moderated by the wood fire upon the hearth, the temperature of the halls and sleeping apartments was such that water froze if left in the room. One can imagine under such circumstances the comfort afforded to the chilled occupant of these apartments by having the bed warmed. A large copper or brass covered pan was used for this purpose. The warming-pan, as it was called, was filled with glowing hickory coals, and when sufficiently heated was passed rapidly to and fro between the sheets, thus taking off the chill from the cold linen, and preparing a grateful warmth for those who had been shivering while undressing in the atmosphere of a room which in midwinter was not many degrees warmer than the open air.

LOOKING-GLASSES.

People generally think that the old Dutch farmers had nothing more than the bare necessaries of life. We should have inclined to believe that they had no looking-glasses whatever, had we not abundant proof to the contrary. The large mirrors of the present day were of course unknown among them, but, as early as 1684, there is mention made of looking-glasses in the colony. In the inventory of the household effects of Nicholas Rutgersen Van Brunt, made at that date, two looking-glasses are mentioned. In 1732 a toll of four pence was imposed upon every looking-glass of two feet high and upward which was carried across the Fulton Ferry.

We find advertised in 1773, " an assortment of oval looking-glasses ; pier ditto ; sconces and dressing-glasses," for sale on Hunter's Quay, New York. So that even handsome mirrors must have been in general use in the colonies at that time. Under the date of 1776 we find the following advertisement :

"An elegant assortment of looking-glasses in oval and square ornamental frames; ditto mahogany, etc., etc. I flatter myself from the assurance of my correspondent in London, when the difference is settled between England and the colonies, of having my store so constantly supplied with the above article as will give general satisfaction."

By reference to the prices upon the bill of sale in 1767, to which we have referred previously, we find that a large looking-glass (een spiegel) sold for three pounds.

In the appraisement of the property of Peter Lefferts, in 1792, there are at least three looking-glasses mentioned, one of which was valued at five pounds, one at one pound ten shillings, and one at one pound.

The glass in the mirrors of a later period was rarely in one plate ; there was usually a division across the top, making it a plate and a quarter ; in some this upper quarter was a gilded landscape, instead of glass. The gilt frames of these mirrors were sometimes elaborately ornamented with gilded balls, chains, eagles, or foliage.

The mirrors which were first used as mantel-glasses had two divisions, one near each end, thus dividing the plate-glass into three divisions, one large and two smaller.

There were also frames of dark wood, or of mahogany ornamented ; these were sometimes adorned with gilt-embossed figures along the borders of the frame.

TABLES.

Of the tables used previously to the Revolution we know little ; there are probably none now remaining in

5

the village which were in use at that early date. The oldest which have come under our notice are not nearly so convenient as the extension dining-tables of the present day.

They had "leaves," which hung down when not used, and were held up, when extended, by legs drawn from under the central portion of the table. These were found to be very heavy when moved, and uncomfortable when in use unless the leaves were opened.

These dining-tables were usually square; the oval and round tables now in use were only occasionally to be seen; there were semicircular tables placed in the halls, or under looking-glasses which were formed to make part of the dining-table, and thus increase its size when needed; these were joined to this table by a small brass fastening made for the purpose.

These semicircular halves, when added to the two extended leaves, formed the largest-sized table around 'which guests could be seated. We can not offer them unqualified praise, for the legs of the table made some of the seats uncomfortable; but they have been the centers of much hospitality, and a genial, true-hearted welcome to the abundance spread upon them was never lacking; neither was there wanting the expression of gratitude to God for the goodness that provided the feast; before and after every meal there was grace said by the head of the household, while the whole family bowed in reverent silence until the blessing, whether silent or audible, had been asked and thanks returned.

There were small tea-tables, the four legs of which were stayed and joined by a cross-piece terminating in claw-feet holding each a ball. The leaves of these tables were semicircular, and could be raised or lowered at pleasure. There were round tables called "stands," of about a yard in diameter; these stood upon a tripod, which branched off from the main pedestal. These could be turned up like a screen, and were in this form placed to fill and furnish a vacant corner.

Smaller tables, known also as "stands," less than half a yard in diameter, were in every family. They were used to hold the candle at night and for the great family Bible. There is one of these little stands still in use which, before the Revolutionary War, served as a rest for the old Dutch Bible.

The Dutch for a table was een tafel; these small stands, on which the candlestick was placed, went by the name of kaers-knaap.

SIDEBOARDS.

The old-fashioned cupboard was replaced in the beginning of this century by the mahogany sideboard, which has in turn given way at this present day to the French buffet of black walnut, an article more graceful than either of its predecessors in the dining-room in shape and appearance.

In the days when the feeling as to temperance had not as yet discountenanced in the household the display of spirituous liquors, the sideboard was usually ornamented with an array of decanters, cut-glass tumblers, china pitchers, and square, high-shouldered glass bottles ornamented in gilt figures. These sideboards had compartments for wine bottles, for china and glass, and also drawers for table-linen; some of them had an arched open space below in the center, in which two or three salvers of graded sizes were placed. The oldest sideboards had high boxes at each end, designed for knives and forks.

The pretty bric-à-brac treasures which adorn the parlors of modern houses were not to be found in our homes in Flatbush many years ago. With a moderate income a room can be tastefully furnished to-day, and made cheerful with the many little knickknacks which it would have been quite impossible to procure in the past age.

APPLIANCES FOR LIGHTING HOUSES.

The candles in common use in the household, prior to 1825 or thereabout, were made in the family. The tallow, which had been collected after preparing the winter's supply of beef, was melted in a caldron ; rattans, on which the wicks, cut of the required length, were hung, were in readiness, and these were dipped in the hot tallow until by repeated dipping and cooling they had acquired the proper size.

Tin molds were in occasional use to make these candles, but generally, when other than this common article was needed, wax candles were purchased.

The lamps in use at that period were made with small tubes, through which the cotton wick ran down to the oil in the bulb below. As these were without shade or chimney, the wick could not be raised very high without smoking.

The lamps which were introduced into general use for the center-table about 1831 had a tall chimney and ground-glass shade to soften the light ; they were called Astral lamps. The wick used in this lamp was circular. The two arms, which served as supporters to the shade, also served as leaders to the oil cup in filling the lamp with oil. As kerosene was unknown at this time, sperm and whale oil were in use.

This style of lamp was superseded by an improved pattern known as the solar lamp, which from some improvement in its construction gave a more brilliant and steady light.

After the discovery and introduction of kerosene oil, this same style of lamp, with very little alteration, was continued in use for the parlor table. Hand lamps, with flat wicks and shades, student lamps, which could be raised or lowered on a standard, and a variety of hall lamps, parlor lamps, and night lamps were invented and improved upon after the discovery of kerosene ; but the introduction of gas into every house, and its use in the streets and public buildings, quickly followed the formation of the village gas-works in 1867.

In the earliest Dutch houses the space between the fireplace and the ceiling was sometimes paneled. The mantel-piece in this paneling was scarcely more than a broad molding ; a wide mantel-piece was rarely seen. Candlesticks of highly polished brass were placed upon this shelf, or, if in the best room, they were of plated ware, sometimes of silver.

A tray of the same metal was placed between the candlesticks to hold the snuffers.

Tenderly as we cling to the memory of the past, we none the less willingly admit the superior advantages of the present. The laboring-man to-day may have his house more thoroughly warmed and more easily lighted, and in many ways made more comfortable, than the richest farmer of that time.

CHAPTER XI.

THERE was more work to be done at home in the housekeeping of earlier days than there is at the present time. This arose from the fact that certain articles of food could not be purchased as they can be now; many things could not be purchased at all, and consequently they were prepared in the family.

All the butter for winter use was made and packed down in firkins, for every farmer kept a herd of cows, which were driven up the farm lane in the morning, or were turned out to pasture in "the wood lot." The oldest in the drove wore the brass bell about her neck; in the evening, on their return, they would stand lowing at the "swing gate" until it was opened, and they were driven into their quarters, to be milked for the night. If, after the bars were let down in the field, a young heifer loitered in the lane to crop the clover, the sharp call of "Cobus, cobus, cobus!" from the farmer, or "Cusha, cusha, cusha!" from the milkmaid, speedily hurried the loiterer into an uncouth gait that raised a cloud of dust upon the narrow farm road.

In the autumn came the busy season called "killing time," which brought with it an amount of labor such as would almost startle the inexperienced housewife of to-day, whose sole duty now is to purchase the articles which at this earlier period were prepared in the family.

In the month of November arrangements were made by the farmer for killing the swine and oxen which he had fattened for the winter's stock of provision.

Sometimes a dozen or more were, by previous weeks of fattening with corn, prepared as one farmer's proportion of the great hecatomb of the season ; but usually some six or eight swine were considered sufficient for the use of a family of ordinary size, with the farm laborers, who might be required as extra help during the harvest season. The day appointed for this purpose by the farmer was a busy one for his wife.

These Dutch people were always early risers, but at this time the dawn of day saw all the family prepared for the work which was before them, as it was necessary that the slaughtered animals should be cold and hard, for they were cut up and salted on the afternoon of the day on which they were killed. The colored servants took a most prominent part in the bustle of the occasion, and, as all the old families employed a large number of these, there was more or less of that hilarity which characterizes that race when engaged in congenial labor.

Before the close of the day the "pickle pork" was salted in huge casks in the cellar ; the hams and shoulders were also laid in salt. After five or six days water was added ; remaining for seven or eight weeks in this brine, they were then hung up in the smoke-house, of which every farmhouse had one, either partitioned off in the garret and connected with the kitchen chimney, or built apart from the house.

The hams, prepared with the greatest care on the part of the farmer as to the feeding of the animals and the subsequent treatment of the meat, were superior to those which we now purchase in the public market.

Sausage-making followed. The Dutch farmer and his wife could never have been induced to purchase sausage from the butcher, even had it been offered for sale (as it was not), for they were particular as to the manner of making it. In the primitive days they did not have the mechanical appliances to relieve them in the chopping and stuffing of the meat which in after-days was afforded them.

Some of the products of their labor were given away by those who were first engaged in it to friends and neighbors who had not yet undertaken it, and they, in turn, gave back of theirs when freshly made. By this interchange the tables were supplied with fresh sausage, spare ribs, head-cheese, and tenderloin of pork, until all the neighbors had prepared each their share of the winter's provision.

It was also the custom, when a calf, sheep, or lamb had been killed, to send what was not needed for immediate use to the neighbors, who, in their turn, felt obliged to return an equal portion upon a like occasion. By this means their diet was varied, and salt provisions were not the monotonous fare they might otherwise have been.

At a period when the coming of the butcher was not, as now, a weekly occurrence, the convenience of this mutual interchange of provisions was an assistance such as we, who do not need relief of this kind, can scarcely estimate. The poor found this a season of plenty, for they were large sharers in the general abundance.

Immediately after the sausage-making was completed, the fatted cows were killed for the winter's supply of beef. The proper pieces for smoked beef were selected to be hung up in the smokehouse, with the hams and shoulders. Some of the best pieces were reserved to be eaten while fresh, and the remainder were kept in brine, to be used through the year as corned beef for the table.

"Head-cheese" and "rolliches" were articles of food so exclusively Dutch that it is doubtful if they were ever seen except in Dutch families, and they have already almost passed out of the knowledge of the present generation.

"Rolliches" were made of fat and lean beef cut in pieces somewhat larger than dice, highly seasoned, sewed in tripe, and boiled for several hours. These were then placed under a press and were eaten cold. When cut in thin slices, and the dish ornamented with sprigs of parsley, its marbled appearance made it not only an attractive-looking dish, but it was justly esteemed by the epicure as being a great delicacy.

"Head-cheese" was somewhat similar, except that it was made of the fat and lean of pork chopped as fine as for sausage-meat. It was then highly seasoned, tied up in a piece of linen and boiled. This also was put under a press, and eaten when cold.

Doughnuts hold such a prominent place on the New England table that they have ceased to be thought a Dutch cake. Under the name of "olekock," they were, however, to be found on all Dutch tea-tables, and we insist that the art of making them was learned by the Puritan housewives while they were in Holland previous to the embarkation of the Pilgrims. We may imagine those

English dames seated at the Dutch tea-table, and asking
for the most approved receipts for making the articles
which they found so nice, and that our great-great-
grandmothers most cheerfully copied off the contents of
their cook-books for their visitors. Thus these receipts
came over in the Mayflower with the many other things
which are supposed to have been brought hither in that
good ship.

There is this difference in the Dutch and the New
England use of doughnuts : our New England sisters
make them in every season of the year, and use them,
at least the farmers' families do, at every meal. Not so
with the Dutch ; they only made them from November
until January, because at that period the lard in which
they were cooked was still fresh. After January they
were rarely, if ever, found in a genuine Dutch family,
and they were never used except on the tea-table, or between meals by the children.

It has been said that " suppawn," or Indian-meal por-
ridge, made very thick, was a favorite dish among the
settlers. As corn was raised on the Long Island farms
in great abundance, this may have been, probably was,
an article of diet much used. But it was not, of course,
a Dutch dish, for, on coming to this country, they were
not accustomed to the use of corn meal. They must
have acquired the knowledge of its use from the Indians.

We incline to believe that even its name was Indian,
unless we derive it from the word sop, broth, or soppen,
to dip in. We do not pretend to a knowledge either of
its derivation or its spelling, and only offer this as a
suggestion.

"Suppawn" was also made from pumpkins boiled,
to which was added wheat flour, making it of the con-

sistency of Indian suppawn ; this, like the other, was eaten with cream or milk, and was often used for a late supper.

A bit of doggerel in reference to this dish, partly in Dutch and partly in English, still clings in memory as many a useless tattered remnant will do, held by its strongest thread—that of being repeated by an aged negro in the chimney-corner introductory to stories of "old times":

> " With their round-scooped ladles they eat their suppawn,
> Calling, 'hoe vaarje Hansem, waar komt ye von daag ?' "

We should not like to be held responsible for the spelling of the above, but we venture to give the lines as showing that suppawn was a dish used by the Dutch settlers at a very early period.

There was a Dutch dish of apples and pork, but how it was made we are unable to say.

Poultry of all kinds was raised on the farms in great abundance for winter use.

The turkey was not so great a favorite with the Long Island farmer as were ducks and geese. Ducks roasted before the fire in the Dutch oven, and brought to the table on a large platter, encircled by raised dumplings, as light as a sponge, were a dish greatly in favor.

Roast goose was the chosen dinner for the winter holidays, Christmas and New Year's day.

Paasch, or Easter, was the season in which the children collected the fresh eggs from the barn-yard and had them colored, to be used freely in the family, both by master and mistress, the children and the slaves.

Easter (Paasch) and Whitsuntide (Pingster) were always kept in old Dutch families.

Large quantities of shad and mackerel were caught in the bays by the farmers in the adjoining towns, who had this right; these were purchased from the boats coming to shore, and were salted to add to the variety of winter provision. As great pains were taken with the preparation of these fish, they were far more rich, juicy, and palatable than the dry, briny material which is purchased now under the name of salt shad and mackerel.

Game was also abundant in former years on Long Island. Wild ducks and wild geese were frequently brought down by the farmer's gun in his visits to his salt meadows, most of the farms in Flatbush having a piece of salt meadow, which was considered as much a part of the farm as if it lay contiguous to it.

If we go back to a distant period, it is probable that game was very abundant on Long Island. A law was passed " for the more effectual preservation of deer and other game, and the destruction of wolves, wild cats, and other vermin" in the year 1708, or in the "seventh year of Queen Anne," as the old law book dates it, which shows what game was to be had in Kings County at that time. It was enacted that no "Christian or Indian, freeman or slave," within the given time for the protection of game, should, under penalty named, kill "any buck, doe, or fawn ; any wild turkies, heath hens, partridges or quails, in the counties of Suffolk, Queens and Kings."

There was a law passed in 1695 forbidding the profanation of the Lord's Day by "shooting, fishing, sporting," etc.

A law was passed in 1717 "to encourage the destroying of wild cats and their catlings, and foxes and their puppies, in the County of Suffolk, Queens County, and Kings County." This was also for the better preservation of game.

Within ten years quail have been shot in Flatbush ; wild rabbits, squirrels, quail and partridges were quite numerous some twenty-five years ago.

At the present time there is no game in Flatbush, unless we except the robins and the migratory birds that in their flight from north to south come within range of the sportsman's gun. The farmers of Flatbush rely upon the markets of the adjacent cities to vary their larder, rather than upon anything they may chance to find in the circumscribed limits of their present farming lands.

BREAD.

When circumstances were such that the housewife herself did not make the bread for the family use, there was usually some well-trained colored cook to take her place in doing this duty. Bread-making was no easy task when a dozen or more loaves were to be made at one time, particularly as one of those loaves was fully equal to two of modern size.

Bread was always raised with a leaven of the dough made at a preceding occasion. It was kneaded in great wooden kneading-troughs. There were loaves of wheat flour occasionally made, but for daily use it is probable that rye bread was the supply of the family until the slaves were all freed, and the size of the family in the kitchen was diminished. Large bins of wheat and rye flour and Indian meal, each capable of holding a quantity equal to the contents of two or three barrels, were kept well filled for family use. The farmers never purchased flour, but sent the grain raised upon the

farm to the mill, the miller retaining a certain proportion for his payment.

The bread was light and nice. The loaves were
large, and the slices were cut alternately from the upper
and the lower half of the loaf. In the kitchen, the servants, who were at that time slaves, used lard instead
of butter on their bread ; it was also used in families
in which poverty made the most rigid economy necessary, for even the poor were unwilling to be dependent
upon public charity, and learned to have their wants
conform to their circumstances.

It will thus be seen that, from necessity, the comfort
of the family depended upon the skill of the housekeeper. For this reason, the Dutch matron gave vigilant oversight, and oftener still took an active part in
the preparation of the meals in her household. She
knew that those whom she loved so well must look to
her for many things which now even moderate means
can purchase. So identified did she become with these
household duties that the language betrayed the fact,
and the word "huysvrouw" was a synonym for our
word wife. Is there not great significance in this fact
as to the domestic habits of the women, that in these
old homesteads the wife and mother stood the central
figure in the home life ? She was the "huysvrouw."

CHAPTER XII.

COOKING UTENSILS.

THE cooking utensils in the old Dutch kitchens differed as much from those in present use as the great open fireplace differs from the modern range, to which, with its various appurtenances, it has given place. The roasting of meats and poultry was done before the open fire, in what was called a Dutch oven. This was cylindrical in form, but stood on four feet, and the joint to be cooked was held in place by a long spit which projected at each end, so that the meat could be turned without opening the door of the cylinder. It was of course open to the front of the fire, and there was a door at the back for convenience in basting. When more than this was needed, then the great brick oven was heated.

For the baking of hot biscuit for tea, or a single loaf of bread or cake, a flat iron pot was used, which was called a "bake-pan" or a "spider." This was placed in the corner of the fireplace upon hot coals, and a layer of hot coals covered with ashes was placed upon the tight-fitting iron lid. A larger "bake-pan" than this, but similarly formed and used, was sometimes called a pie-pan. For boiling meats and vegetables cast-iron pots were used.

A large-sized iron pot at one side of the fire was always kept filled with hot water, as the pipes at the back of the chimney, which now supply that need, were then unknown. From a long iron crane, which was fastened in the brickwork of the chimney, there were links of heavy iron chain, known as trammel and pot-hooks, on which the vessels for cooking were hung over the fire. These vessels were of iron, copper, or brass; usually they were of iron. The tin or the porcelain-lined kettles, such as are now used on the modern range, were not known. The great brick ovens of those days were quite different from the small stove and range ovens in present use. They filled the corner of the kitchen next to the fireplace, and when the fireplace took up more space than usual, instead of contracting the size of the oven, it was placed in a shed adjoining the kitchen. The Dutch housewife expected to have at least a dozen loaves of bread baked at one time, with, perhaps, as many pies, before these brick ovens cooled after being heated. The loaves of bread were not baked in pans, but on the stone floor of the oven. There was this large baking of bread, cakes, and pies every time the oven was heated, because the families, including the slaves, were large, and there was no bakery to supply a deficiency, should there be such.

In order to heat these ovens, the farm hands brought in a quantity of light wood which had been thoroughly dried for oven wood. This was lighted in the oven, and when it was entirely consumed the ashes were swept out, and the floor was cleansed with a wet towel fastened on the end of a pole, forming a sort of mop which was kept for that purpose, or with a brush called a "boender"; for the Dutch women were neat to an extreme.

Every family owned a waffle-iron ; these were larger and deeper than those now made, and had two long handles for the purpose of holding them with more ease over the beds of hickory coals on which the waffles were baked.

We find in an old newspaper of March 16, 1772, an advertisement, as follows :

Hard and soft waffle-irons for sale by Peter Goelet, at the Golden Key, Hanover Square, New York.

There was another tea cake which we must consider exclusively Dutch, as we have never seen the irons for cooking them anywhere except in families who are descendants of the Dutch settlers. These cakes were so thin as sometimes to be called wafers ; they were also known as split cakes, because, thin as they were, they were split open and buttered before being sent up to the table. The name by which they were correctly known was " Izer cookies " ; this might have reference to the iron in which they were baked—Yzer, or it may be a corruption of " Eitzaal," a dining-room. On going to housekeeping, it was customary to have one of these wafer-irons made with the united initials, and the date upon it, so that the impression of the letters and figures was made on the cakes when baked. The letters P. L. and F. L., with the date 1790, are to be seen in an iron which is still in use among the great-grandchildren of P. L. and F. L.

From what we have said, it will be inferred that the Dutch enjoyed the good things of this life, and that their household arrangements were such as to provide the table with abundant and wholesome food. This is strictly true, with only the limitation of that proper moderation which is characteristic of the Dutch under all circumstances.

A letter quoted in Stiles's " History of Brooklyn " gives such a false representation of the Dutch manner of living that simple justice should have impelled the historian who published the letter to follow it with an explanation, instead of offering it as a " portrait of most of the Dutch families of that day." It seems that an officer who was billeted in Flatbush during the War of the Revolution wrote a letter complaining of his very poor fare and the extreme poverty of the table appointments. The letter is called by Stiles " a humorous sketch," and he leaves his readers to infer that the mode of living and the food offered at that period in Flatbush were hardly those of civilized life. As the historian quoted the letter, he should have followed it with the explanation that Flatbush at that period had been ravaged by the lawless hordes that follow an army ; that their crops had been burned, and their cattle driven away, while they were left with scarcely subsistence for their own families ; and that these soldiers were billeted upon them not only against their wishes, but in spite of their representations as to their poverty. The board promised for the support of each soldier was two dollars per week, or a little more than nine cents for each meal, and the payment of even that was doubtful. We are glad that the writer of the letter is obliged to notice the "extreme neatness of the house and beds," and that there was grace said over their food, although this admission is accompanied with a sneer. But it is obviously gross injustice to take a period in which all their resources were exhausted as the typical one of the Dutch manner of living.

CHAPTER XIII.

EVERY Dutch family in Flatbush owns some piece of silver which has been handed down as an heirloom ; to one, the family tankard has come through many generations, passing to the oldest son or the only daughter ; to another, it may be only some quaint old spoon, a cream-jug, or a sugar-bowl.

Upon the marriage of a daughter it was quite customary to purchase, in connection with her wedding outfit, and as a wedding present for her, a tea service, consisting of a teapot, cream-pitcher, sugar-bowl, and slop-bowl. These were usually of heavy, solid silver, and varied in price according to the means of the family.

The old farmers have had the reputation of being very close in their expenditure, except for the mere necessaries of life. This is unjust, and the charge has been made by those who do not understand the character of the Dutch people nor appreciate their economy, prudence, and wise provision for an unforeseen exigency in the future. They were generous to their children and relatives, helpful and kind to their neighbors ; because they were not wasteful, they had the more to give, and when they gave it was not grudgingly.

They were fully capable of appreciating that which was beautiful and ornamental, but their preference lay in the direction of that which was solid and substantial, and their selection in the way of gifts was always in favor of that which was supposed to be durable. This was characteristic, for they abhorred shams and cheap imitations, and, when an article was purchased in accordance with their taste, it was the best of its kind, and that which would last. We can easily see, therefore, why they gave plate the preference, and why almost every family has some silver heirloom in possession.

There are still bills to be found among old papers, which we give to show the cost of such articles at time of date. There are silver pieces of an earlier period than these, the value or age of which we do not know. As money was more scarce then than now, the sums paid indicate a larger amount compared to their general expenditure than the same outlay would at the present day.

NEW YORK, 25th July, 1792.

PHEBE LEFFERTS

Bo't of JOHN VERNON,

1 silver teapot, engraved in cypher..........£16 5<i>s</i>. 8<i>d</i>.

Received the above in full,

JNO. VERNON.

NEW YORK, Oct. 8, 1787.

JUDGE LEFFERTS, Esq.

Bo't of THOS. DAFT,

	£	s.	d.
1 silver teapot	12	0	0
Sugar basin and engraving	9	13	0
Milk-pot	4	12	0
	26	5	0

Received at the same time the full contents,

THOS. DAFT.

NEW YORK, *Sept.* 4, 1802.
JOHN LOTT, Esq.,
   Bo't of JOHN VERNON,
          £ *s.* *d.*
1 teapot, sugar-dish, and milk-pot........... 45 0 0
1 dozen table spoons, engraved in cypher..... 16 5 4
¼ dozen tea "   " " "   2 12 8
1 sugar-tongs............................ 1 6 0

          65 4 0
   Received payment.
       JNO. VERNON.

In an inventory of estate, dated 1776, we find nine silver spoons valued at nine pounds ; six small teaspoons at eighteen shillings.

We find, from a record which has been preserved, that at a private sale of the household effects of Rev. M. Schoonmaker, June 9, 1824, the following prices were paid for a silver tea service :

1 silver teapot, sugar-dish, and milk-pot, weighing
  41½ oz., at 9s. per oz. $46.69
6 silver teaspoons, 2¼ oz., at 8s. per oz........... 2.25

A silver tankard was at one time in possession of almost every family in Flatbush. These were sometimes not only heavy but were of curious workmanship, and it is probable that they were brought from Holland. It is much to be regretted that some of these valuable pieces have been exchanged for modern silver. Others have been stolen or lost through the many vicissitudes which time brings to every family.

The following advertisement, taken from the "New York Gazette" of October 8, 1733, shows that such property was not safe from the predatory tramp even at that early period :

Stole at Flatbush, on Long Island : One Silver Tankerd, a piece of money in the Led [lid] of King Charles II, and the led all engraved. A coat of arms before (in it a man on a waggon with two horses), marked on the handle L. P. A.

One silver Tankerd, plain, with a piece of money in the led, marked on the handle A. P., or A. L.

One cup, with two twisted ears, chased with 'scutchens, marked L. P. A.

One tumbler marked L. P. A.

One Dutch Beker, weighs about 28 ounces, engraved all round.

(This word " Beker" is a Dutch term, signifying a cup, a chalice, the same as the English word " beaker.")

All the above was made by Mr. Jacob Boele, stamped J. B. (trade mark).

One large cup with two cast ears, with heads upon them, and a coat of arms engraved thereon.

One cup with two ears ; a small hole in the bottom.

Two pairs shoe-clasps, new cleaned.

For the above a large reward is offered and no questions asked.

By reference to the sales for division of property, already given, it will be seen that, in 1792, silver tankards, sugar-cups, milk-pots, tablespoons, etc., were among the articles in household use. The price of the tankard upon the bill is given as £15. The price of a tankard on the inventory of an estate, bearing date March 11, 1776, is given as £22.

There was formerly a great deal of blue china in Flatbush. There are still single pieces which are duly authenticated, and known to be a hundred years old, and are probably older. There are also pieces of Spode bearing the name of the maker.

Some articles of old china have outlasted the tradition of their purchase or their age.

For ordinary use at the dinner tables of two hundred years ago, pewter plates and platters served the family. They varied in price. Upon a bill of sale we find that a pewter platter brought four shillings and sixpence (English). Another, at the same sale, brought seven shillings and sixpence. Six pewter plates sold for nine shillings and ninepence ; an earthen dish for three shillings and ninepence.

At the appraisement of the property of an old inhabitant, Peter Lefferts, born 1680, we find that the value of his table service of dishes and plates was as follows :

	£	s.	d.
Twenty-five pewter plates	1	5	0
Thirty-seven earthen plates	0	10	0
Nine pewter dishes	1	16	0
Eight earthen dishes	1	0	0
Six setts china cups and saucers	3	0	0
Twenty-seven Delft plates	0	13	6

We find by an appraisement, made 1714, in a neighboring town, that one china dish and cup were valued at seven shillings and sixpence, and one pewter dish at five shillings. From these prices we infer that the plates and dishes in daily use were not very expensive, although the sums given implied a greater relative amount of wealth than the same sums would at the present day.

Tall china vases were very frequently the ornaments of the mantel-piece. Some of these which have been preserved are now very valuable.

They were generally of dark blue, or of white ware ornamented in various ways. The antiquarian or the learned in ceramics would be delighted with many a tall vase which we remember to have seen consigned to the kitchen, or, hidden in upper shelves, disappear for ever in that mysterious manner which inanimate matter seems to have the gift of doing when not closely watched. These tall vases were sometimes cylindrical and without covers, at other times they were more curved and swelling in their outlines, with dragons at the handles and on the cover. Sometimes five of · these vases constituted a set, or if they were large there were but three.

It is to be regretted that so few of these china jars have outlasted the changes of fashion, as they were undoubtedly of more value than many of the mantel ornaments by which they were displaced.

CHAPTER XIV.

WE have no knowledge as to the musical taste of the early colonists. It is doubtful if it was developed in any direction except that of church psalmody; even their best efforts in that line would probably have not been considered a success by the connoisseurs of this day. In the silver-tipped Psalm-books, which they carried to church every Sunday, the words were interlined with quaint-looking bars of musical notes, from which they sang.

Legends and traditions place the violin in the hands of the negro, and tell how the children gathered around him in the summer evening or the winter "schemeravond" (twilight) to listen to the tones which he drew from its strings.

When we come down to Revolutionary days, we have authority for a band of music in the town, but that was not native talent or property. The young people danced to the band of the regiment, and the pretty girl who was selected by Ethan Allen as his partner in the dance transmitted the knowledge of that fact

6

to her grandchildren, and with it the very natural opinion that the music on the occasion was the best in the world. How much an opinion given under such circumstances is worth we do not venture to decide.

In a number of the "Daily Advertiser," New York, dated Saturday, May 10, 1788, we find the following advertisement :

Jacob Astor,

No. 81 Queen Street,

Has just imported an elegant assortment of PIANO-FORTES, which he will sell on reasonable terms.

He also buys and sells for cash all kinds of furs.

We do not cite this as a proof that "piano-fortes" were numerous in our village at this period, but, as the full cup overflows, so we may conjecture that the adjoining towns were not entirely without these instruments if Mr. Jacob Astor could offer such an elegant assortment on reasonable terms.

While exploring in childhood the recesses of an old garret, we found under the eaves the dilapidated remains of what was once a harpsichord. It was larger than the melodeons in present use, and resembled them somewhat in general appearance, except that it was a stringed instrument.

We find in an old newspaper, printed in 1773, the following advertisement :

John Sheybli, Horse and Cart Street, New York, makes, repairs, and tunes all sorts of organs, harpsichords, spinnets, and forte-pianos on the most reasonable terms.

The sparsely settled miles between Horse and Cart

Street, New York, and the little town at the foot of the hills beyond Breukelin, must have made a journey which might well have deterred Mr. Sheybli when called upon to tune the spinets there "upon reasonable terms."

It is probable that there were but few instruments in Flatbush. The ivory keys of this one were yellow and loose, and, as with childish fingers we ran over the scale, the keys rattled to the touch without a sound, save as one or two, still connected by a rusty wire, jingled and vibrated in most unmusical sibilant echoes. The fingers that once brought melody from these time-stained keys have been motionless for more than ninety years. It almost seems as if no musical sound should linger upon the broken strings, when it was written upon her tombstone who once sang to the accompaniment of these notes that she died August 30, 1786, aged twenty-four years.

There were pianos in Flatbush about 1812, if not earlier. We speak from knowledge of one which we remember to have seen in its old age. It was scarcely six octaves in length, and had a spindling, attenuated appearance, arising from the shallowness of the body and the thin gilded legs. On the front, above the key-board, were inscribed the name and residence of the maker, "Geib, New York"; this was surrounded with a wreath of painted rosebuds.

A drawer to hold music opened below the body of the instrument. It is needless to say that no great volume of sound was produced from these pianos, and that their notes were thin and weak.

The price of this instrument we are enabled to give, as the bill has been preserved.

Mr. L——.

To John Geib & Son, Dr.

1812.

Sept. 19.

To an Elegant patent Piano-forte with drawers
and two pedals.......................... $270 00

                                          $270 00
            Received payment,
                        John Geib & Son.

To show what money it cost to take lessons in music
seventy years ago, we copy the following from the
"New York Weekly Museum," of March, 1809 :

LESSONS ON THE PIANO-FORTE.

Frederick W. Dannenberg

Proposes to give Lessons on the Piano-forte, at his residence,
No. 60 Maiden Lane, on the following

Terms.

1. To enable him to pay the utmost attention to the progress of his Pupils, he will engage with only twelve scholars.

2. Six scholars to form a class, and to be taught at a time.

3. Each class to receive their lessons twice a week, from 10
A. M. to 1 P. M.

4. Each class to consist of scholars of equal capacity, so as to
render the instructions in their progress equally beneficial to all.
Terms, $12.50 cents per quarter for each scholar.

A musical instrument maker from London advertises
that he makes and repairs "all sorts of violins, tenors,
base violins, guitars, kitts, mute violins, æolian harps,
spinnets, and spinnet-jacks."

The "New York Gazette" of the same year (1772)
also sets forth that a maker from Philadelphia "makes
and repairs all kinds of organs, spinnets, harpsichords,
and pianos." But this man apparently had no shop in

New York, for, to use the words of his advertisement, "he is to be spoke with at Mr. Samuel Prince's, Cabinet Maker, at the sign of the Chest of Drawers in New York." He concludes his advertisement with a postscript to the effect that he makes "hammer spinnets that never wants quilling as other spinnets do."

PAINTINGS.

It is doubtful if there were any works of art worthy of the name in Flatbush for many years after its settlement.

Family traditions tell us that some of the old houses burned down in the Battle of Long Island contained oil paintings which had been sent from Holland; how valuable these were there is no means of knowing.

There were at one time in the village many small pictures on glass; these were of dark colors, and have been in possession of the families who own them for very many years. They are, however, more valuable as relics than for their skillful workmanship. The glass seems to be gradually scaling off, and, as the painting is upon the glass, the pictures are slowly disappearing.

We know of one miniature painted about 1780, and there are others of more or less value; but we have seen none which are worthy of mention as works of art.

In a number of the "Daily Advertiser" for 1788, we find that an artist of that day in New York was not above advertising his skill. We would draw attention to the fact that he, singularly enough, offers to "take back the likenesses should they not meet with approval." Remembering some old, stiff portraits, we wonder that such permission was not taken advantage of :

Lately arrived from France,

Presents his respects to his friends and the public in general, and informs them that he draws likenesses of ladies and gentlemen at the lowest price, and engages the painting to be equal to any in Europe. Should the likeness not be approved of after drawing, it will be taken back.

This artist gives his residence as "42 Hanover Square, opposite Mr. Peter Goelet's." On inquiry we gain traces of portraits which have been lost through the lapse of time, and pictures which have been destroyed; but there are none old enough to be valuable as relics or worthy of notice.

CHAPTER XV.

DRESS.

OF this chapter on dress we must say, as we did of that on furniture, that we describe nothing peculiar to this locality; it is the fashion of the period, and not of the Dutch people, which we here attempt to portray.

DRESS OF GENTLEMEN.

The dress of gentlemen about the year 1770 was in the style with which we have been made familiar by the pictures of General Washington. In full dress, gentlemen appeared in long coats, often of a light color, velvet breeches, silk stockings, and knee-buckles; they wore low shoes, which were fastened with shoe-buckles. The hair was powdered and tied in a queue. Some of these knee-buckles and shoe-buckles are still preserved in Flatbush, as also some other portions of a dress of this style.

We find a tailor's advertisement in the "New York Gazetteer" for May 13, 1773, which glitters like a rainbow. Behold what is offered as the fashionable spring colors for gentlemen:

A general assortment of scarlet, buff, blue, green, crimson, white, sky-blue, and other colored superfine cloths.

Superfine scarlet, buff, sky-blue, garnet, and green cassimirs.

Superfine Genoa velvets; striped velverets for breeches of all colors. . . .

A neat assortment of gold and silver lace, gold and silver spangle buttons; gold buttons with loops and bands; silver-ground gold brocade for hats. . . .

Any gentleman that chooses to have his buttons made of the same cloth can have them worked with pearl and spangles, with any sprig or flower he may choose, as neat as those made in London.

All these elegant things are offered for sale by John Laboyteaux at his fashionable establishment at Beekman's Slip.

We can not say if our Flatbush ancestors were rowed in a small boat over the ferry to purchase any of these flashy dresses, for, if they ever owned such finery, it has as entirely disappeared as the rainbows of that summer.

The hats worn at this period by gentlemen were cocked hats. In the same newspaper a hatter advertises his stock as excelling all others in "cut, color, and cock."

If we may judge from the advertisement of a fashionable tailor at the corner of Wall Street, in the year 1773, the vests worn by gentlemen in full dress must have been showy. He offers for sale a "curious assortment of vest patterns," such as :

White and buff tambour embroidered cassamar.
White silk, embroidered with gold.
White silk,   "   "   silver.
White satin,   "   "   gold.
White satin,   "   "   silver, etc.

Since gentlemen assumed the style at present worn they have only varied their dress slightly. Sometimes the coat-collar has been cut to stand higher in the neck or to roll farther back ; the waist has been made shorter or longer, or a button has changed its place here and there ; otherwise there has been no perceptible differ- ence in the dress of gentlemen for many years.

For a long time it was considered very foppish and undignified to wear a beard. A mustache allowed to grow was the sign of a dandy ; a gentleman must be smoothly shaven, unless he chose to be looked upon as foppish or eccentric. A full beard was never seen in the pulpit, never in general society, except when worn by foreigners or those aping foreign manners and customs.

Incredible as this seems, now that gentlemen allow their beards to grow as nature intended, yet it is true that an elderly gentleman some thirty years ago would not have appeared in church or in the street unless he was fresh from the process of shaving. It would have been the subject of censure from the consistory had the clergy appeared in the pulpit as they do now with whiskers, mustache, or beard.

We have Richard Grant White for authority in say- ing that "from 1700 to 1825 the appearance of a beard on any part of an Englishman's or an American's face was, strangely enough, so rare as to be regarded as a monstrosity."

DRESS OF LADIES.

At the early settlement of Long Island it is proba- ble that the short gowns and petticoats of our great- great-grandmothers were made of material spun and woven in the family. Durability rather than beauty was the chief consideration in preparing the cloth. They were fond of gay colors, and, as they were not confined to somber hues because of the simplicity of their dress, bright red and dark blue must have given a pictu- resque effect to their costume.

Up to the time of the War of the Revolution the ordinary dress of the women when engaged in their household duties was a short gown and petticoat, of a color and material to suit the taste of the wearer.

The full dress of that period was that which is seen in representations of the costume of Mrs. Washington. There are some dresses of this style in Flatbush, still preserved by those whose ancestors wore them about ninety years ago. One of these dresses, worn as a bridal dress, August 7, 1780, is a fawn-colored satin-damask, without a train, and open in front; it was worn with a blue satin-damask petticoat. The vest of the bridegroom was made from the same piece of blue satin-damask. The sleeves of the bride's dress reached to the elbow, and were probably trimmed with a deep ruffle of lace falling over the arm. Another of these dresses of the same age is of silk, embroidered, and with a train.

After that style of dress, also well known through the pictures of Mrs. Washington, had passed out of fashion, it was followed by another, its opposite in almost every respect; the ladies of the next generation wore absurdly short waists and scant skirts. This French fashion did not retain its hold upon the taste of the ladies as did that which had preceded it.

There are some of these scant, short-waisted dresses still preserved by the descendants of those who had worn them in the early part of this century.

After this, dating from 1825 or thereabouts, a more simple style of dress came into general use. The skirt and waist were united, forming one garment; this was called a frock, a word which has almost passed into disuse, except that in a gentleman's dress it is used to designate the garment called a "frock coat." At this date,

also, there was a marked difference in the dress of young
people and of elderly people. ·

Old ladies wore silver-rimmed, round-eyed spectacles, and Swiss-muslin caps, with narrow borders neatly
crimped. A white lawn kerchief was crossed over the
breast, with a black silk one neatly folded above it.
They wore plain skirts without tucks, flounces, or trains,
and by their simple and unostentatious garb impressed
the beholder with the idea of a serene and placid old
age. That they showed no wish to adopt a youthful
dress seemed significant of a peaceful acknowledgment
of the age they had reached, with no frivolous longing
for the youthful pleasures unsuited to their years. Their
old age was not one of idleness ; every moment not otherwise occupied was employed in knitting ; this work was
always close at hand, and the needles moved briskly and
mechanically without the necessity of watching them.
A knitting sheath was used by these old ladies, pinned
at the waist, and their method of holding their needles
differed from that of the knitting of the present time
in the use of this knitting sheath. A remnant of the
style of a bygone age also remained in the round, ball-
like pincushion which hung suspended at the side, unless they were dressed for visiting or for church-going.

Perhaps we credit these old ladies with a simplicity
of dress which was, after all, nearly as much the fashion
of the period as their own peculiar selection, for the
dress worn by ladies of whatever age was more simple
fifty years ago than it is to-day. New dresses were not
so frequently purchased, and, as fashions did not vary so
constantly, an expensive dress could be worn longer
without getting to be out of fashion.

The ordinary dress of a lady in her own home was

not as costly as it is now, because, being simpler, it required less material, and, as it was less elaborately trimmed, it did not require so much of a dressmaker's time ; consequently a lady could be tastefully and prettily dressed at much less expense. This is going back some thirty or forty years ; at that period the variations in the style of dress were for a long time very slight. Sometimes a belt was worn in the dress, sometimes it was a bodice ; for one season the sleeve was loose and flowing, the next it was tightly fitting ; the bishop sleeve was adopted in one year, and the "leg of mutton " in the next. This name had reference to the shape, which fitted closely to the arm from the wrist to the elbow ; above the elbow it puffed out, and was sustained in this form either by stiff muslin or by down undersleeves. These large down or feather undersleeves, fastened in the armholes of the dress, were very warm and uncomfortable.

For young ladies, the dress was then worn low in the neck ; a round or a pointed cape of the same material as the dress was worn with it if needed. The waist was always buttoned or hooked up at the back. The intricacies of overskirts had not yet been adopted, except in thin material worn as ball-dresses. The skirts of the walking-dresses were not gored, but were worn full, often without trimming. A dress could be made by one person without a sewing-machine in one day ; sometimes assistance was given by the young ladies in the family, but, even without it, it was not unusual for the entire dress to be completed between the hours of 7 A. M. and 6 P. M. Sometimes the skirt was tucked, or folds were laid on it, or it had ruffles upon it, or it was flounced up to the hips ; such dresses of course required more time in the making. Bows of the same material or of ribbon were worn, or any other ornament, to vary the skirt ; but the weighty overskirt of heavy material, with its tight tieback, interfering with the free motion of the limbs, is an invention of a later day. Anything more entangling and illy adapted to free and easy movement than this it would be difficult to suggest. Upon every style of sleeve except the "bishop" and the "leg of mutton " a cap was worn. It was of the same material as the dress ; sometimes it reached from the armhole, into which it was sewed with the sleeve, nearly to the elbow ; generally it was three or four inches in length, and was trimmed to match the skirt. This finish to the sleeve has been so long out of date that now it seems useless, but, undoubtedly, it was introduced · because young ladies often wore short sleeves, and by this device the long sleeve could be ripped out, and the cap, which remained, formed a short sleeve complete in itself.

The custom of wearing low-necked dresses and short sleeves was very common with children ; their frocks were always worn thus. Little girls, those who were such between 1825 and 1845, wore very short dresses and long pantalettes reaching below their ankles. Infants appeared with bare neck and bare arms. They were very lovely, and the child looked much prettier ; but this fashion began at last to be carried to such an unhealthy extent that the evil corrected itself, and children are now more comfortably and healthfully attired in long-sleeved and high-necked dresses. Proud mothers, anxious to exhibit the fair white necks and dimpled shoulders of their little ones, often made their dresses so low that the wonder was how the child ever kept the dress on. They seemed almost able to slip out of the bit of garment altogether, had it not been tied on at the waist by a sash, which, in its amplitude, seemed broader and larger than the dress itself. This was carried to such an extreme by foolish mothers that infants often seemed smaller than the huge sash-bow to which, apparently, they were tied.

Some thirty years ago, infants always wore caps with a lace ruffle surrounding the face. This was a pretty and a becoming fashion. There is no style of dress so unnatural and unhealthy but there are found some foolish women who accept it, and it is a sad truth that many fond but weak mothers have sacrificed the health and strength of their little ones to some of these foolish fashions.

We claim for the present style of dressing children in moderately long dresses without tieback or sash, high at the neck and with sleeves reaching to the wrist, that it is the most sensible fashion which parents have ever adopted. Let us hope it may long continue, and that we may have healthier girls and boys, and stronger men and women, in the next generation.

The corsets worn by the ladies of the present day are certainly an improvement as to health and comfort upon the "stays" which were worn by the ladies a hundred years ago, and, strange to say, were worn also by children. An advertisement of a stay-maker in an old paper is so curious that we copy it in confirmation of our statement as to the article being worn in 1772 by children :

JOHN BURCHETT,

From London and Paris,

Takes this method to inform the ladies and the publick in general that he has removed to Burling's Slip at the sign of the

Crown and Stays, where he makes all sorts of stays, jumps, packthread, turned and single; likewise children's stays (to give and preserve a shape truly perfect, and not drooping or falling in before) in the neatest and newest fashions. He has also a number of good ready-made stays of the best quality, cheaper than can be imported, prices from ten shillings to five pounds, and by a system to himself to exceed in fineness and quality. Farther, said Burchett will take from any lady who shall employ him half cash for stays and the rest in dry goods. He also returns his most hearty thanks to all who have countenanced him with their esteem, *tho' undeserved ;* but for the future will use all possible endeavors to merit their interest, and as he has obtained a certificate from the Queen's stay-maker, London, he flatters himself fully capable to satisfy any ladies who shall please to favor him with their commands.

A dress-maker was called formerly a mantua-maker. The dictionary gives the meaning of the word mantua as "a gown or dress worn by females." As no part of the dress of the present day is so called, the change of name has followed both the maker and the thing made.

We here insert a genuine bill of a mantua-maker of seventy years ago :

Mrs. —— Dr. to JANE WHITE:

	£	s.	d.
For cuting and making three frocks, 9s.	0	9	0
For cuting and making two frocks	0	4	0
For cuting two under coats.	0	2	0
[*Illegible*]	0	3	0
Two pair wooling stockings	0	7	0
For cuting and making a great coat.	0	4	0
	1	9	0

As we read the descriptions accompanying the fashion plates of the present day, or if we turn to the magazines which furnish the names of the material for the latest style of ladies' dresses, the variety of goods in the market seems almost incredible. But the ladies of the olden time were certainly not the less favored as to variety in their choice of material. We do not recognize the goods comprised in the following list, but we copy it as advertised under the head of "India Goods," offered for sale by the firm of Francis Lewis & Son, "near the Fly Market," New York (1775). We copy the advertiser's list :

Taffeties, Persians, Damasks, Lutestring, Padusoys, Sattens, Amozeens, Modes and Peelongs Dowlas, Garlix, Tandems, Plattilas royal, Pistol lawns, Minionets.

Also in Horse and Cart Street, a large assortment of Printed Linens, Shalloons, Rattinets, Kentings, Tamies, Durants, Callimancoes, Alapeens and Silverets.

We surely can not say, after this list of material, that our grandmothers had no choice of the wherewithal to make their dresses and petticoats.

HOOP-SKIRTS.

History tells us that in the year 1709 the petticoats worn by the ladies of fashion in England had attained an enormous size. The "Tatler," the great "censor of the morals and manners of the day," jestingly speaks of it as a "silken rotunda, not unlike the cupola of St. Paul's."

This fashion seems to have reached its most absurd height in 1745. A pamphlet was at that time published against the fashion, entitled, "The Enormous Abomination of the Hoop Petticoat," because the garment "had become of so enormous a circumference that it could not be longer endured."

Slowly and gradually this unnatural fashion passed away, but its extinction was not to be final. Somewhere about 1858 it was revived in a more moderate form, and hoop-skirt making became an industry that gave employment to thousands of workmen. There were manufactories in all the large cities. The ribs were made of steel or tin, with a woven cover over each rib. They were pliable and not expensive.

It is probable that through the invention and improvement of machinery the hoop-skirts of this century were much lighter and less cumbersome than the "stiff hoops" which Pope denounces in his "Rape of the Lock."

The fashion held sway for nearly twenty years, only varying in the size and shape of the framework. Then the modern hoop-skirt passed into disuse, and woman once more presents herself in the size of her natural figure.

STOCKINGS.

Even articles so simple as stockings have been subject to the mutations of fashions. We read that Queen Elizabeth had them "of black knitted silk." There is little doubt but that at an early period they were of bright colors. In 1737, or thereabout, white stockings were first worn. At first they occasioned some dispute as to whether they were modest and lady-like. White stockings, however, continued to be worn, even in the deepest mourning, we are told, until 1778 ; at that time black silk stockings were introduced as the usual wear in England.

Black silk stockings were always worn in our recollection in this country by ladies in mourning until about 1855, when the fashion of wearing high boots hid the stocking, and unbleached cotton hose were worn with all dresses, whether dark or light. At that same period, also, children always wore white stockings with white dresses ; a dark stocking with a white dress would have been considered in very bad taste. At present that has been changed ; colored hose of the deepest, or of the most brilliant, dye are worn with white dresses, and white or unbleached cotton hose are worn only at the will of the owner.

The knitting of stockings was an important industry in the family in the last century and in the beginning of this. The ball of gray and dark-blue woolen yarn was always in the knitting-basket ; the stockings for the whole family were knit by hand at that time ; the children's were often of red yarn ; the men's were of gray or blue, and the women's of any color to suit the fancy of the wearer. To-day, when a good pair of unbleached cotton hose can be purchased for twenty-five or thirty cents, and coarse cotton at even a less price, we can not advise the resumption of the knitting-needle, although it seems like a pleasant, home-like way of spending the long winter evening, when conversation, or even reading, offers no interruption to the industrious fingers.

SHOES.

If Fashion stoops to select the color of the stocking, we can not expect to have the shape of the shoe exempt from her tyranny.

With the bridal dress, to which we have referred as having been worn in 1780, there were also preserved two pairs of shoes. We may judge from these of the style worn in full dress at this period. One pair was of dark, maroon-colored silk, embroidered ; the other was

of pink satin. Both pairs were very pointed at the toe,
and the heels were at least two inches high, and somewhat in shape of a flattened hour-glass.

Probably that shape was out of fashion for some
eighty years ; to-day we find an approximation to it in
the high heels placed almost under the instep, which
one sees in the window of the fashionable shoemaker.
High-heeled shoes passed out of fashion when that extreme was reached.

Slippers were always worn in full dress some thirty
years ago, and high boots were only used in the street.
Afterward boots for ladies were made with paper soles
and of handsome material to match the dresses, and
then slippers were for a time out of fashion. These thin
boots were laced up at the side. Buttoned boots were
first used some fifteen or twenty years ago.

The thick, coarse shoes worn before India-rubber
overshoes were made were not sufficient to keep the
feet dry in stormy weather, and it is only since the present perfected use of gum overshoes that there is entire
protection afforded.

India-rubber shoes and boots were unknown in the
time of our grandmothers ; they are comparatively a
recent invention. They were at first bulky and stiff,
but now such a degree of elasticity has been attained
that, whether in the shape of sandal or high shoe, they
are pliable, light, and strong.

Before and even a few years later than 1800, the
shoes for the farmer's family were made in his house.
The skins of the calves killed on his farm were sent to
the tanner, who reserved a certain share for his own
pay, and of the remainder the boots and shoes were
made by a shoemaker who came to the house for that

purpose. At such times the whole family, including master and mistress, children and slaves, were supplied with common shoes for ordinary use.

APRONS.

About the close of the last century fancy aprons were not considered out of place even in full dress, although it is not probable that they were worn at balls and parties.

We find in a newspaper bearing date April, 1773, an advertisement in which there is a great variety of these offered for sale :

Spotted and figured Scots lawn..............aprons.
Spotted and figured silk...................   "
Plain and flowered, figured and spotted, black
    gauze.....................................   "
Figured and flowered black and white silk....   "
Needle-worked lawn.......................   "

Fancy aprons, more or less trimmed, were worn by young ladies, and formed a very pretty addition to their afternoon dress. Until within some ten or fifteen years they were not considered inconsistent even with a silk dress. At present they are only worn by children, or, if used by ladies, only to serve the temporary purpose of neatness, and not an ornamental part of their general costume.

GLOVES

are an expensive and necessary part of a lady's equipment, but they have not, from the nature of things, been subjected to the same changes as have other articles of dress, except as to improvement in color and quality.

The buttoned gloves worn in full dress were not so common a few years ago as they are now.

When children and young misses all wore short sleeves, there were long kid gloves which could be drawn up above the elbow; for school-children these long gloves were made of "nankeen." For weddings and parties, long kid gloves reached half way to the elbow, and were trimmed with lace, swan's-down, or quilled satin ribbon; when they were not worn so long, then buttoned gloves came in fashion.

Silk gloves and mitts were in more general use formerly than they are at present. As long ago as in the past century they were worn of colors selected to match the rest of the dress.

We copy the following advertisement from a newspaper published in 1773:

Women's	silk and worsted	gloves	and	mitts.
"	white and purple kid	"	"	"
"	purple............	"	"	"
"	crimson...........	"	"	"
"	blue..............	"	"	"
"	black.............	"	"	"
"	white.............	"	"	"
"	cloth-coloured......	"	"	"

This last-named color is as much a puzzle to us as some of the fancy names which are now given to various colors may be to those of the next generation.

WORK-BAGS.

A work-bag, or reticule, carried on the arm, was at one time fashionable; the article itself seems to be revived at this present time, but it is now most frequently worn appended to the waist, upon the belt.

Bead-bags were made of canvas entirely beaded over in designs of flowers, etc.; others were of velvet, silk, or of cloth to match the rest of the dress.

These bags were used for the pocket-handkerchief, instead of a pocket in the dress ; perhaps they also held the snuff-box when that habit was indulged in.

JEWELRY.

If there was much jewelry worn by the young men and maidens in Flatbush before the Revolutionary War, there is very little of it now remaining except some few rings, brooches, and the knee- and shoe-buckles which formed so important a part of the gentlemen's dress.

The jewelry worn in New York in 1770–1780 may be judged from the jewelers' advertisements, one of whom speaks of himself as "the only real Maker in this city of Ladies Sett Shoe buckles, Ear rings, Egrets, Sprigs and hair pins, Seals, Necklaces, Combs, Crosses and Lockets, Sleeve buttons and Braslets, etc. Gentlemen's Setts shoe, knee, and stock buckles, Seals, Brooches, Buttons and rings. The above articles done in the neatest and best manner and sold as cheap as in London, wholesale or retail."

HATS AND BONNETS.

There is in this present day an improvement in the covering worn upon the head. Hats and bonnets are more tasteful and pretty than those formerly worn. For children the Normandy cap is comfortable and child-like, as also are the round straw hats worn in summer. The shade hats used by young ladies, and the stylish shapes of their dress hats, are also very picturesque and becoming. Even the bonnets of elderly ladies, when not overladen with trimming, are more tasteful than the poke bonnets formerly worn.

When children were out at play in the summer they wore gingham sun-bonnets; as these were made over stiff pasteboard, they were heavy and very uncomfortable. A child has been many a time punished for throwing off these scoops in its out-door games, when the fault really lay with the parent who required the child to wear such an uncomfortable covering upon the head.

The elaborate bonnets worn some thirty years ago consisted of a front piece, a crown, and a cape at the back of the neck; they were varied in their general outline every season—the front flared more or less, the crown was at a greater or less angle of inclination, the cape was very full and deep, or it was scant; it was plain, or it had frill trimming. The face trimming in these fanciful results of the milliner's art was an elaborate semicircle of lace, ribbons, and flowers. There were generally tabs of lace against the cheeks, and flowers above the forehead; or there were lace and flowers intermingled at the sides, and bows of pink, blue, or yellow ribbon above, like the keystone uniting the arch. These bonnets met under the chin, and were tied there with broad ribbon, but, in some of the senseless changes of fashion, were worn so far back upon the head that the strings were useless; the bonnet almost rested upon the back of the neck, and if it was not apt to drop off, it had at least that appearance.

There is a picture of Queen Victoria in one of these large bonnets, of the style when they were drawn forward over the face.

On or about 1835 a covering for the head, known as a caleche, was much worn while walking or driving. These were somewhat in shape of a gig-top. They were made of reeds covered with silk; black was the color for elderly ladies, green for young ladies; they were lined with white. When laid aside, they were perfectly flat; when worn, they were drawn forward over the face with a ribbon fastened on both sides about three inches from the top, which was held in the hand.

A writer in "Scribner's Magazine" for August, 1879, on New York fashions in 1814–1830, says : "Chip and Leghorn bonnets were the favorites for summer wear. Twenty dollars, or even more, were paid for an untrimmed Leghorn bonnet. But then we expected a nice thing, once bought, would last a long time ; our bonnets were done over and retrimmed, and came out again as good as new next season—or, if we were of a frugal mind, for several seasons.

". . . . Merino or raw-silk underwear, or anything resembling it, had not yet been heard of.

". . . . Merino long shawls, with a broad border at the ends, and a narrow one along the length, came up during the war, and were considered a part of a nice toilet. At first they were white, but black and scarlet soon appeared.

"Tortoise-shell combs and thread-lace were among the desirable possessions of ordinarily well-dressed people ; of jewels we heard but little. A person had a set of pearls, perhaps, or sometimes you saw a ruby or a diamond finger-ring, but precious stones of a high rank were very infrequent."

Water-proof cloaks, whether of the rubber silk or the water-proof cloth, were unknown until within the last twenty years. They are now almost a necessary part of a lady's outfit, and we hope there may be some significance in the fact that these modern inventions of women's wear are in the direction of the comfortable and the useful.

The long trains and tieback style of overskirt which are at present worn may soon be followed by some other absurdity; but it is, at least, a cause for congratulation that that which is fantastic and arbitrary does not retain its hold as long as that which is natural and graceful.

Now that intercourse between this country and Paris is so easy and frequent, the fashions of France are adopted almost as quickly here as they obtain favor abroad.

In the beginning of this century, instead of the fashion-plates, with their full directions as to the changes in costume, a doll was dressed in Paris in the height of the prevailing mode, and sent by the " regular fast-sailing packet" to the mantua-makers in New York as a model to be copied.

As early as 1712, these dolls, dressed in the fashion of the period, were sent from Paris to London ; it was by this means that the changes of fashion were introduced before steam opened up the facilities for constant intercourse. We have a vivid remembrance of the old age of one of these fashion-dolls which had been sent from Paris to a fashionable mantua-maker in New York. When the dress had changed as to style, the dressmaker sold the doll to one of her customers, and " Miss Nancy Dawson" passed into the obscurity of humbler dollies who had never been sent as ministers plenipotentiary from the court of fashion.

7

Let us hope that in time women will not be subservient to the dictates of French modistes, but will select for themselves that which is healthful, becoming, tasteful, and simple.

To spend so much thought, time, and money upon the garments which we wear is a wasteful expenditure of time which might be better employed, and of money which might be better spent, especially if the result is the cumbersome and tasteless dress which women, in some seasons, have been led by fashion to adopt.

We here insert an extract from a historian of the Dutch in New York, which may be of interest in this connection :

"Every household had from two to six spinning-wheels for wool and flax, whereon the women of the family expended every leisure moment. Looms, too, were in common use, and piles of homespun cloth and snow-white linen attested the industry of the active Dutch maidens.

"Hoards of home-made stuffs were thus accumulated in the settlement, sufficient to last until a distant generation. . . .

"There was a good deal of wealth and intelligence here, and the necessities of their occupations did not prevent them from devoting time to mental, social, and religious matters. . . .

"The Dutch ladies wore no bonnets, but brushed their hair back from their foreheads and covered it with a close-fitting cap; over this they wore, in the open air, hoods of silk or taffeta, elaborately quilted. Their dress consisted of a jacket of cloth or silk and a number of short petticoats of every conceivable number or material, quilted in fanciful figures. . . . The wardrobe of a fashionable lady usually contained from ten to twenty of these, of silk, camlet, cloth, drugget, India stuff, and a variety of other materials, all closely quilted, and usually costing from five to thirty dollars each.

"They wore blue, or red, or green worsted stockings of their own knitting, with parti-colored clocks and high-heeled shoes.

"Considerable jewelry was in use among them in the shape of rings and brooches. Gold neck and fob chains were unknown. The few who owned watches attached them to chains of silver or steel, though girdle chains of silver or gold were much in vogue among the most fashionable belles. For necklaces they wore strings of gold beads."

In an autobiography of Mrs. Sigourney, she describes the food and clothing of children in New England during her childhood. Her description agrees in every particular with the manner in which the children on Long Island were trained during the same period. We prefer to give her words, rather than our own, for we could not reproduce a more perfect picture of household life such as it was with us than that which she shows us of her New England home :

"The diet allotted to children in those days was judicious and remarkably simple. Well-fermented and thoroughly baked bread of the mingled Indian and rye meal, and rich, creamy milk were among its prominent elements. I never tasted any bread so sweet as those large loaves, made in capacious iron basins. Light, wheaten biscuits, delicious gold-colored butter, always made in the family, custards, puddings, delicate pastry, succulent vegetables and fruits, gave sufficient variety of condiment to the repasts allotted us. The extreme regularity and early hours for meals—twelve being always the time for dinner —obviated in a great measure the necessity of intermediates, and saved that perpetual eating into which some little ones fall until the digestive powers are impaired in their incipient action. If sport, or exercise in the garden, led me to desire refreshment between the regular meals, a piece of brown bread was given me without butter, and I was content. Candies and confectionery were strangers to us primitive people. The stomach, that keystone of this mysterious frame, not being unduly stimulated, no morbid tastes were formed, and no undue mixture of saccharine or oleaginous matter caused effervescence and dis-

ease.   The name of dyspepsia, with its offspring stretching out
like the line of Banquo, I never heard in early years.   Spices
were untasted, unless it might be a little nutmeg in the sauce of
our nice puddings, which I still counted as a foe, because it
'bit my tongue.'   When seated at the table I was never asked
whether I liked or disliked aught that appeared there.   It never
occurred to me whether I did or not.   I never doubted but what
I should be fed ' with food convenient for me.'   I was helped
to what was deemed proper, and there was never any necessity,
like poor Oliver Twist, to ask for more.   It did not appear to
me, from aught that I saw or heard, that the pleasure of eating
was one of the main ends of existence.

   " My costume was simple, and unconstrained by any ligature
to impede free circulation. Stays, corsets, or frames of whalebone
I never wore.   Frocks, low in the neck, and with short sleeves,
were used both winter and summer.   Houses had neither furnaces nor grates for coal, and churches had no means of being
warmed, but I can not recollect suffering inconvenience from
cold.   Thick shoes and stockings were deemed essential, and
great care was taken that I should never go with wet feet.
Clear, abundant wood-fires sparkled in every chimney, and I
was always directed, in cold seasons, to sit with my feet near
them until thoroughly warmed, before retiring for the night."

CHAPTER XVI.

WEDDINGS among the old Dutch people were celebrated at the house of the bride's parents. There may
have been instances in which the ceremony was performed in the church, but we have never known of
such. It was not until some twenty years ago that a
bridal party assembled in the church for the marriage
service. It is now quite common.

Furman says that the marriage fees were not the
perquisite of the minister, but were paid over to the
consistory. Dominie Solyns paid 78 guilders, 10 stivers,
as the sum which he had received officially for this
duty, this being the amount of fourteen marriage fees.
In the account of subscriptions received for the building
of the first church in 1660, we find an item which is ex-
plained by this fact, viz.; "43 guilders for marriage fees."

As far back as we have any personal recollection of
the matter, or as we have been informed by others, the
service was performed early in the evening, in the presence of the immediate relatives of the bride and groom ;
the invited guests assembled soon after.

A table was bountifully spread with very substantial
refreshments, and as no expense was spared to entertain
the wedding guests, the good things prepared were in
characteristic abundance. The elderly people left at a

comparatively early hour, but the younger guests continued the festivity until after midnight, as they are wont to do even at the present day.

The office of groomsman and bridesmaid was not the sinecure then that it is now ; they were expected to assist at the serving of the supper, to carve, to see that the guests were all helped, to entertain the company, and to feel a certain responsibility that everything went off well. The cutting and giving the guests the bridal cake was also the work of the bridesmaids, and the guests all expected to be provided with a piece to take home.

The custom of having a large circle of friends and relatives present at a wedding was very general, particularly if the choice of the young couple about to be married was acceptable to the parents. It was considered as the proper time for rejoicing and merry-making, for the Dutch, although quiet and sober in their family life, were not as austere as their Puritan neighbors ; they were very willing upon the proper occasion to throw open their houses for festivity and rejoicing, and a wedding was considered very emphatically as the proper time.

There were no wedding journeys undertaken by the bridal party whose marriage was celebrated before steam made traveling easy and opened so many places of resort. The day after the wedding the bridal party went, accompanied by the bridesmaids and groomsmen, to the house of the parents of the groom, where the bride was welcomed by her husband's parents, and where it was very frequently the case that the festivity of the previous day was continued.

A great deal of visiting followed upon the occasion

of a wedding ; at one time it was customary for the bride and groom to drive about on horseback, the bride upon a pillion ; the happy couples of a later date paid and exchanged their visits in a chaise. They were invited by their relatives and friends, and entertained at tea-drinkings and evening suppers in a continued round of gayety.

It was customary for the bride to wear her bridal dress to church on the Sunday following her marriage. The young couple were accompanied to church by the bridesmaids and groomsmen, who took seats with them.

Some rich and handsome fabric was chosen for the bridal dress, which could be worn upon other occasions, this practical view of everything showing itself among our Dutch ancestors even in their festivities. We refer now to the customs of the last century. As bright colors and rich fabrics were worn by gentlemen as well as by ladies in that age, it was considered a delicate compliment to the bride for the groom to recognize her taste in dress by adopting the same color in his. In the wedding dress to which we have referred as being worn in 1780, the petticoat of the bride and the waistcoat of the groom were from the same piece of blue satin damask.

To the full bridal dress of a more recent date orange blossoms and the bridal veil are indispensable, and white must be the only color worn by the bride.

The engagement ring which the maiden expects from her lover in this age was not looked for in the last century, or it was left optional as to whether it should be given or not. A gold ring was generally a wedding gift, although it was not used in the ceremony of the Dutch Church.

CHAPTER XVII.

FUNERALS.

THERE are certain fragrant flowers which have become associated with funerals from their constant use on such occasions ; we are sometimes inclined to turn away from them for the painful memories they bring. Still, the custom of placing floral offerings upon the coffin and on the grave is a very beautiful one, and it is to be regretted that, from their indiscriminate profusion, the sentiment that might be expressed is so frequently lost. Equally at the funeral of the aged saint and the little child, we find the cross, the anchor, the harp, or the crown, and these emblems of love, hope, faith, and victory have nearly lost their significance in their promiscuous use, and are too often objects of display rather than touching tributes of affection. But the practice of sending flowers as gifts *in memoriam* at the time of a funeral is so touching and beautiful that, even when carried to excess, it is like some lovely but untrimmed vine, over which we express regret, not at its existence and growth, but rather that its wasteful luxuriance has not been pruned and trained, so as to be kept within its proper limit.

There was a custom which formed part of the fu-

neral preparations of the last century that was as baneful
as this practice of sending flowers is beautiful, and
which grew in proportionate rankness, like the noxious
growth of some poisonous weed. We have reference to
the amount of liquor provided by the family of the deceased at the time of a funeral. It seems almost incredible now that it should ever have been done, so entirely
has the custom passed away, leaving nothing but the
tradition of its existence and the corroborating bills
among the items of funeral expenses.

When the country was thinly settled, and friends and
relatives came from a distance to pay the last tribute of
affection to the dead, some refreshment was necessary
for them, and thence arose the custom of setting a table
and preparing a bountiful supply of provisions for such
as lived at a long distance. There was the free use of
liquor on all occasions at that period ; the decanter was
always filled on the sideboard, and it was considered
inhospitable not to offer it to visitors. We need not
wonder, then, that it was abundantly offered on wedding
and funeral occasions.

The following is an exact copy of a bill of certain
funeral expenses of a wealthy and highly respected resident of Flatbush, whose death occurred in 1789 :

An account of Funeral Expenses of P. L——, Esq.
  20 gallons good wine.
  2   "   spirits.
  1 large loaf of lump sugar.
  ½ doz. nutmegs.
  ½ gros long pipes.
  4 lbs. tobacco.
  1½ dozen of black silk handkerchiefs.
  6 loaves of bread.

Probably the bread referred to was wheat bread purchased for the occasion ; the rye bread was baked in the house at the same time that the other provisions were made ready.

It is certainly significant of a marked change for the better that while in 1789 such articles were deemed absolutely necessary and respectable, not a single item on that bill would be called for on a similar occasion by those of the same social status at the present date.

It has been said that the very choicest wines were held in reserve for funeral purposes.

The funeral services were never held in the church in the past century, and rarely until after the middle of this; but always at the late residence of the deceased.

Upon the occasion of a death in the family, the sexton of the church was immediately sent for, and to him was committed the business of inviting the friends to the funeral. He went from house to house and personally gave an invitation to every family. If any one was known to be seriously ill, the distant approach of the sexton, as he proceeded on his melancholy errand, was as certain an indication of death as if he had already announced the summons to the funeral.

The news of a death and the invitation to friends at a distance were generally given through the assistance of the neighbors. Two or three young men volunteered for this purpose, and divided between themselves the routes through the different county towns to which they were requested to drive and deliver the announcement.

After the funeral a notice of the death was inserted in the weekly newspapers, there being no daily papers taken by the people in the country. The daily distribution of morning and evening papers is part of the progress of the last twenty years.

There was at that time no undertaker prepared to furnish all the requisites for a funeral. The cabinet-maker was called upon to make a coffin, and he came to measure the dead for that purpose. Some woman in the neighborhood was expected to make the shroud, if it was not in the house, ready made years before, as was often the case. This may seem remarkable, but it is nevertheless strictly true that most persons having reached middle life felt it to be their duty to see that they had a shroud made, so that in case of their sickness or sudden death their family would not be obliged to have it made in haste for them. We have known persons to have a shroud laid by for so many years that it became so discolored and yellow by age as to have it thrown aside and replaced by another.

The announcement of death in a house by a drapery hung upon the door-bell, of white for a child and of black for a grown person, was not customary until a recent period.

Funerals were very generally attended, to show respect to the deceased, so that the houses were on these occasions much crowded. On the morning of the funeral, chairs were carried in from the houses of the families living near, to seat the numerous relatives and friends who were expected. Long after the services of the undertaker provided the necessities in other directions, the chairs were supplied by the neighbors, for the convenient camp-chairs which now it is a portion of the undertaker's duty to provide were then not known.

Neither the casket nor the oblong burial-case, with its heavy silver handles and rich mounting, was then in use. The coffins of those primitive days were more in the shape of the human frame, broad at the shoulders and tapering toward the foot. The pall-bearers, of whom there were eight, and who were usually friends of the same age as the deceased, carried the coffin out to the hearse, and from the hearse to the grave ; now, the coffins being so much heavier, that work is performed by paid assistants. In case of the death of elderly persons, white linen scarfs containing three yards of linen were presented to the pall-bearers. When scarfs were not presented, the gift consisted either of black gloves or black silk handkerchiefs. The clergyman officiating at the burial service, and the family physician who had been in attendance, were included in the number of those who received these gifts.

Not only were the ladies of the family clothed in crape upon the death of a friend, but the gentlemen wore heavy bands of crape upon their hats. This was not, as now, merely a close-fitting band, but, after encircling the hat from crown to brim, a long piece of the same was left hanging to reach almost to the shoulder. As time passed on this was shortened by pinning it into a fold at the back, which fold stood out at a right angle to the hat, and, finally cutting off all superfluous length, it appeared only as the band of crape at present worn.

Interments were usually made the third day after death, as the preserving of the body on ice was not then practiced. A bier was used to carry the dead when the funeral was not too far from the village graveyard.

There was a strange, superstitious custom said to have been prevalent generations since. It has only survived in its practice among the colored people in this neighborhood at the present day. All the looking-glasses in the house were carefully covered at the time of a death in the family. It is within the memory of those now living that this has been done.

There was another superstitious custom of which we have heard, but, as it was told by one who has since died at a great age, there is no means of ascertaining if it was very general, and how long ago it existed. For those who owned many hives of bees, it was usual, in case of a death in the family, to knock on the hives and inform the bees of the fact, "lest," said the narrator of this superstition, "the bees should leave."

It has been said, also, that a coffin was never placed near a mirror; but this may have been an individual rather than a general superstition. The diffusion of light and knowledge has driven these old notions skulking into the dark corners where they properly belong, and it is difficult now to trace them distinctly, even in their outlines.

CHAPTER XVIII.

DR. STRONG says that in 1698 a document was prepared containing certain laws and ordinances, among which were regulations and restrictions in regard to interments in the church, a practice which seems to have been quite general. Those whose friends could afford to incur the extra expense connected with this privilege were laid to rest beneath the church in which they had worshiped.

"This accounts," says Dr. Strong, "for the fact that the graveyard contains so few tombstones of ancient date."

The custom of burying the dead under the church was common formerly in Holland as well as in England; the Dutch settlers had therefore a precedent in the usage of their fathers for placing their dead within the inclosure of their place of worship, but they had also an additional reason for doing so in the security it afforded them at that period from molestation; the Indians were said, we know not with how much truth, not infrequently to disturb the graves.

There are very few tombstones which bear the date of Revolutionary times, because this part of the country was in a very disturbed state, and it was difficult to obtain the brown stone slabs which were then used.

Long ago the consistory refused permission to disturb the ground immediately surrounding the church, on account of the bones which were disinterred in doing so, for the graves are far more numerous than the gravestones in this old burial-place, and the irregular surface of the ground indicates many an unmarked grave.

More recently the consistory resolved to refuse permission for interments in any part of the ground; exception was only to be made in case of elderly persons whose relatives were sleeping there, or for whom vacant spaces had been reserved at their own request.

A substantial iron railing has replaced the wooden fence which formerly inclosed the graveyard, and it is kept in good order. The weeds are not allowed to grow, or the grass to cover the mounds in tangled masses, as is sometimes the case in old burial-grounds.

This churchyard has been enlarged from time to time, as the passing away of successive generations required more room, but it would not now be desirable to change its limits, as most of the Flatbush families have purchased plots in Greenwood Cemetery.

There are no monuments in this graveyard expressive of a desire for ostentatious display, and no inflated epitaphs upon the old tombstones exaggerating the virtues of the deceased. It is noticeable that a large majority of these tombstones only give the name and age of those who sleep beneath; sometimes this is so worded as to express a belief in immortality, or to the inscription is added some simple expression of faith and hope. There is a certain solemnity about these old Dutch words, a dignity that is impressive; it may be the reflection of the graves which they overshadow, or it may be that the silence of the long years since they were the written or the spoken language invests them with the somber grace and tenderness which characterizes the record of that which has for ever passed away.

" Hier leyt begraven " (" Here lies buried ") are the simple words that precede the name, and then the age follows ; or the wording is this: " Hier leydt het stoffelyk deel —— " (" Here lie the earthly remains of —— "). Sometimes the expression is, " Hier rust het lighaam " (" Here rests the body ") ; or it is thus: " In den Heere ontslapen " (" Sleeping in the Lord ").

These words, simple and unaffected, seem a pleasing contrast to the pompous eulogies and epitaphs which are so often found engraven on tombs.

" Gedachtenis," in remembrance, from gedacht, thought, is a word which frequently appears on these headstones.

The birth and death of a young girl are thus expressed :

Zy kwam in de waereld ——. Zy es wader uyt verhuysden ——. She came into the world (date); she removed to another home (date).

The ugly skeleton heads and cross bones which may be found in some old graveyards are not found here, but, instead, upon nearly every stone are carved a head and wings, supposed to represent a cherub ; more crude and grotesque representations it would be difficult to find.

Time, for so many years weaving through long summers her green coverlet over the beds of the silent sleepers, has also been slowly hiding these hideous faces under her mosses and lichens, until they seem to appeal, through their very indistinctness, to our forbearance. So we will not criticise the skill that carved, but acknowledge the love that decorated with tenderness, a memorial to the husband or to the "huysvrouw" who here in "den Heere ontslapen."

Some of the inscriptions are scarcely legible from the crumbling of the brown stone and the growth of moss and lichens upon the lettering.

The following are copies of the Dutch headstones. Should mistakes appear, they must be attributed to the defacement of time upon the yielding surface of the gravestones :

Hier leyt begraven het lighaem von Hendrick Suydam, overleden den 9de July 1805 oude zynde 73 jaren, 3 m., en 20 d.

Hier is begraven het lighaem von Adrieantie Hubbard Huysvrouw von de overleden Adriaen Voorhees, overleden de 23ste dag von July 1810. In het 80 Jaar haar levens.

Hier leyt het lichaem von Gerrit Lefferts overleden den 14 May 1773. . . . [illegible].

Hier leght t' lighaam von Rebecca Emons huysvrouw von Hendrick Suydam geboren 1729. Sept. . . . overleden Oct 1797.

Hier leyt Begraven t' lighaam von Englebert Lott, Sen. Overleyden de 17 daag von Nov. 1779. . . . Out synde 60 jaar.

Hier leydt begraven het lighaam van Marytie Ditmas huysvrouw von de overleden Englebert Lott, Sen. overleyden de 27 dag von April 1797.

Hier leyt het Lichaam von Abraham Lott Overleden op den 29 July 1754. In t' 70. . . .

Hier leyt begraven het Lichaam von Hendrick Suydam overleden den 16 May 1792 oudt zinde 60 Jaaren 3 maanden en 7 dagen.

Hier rust het lighaam von Maria Amermon huysvrouw von Hendrick Suydam, geboren May 29, 1755 overleden Nov. 14 1795 out synde 40 jaaren 5 maanden, 16 dagen.

Hier Rust het lighaam von Leffert Martense geboren in het jaer 1725 den 17ste Janunare. Overleden den 6de September 1802 oudt synde 77 Jaaren 7 maanden de 20 dagen.

Hier leyt het lighaam von Hilletie Van der Bilt huysvrouw von Leffert Martense overleden 26 Sept anno 1779 oude zynde 58 jaaren.

Hier leydt het lighaam von Adriantie Ryder, Huysvrouw von Adrian Martense Es geboren in het jaar 1747 den 2 Feb. Es overleden den 27 May 1776.

Hier leyt begraven het lichaam van Joris Martense, Geboren Mey 27st 1724 O. S. Overleden Mey 23st 1791 oudt zynde 66 Jaren 11 maanden, en 15 dagen.

Hier Lyt het lighaam van Rem Martense Geboren Den 12st von Dec' 1695. Gestorven den 14de von June 1760. Out zynde 64 jaaren 5 maanden en 21 dagen.

Hier rust het lighaam van Garret Martense geboren den 30 Jannuwary 1745 overleden den 1 June 1808 oudt synde 63 jaaren 4 maanden en 2 dagen.

Hier leyt begraven het lichaam von Adrian Martense geboren den 9de December A. D. 1742 overleden den 13 March A. D. 1817 oudt zynde 71 jaaren 3 maanden 7 dagen.

Hier leyt het lichaam van Jannetie Monfoort huysvrouw von Adrian Martense overleden den 28 dagh Oct. A. D. 1804 en es geboren den 27 dagh Dec. A. D. 1750.

Hier leyt het lichaem von Joris Martense Overleden den 9de dagh von Nov. A. D. 1804 en es geboren de 8de dagh von Maert A. D. 1737.

Hier rust het stoffelick diel von Philipus de son von Johannes & Jannetie Ditmas overleden den 20 October 1797 oude zinde een jaer ses maanden 13 dagen.

Hier leydt Begraven het lichaem von Jeremyas Von Der Bilt overleden den 12d dag von November 1785 oudt zynde 70 jaer.

Tot gedachtenis van Leffert Lefferts die geboren es den 20ste February 1723 en overleden . . . . oude zynde 77 jaaren 7 maanden 4 daagen.

Hier leyt het lichaam von Catharina VanderVeer Huys-

vrouw von Jacob Lefferts. Zy es overleden den 2ᵈ Nov. en t'
yaer 1773. . . . [illegible].

Hier leydt het stoffelyk deel von Adriantie Lefferts dochter
von Jacob Lefferts. Haar ziel zy hemels waarts heeft Begraven
Zy leyt hier zonder pyn De ziel is in haar rust. Zy kwam in
de waereld den 3 Maert 1701. Zy es wader uyt verhuystden 2
Miey 1775. Memento Mori. U. V. S.

Hier leyt begraven het lighaam van Cornelius Vanderveer.
Geboren den 5ᵈᵉ Dec 1731 O. S. Overleden den 13 de Feb.
1801 oude zynde 72 jaaren 1 maand en 21 dagen.

Hier leyt Begraven het lighaam von Jannetie Wyckoff, Huysvrouw von Cornelius Vanderveer overleden den 31 Oct 1774
oude zynde 73 jaer . . . . [illegible].

Tot Gedachtenis van Femmetia Vanderveer Overleden den
3ᵈ June 1801 oude synde 79 jaaren 7 maanden en 3 dagen.

Hier leyt begraven het Lichaam von Cornelius Vanderveer
Overleden de 22ˢᵗᵉ Jan, anno 1782 Oudt zynde 85 jaren . . . .

Hier leyt het lighaam von Gilijam Cornel geboren den 23ˢᵗᵉ
Augustus 1679 Gestorven den 1ˢᵗᵉ Augustus 1754 Oude zynde
74 jaren 11 maanden en 9 dagen.

Tot godachtenis von Jacobus Van Deventer overleden den
14ᵈᵉ Nov, 1799 oude zynde 67 jaaren 5 maanden en 24 daagen.

Hier leyt begraven het lichaam von Michael Stryker geboren
den 1 March 1725. O. S. overleyden den 26 September 1807
oude zynde 84 jaaren 6 maande 21 daagen.

Hier leyt begraven het lighaam vou Johanna Stryker huysvrouw von de overleden Michael Stryker geboren den 13 Feb.
1733 O. S. overleden den 1 Oct. 1807 oudt zynde 74 jaaren, 7
maanden, en 18 daagen.

Hier leyt begraven het lighaam von Femmetia Schenck huysvrouw von Peter Stryker geboren den 29 July 1740 Overleden
den 14 Dec 1814 oude zynde 75 jaaren 4 maanden en 16
daagen.

Hier leyt begraven het lighaam von Peter Stryker geboren
den 22 December 1730 overleden den 14 December 1814 oud
zynde 84 yaaren 11 maanden en 22 daagen.

Hier leyt het lighaam von Seytie Suydam huysvrouw von

de overleden Evert Hegeman overleden den 11 July 1802 oude 76 jaaren 9 maanden en 13 dagen.

Hier leydt het Lichaam von Jan Leffertse Jun. overleyden den 28 October, Anno 1776 oude zynde 19 jaer 10 maanden. 13 dagen.

Hier rust het lichaam van Jan Lefferts in den Heere ont-slaapen October 20 1776 oude synde 57 jaaren 7 maanden en 4 dagen.

Hier est begraven het lichaam van Sara Martense huysvrouw van Jan Lefferts overleden in het 36 jaar . . . . [illegible].

Hier leyt het Lichaam van Peter Lefferts overleden den 13 March 1774 oude zynde 94 jaaren.

Hier rust het lichaam van Peter Lefferts geboren Dec 27. 1753 in den Heere ontslapen Oct 7. 1791. Voorbeeldig in syn leven heest hy de welvoort van Landt, en Kerk bevorderd: en in syn laaste uuren (die hy met lydzaamheyd heest vervult) syn geist Godt aanbevolen in de hope van een salige opstandinge.

The following is the inscription upon the brown stone over the grave of Dominie Rubel :

Tot gedachtenis van Joh' Casp' Rubel V. D. M. Geboren den 6 Maert O. S. 1719. Overleden den 19 Meii 1797.

In "Furman's Notes" we read that there is in this graveyard a tombstone of some Helen Vanderbilt, the wife of a Martense, which cost £10, a sum at that time equal to the year's salary of the county clerk of Kings County. We have found nothing that answers to this description, unless it be the following :

Hier leyt het lichaam von Hilletie VanD'Bilt, huysvrouw van Leffert Martense overleden den 26 Sep' Anno 1779 oude synde 58 jaar.

This is, however, only a neat granite headstone, with nothing to indicate that it was costly, unless it might be that, at that period, gray granite slabs were rare. All the old tombstones are of brown stone ; some of

the older ones slowly disintegrate, so that it is difficult
to trace the lettering; others split lengthwise. Time
has set his strongest workman here; the winter raindrops lodge in the crevices, and the hammer of the
frost king enters after them. These old memorials will
not much longer withstand the defacement; they are
yielding to Time the conqueror, more slowly, but none
the less surely, than those whose names they vainly
strive to commemorate. We give a few inscriptions in
English of a later date.

There are four large white marble tombs in this old
graveyard, two of which are over the graves of John
Vanderbilt and his wife, and two are over the graves of
his daughter and son-in-law, N. R. Cowenhoven.

On the tomb of John Vanderbilt, who died in 1796,
in the fifty-seventh year of his age, is the following inscription :

He was a merchant of distinguished probity, a real patriot,
an affectionate relative, a sincere friend, and a worthy man.
Blessed with affluence, he displayed a spirit of munificence in
promoting the interests of his country, of religion, and virtue.
The moderation and conciliatory disposition which accompanied
and conducted his virtues secured him through life an esteem
almost unrivaled, and rendered his death a great loss to the
public, and to his family irreparable.

On the tomb of N. R. Cowenhoven is the following
inscription :

Sacred to the memory of Nicholas R. Cowenhoven, Esquire.
Born April 14, 1768. Departed this life Aug. 25, 1809, aged
41 years, 4 months, 11 days.

> Calm conscience first his soul surveyed
> And recollected toils endeared his shade,
> Till Nature called him to the general doom,
> And Virtue's sorrows dignified his tomb.

Beside this is the tomb of his wife, on which the following is inscribed :

In memory of Catharine Cowenhoven, the beloved wife of Nicholas R. Cowenhoven, of Brooklyn, by whom her earthly remains are here deposited. She was born Oct. 3, 1768. Amiable in manners, gentle in deportment, affectionate to her relatives, and kind to all, her virtues acquired her universal esteem. She long and patiently endured a complication of bodily infirmities, and exchanged a mortal existence for an immortal life Aug. 23, 1801.

Here lies the body of Philip Nagle, Esq. Born 1ˢᵗ January O. S. 1717, and died the 11 of May N. S. 1797, aged 80 years and 4 months.

> Behold and see as you pass by,
> As you are now so once was I.
> As I am now you soon will be :
> Prepare for death and follow me.

The name of Philip Nagle appears frequently in Dr. Strong's history ; there are none of that name at present in Flatbush.

To the memory of John Hegeman, who departed this life the 16ᵗʰ of Sept. 1769, aged 66 years. This stone was erected by his friend Andrew Gautier as a testimony of his regard.

Explanatory of the above, we remember to have been told, when a child, that John Hegeman was never married, and left his property to his friend Gautier, who, however, only reserved sufficient to erect this stone "as a testimony of his regard," and returned the remainder to the brothers and sisters of the deceased, who were, he thought, in need of it. It was an unselfish act, to which we would pay the tribute of this notice.

Beyond the western boundary of the graveyard,

separated by the high fence, is a small inclosure not much larger than the grave itself, where lies buried a colored woman by the name of Flora, who lived to a great age in the family of Mrs. A. L. Loyd. The following inscription is upon the tombstone :

Sacred to the memory of Flora, a colored woman, who died Jan. 5, 1826, aged 104 years. Strong faith . . . trusting in her Saviour . . . [illegible].

Two other colored persons, Diana and Cato, are buried in this inclosure, who were also domestics in the same family.

A small building, known as the guard-house, formerly stood on the northern boundary of the graveyard. Near the close of the last century, or about the beginning of this, some of the graves had been disturbed in this and the neighboring villages, and in consequence great excitement had prevailed ; and an act of the Legislature was passed in 1796, authorizing the inhabitants of Flatbush to establish a night watch. For this reason a building was erected, in which watch was kept for a time over new-made graves.

In some of the adjacent towns, instead of a guard-house, such as was built in Flatbush, a structure was erected which required a dozen men in order to raise it, and this was placed in turn over each newly made grave.

After a time all cause for alarm in this direction abated ; the guard-house was then diverted from the use for which it was originally constructed, and used to hold the bier on which coffins were carried.

Some aged colored people, who were supported by the town, were at one time allowed to live in this building, there being no almshouse in Flatbush until 1830. It would seem a melancholy fate to live in a church-yard with a bier in the house !

Subsequently it was converted into an engine-house for the protection of the first Flatbush fire-engine, before the present house of the company was built.

CHAPTER XIX.

ALTHOUGH, like most other country towns in this State, there are seasons when cases of fever and ague occur in Flatbush, yet it would be difficult to find a town of the same size in which so many persons have attained a great age. In 1876 there were five aged couples living south of the church, each individual being over seventy years of age ; these had always enjoyed good health, were all born in Flatbush, and had always lived there. One old gentleman and his wife living in this town had each of them attained the age of ninety-four years, when the wife died, apparently of old age ; the old gentleman is still vigorous.

Looking back through many years, we can not recollect a family in which we do not remember an aged person as being one of its members.

We can recall by name forty-nine persons whom we knew personally, each one of whom reached the age of seventy years, and many of them were more than eighty years old at the time of their death. They were all old residents of the town, and were born, lived, and died here.

8

The physicians in practice some fifty years ago were Dr. Adrian Vandervccr and Dr. John Zabriskie. These were succeeded by Dr. John L. Zabriskie, son of Dr. John Zabriskie, Dr. II. L. Bartlett, and Dr. T. Ingraham. The adjoining towns were included in their practice, there being for many years no resident physician except in Flatbush, this village being central in the county and also most thickly populated.

In Revolutionary times and after that period the physicians were Dr. Samper, Dr. Van Buren, Dr. Sage, and Dr. Schoonmaker. Among a file of old papers we find some bills, which we give as being curious, and showing what was paid for professional skill at the dates given.

The bills were evidently those of physicians sent for from New York in consultation with the village doctor. As the country road was at the date of visit unpaved from Fulton Ferry to the village, and as the wide river running between was crossed in a skiff or a rowboat, the bills for professional services were certainly not extravagant.

Mr. ———, Deceased, his heirs,
To Dr. Benjamin Lindner, Debt.

£   s.   d.

1767. Feb. 28th.   To Visiting to Flatbush........ 2 10 0

    April 23.   Received the above sum in full by me,
Benjamin Lindner.

Feb. 28th, 1767.
    Mr. ———, Dr.

       To Dr. Peter Middleton, New York.   £   s.   d.

       A visit to Flatbush..................... 3 4 0

       Received the above in full of all demands,
Peter Middleton.

Mrs. ——

To A. Bainbridge, Dr.

Sept. 1779.

Visiting your husband, and consultation with   £ *s. d.*

Doctor Samper........................ .... 1 17 4

Madam: Above you have your account, hope it will prove agreeable.

I am yr Humble Servt,

A. Bainbridge.

A bill for medicine and attendance from August 14, 1789, to April 17, 1790, in which twenty-eight items and visits are mentioned, amounts to £4 9s. The date of each visit and the amount due on each mark the difference between the custom of the medical faculty at the period in which this old time-stained bill was presented and that of the brief summing up of the bills "for professional services" to-day. There seems to have been no regular price for each visit, but the amount charged was regulated by the requirement of the occasion. It is also in marked contrast to the present treatment of diseases that this bill is principally made up of items such as this :

	£	*s.*	*d.*
To bleeding in the arm.....................	0	2	0
To a purge...............................	0	2	0
To an emetic.............................	0	2	0

Etc., etc.

Not only are the healthfulness of the village and the longevity of the inhabitants noticeable, but the moral sentiment of the community is such as conduces to the prevalence of virtue and good order. Great crimes in the past were unknown. There is no record of a single instance of deliberate murder, or of homicide, among the old settlers in Flatbush or their descendants, through a period of a hundred or a hundred and fifty years.*

Filial love and obedience have always been shown, and the family life has been peaceable and harmonious. The standard of domestic virtue has been so high, and the marriage relation so honored and respected, that we can not recall one single instance of separation or legal divorce, and we know of no record of such through the annals of the past century.

Between man and wife there has been the exhibition of love and respect, the display of mutual confidence and kindness, and that deep sympathy for each other in all the cares and anxieties of life which makes the marriage relation a realization of what God intended man and woman should be to each other.

* Says Thompson, in his " History of Long Island," published 1843, speaking of Kings County : " In 1786 a man was hanged in this county for forgery, and was the last person executed in a community so populous, which, considering the mixed character of the inhabitants, and their proximity to one of the greatest commercial cities in the world, is quite a phenomenon in the history of morals, while the more distant and proverbially peaceful county of Suffolk has exhibited five capital executions in the same period."

The writer of a historical sketch, published 1840, says : " E. Hubbard, Esq., of Flatlands, states that he has held the office of justice of the peace therein for more than twelve years, and during that period has transacted most of the judicial business for Flatlands, Flatbush, New Utrecht, and Gravesend, and during the whole time he has scarcely had a dozen trials, and only two suits at law in which a jury was demanded ; that another gentleman held the office of justice in the town of Gravesend for eight years, and during that period there was but one trial by jury, and even in the case alluded to the difference was compromised by the parties before the jury had delivered their verdict into court. Such a peaceable disposition in the people is highly creditable and honorable to them."

It speaks well for the religious and moral sense of the community that entire peace and harmony in the household were taken for granted ; it was the normal condition of things. The reverse would have been commented upon as something of unusual occurrence.

There have been aged couples who have lived together through their silver to the date of their golden wedding whose love and tenderness for each other have been beautiful beyond expression ; there is even an element of pathos in their feeble endeavors to assist each other in the feebleness of old age, and a protest against the charge of fickleness when such a feeling can thus outlive all outward change.

The business men of the town have been characterized by honesty when intrusted with public funds, and fidelity in the discharge of their duties, together with that steadfastness of purpose, that stability, and that strict adherence to what they consider right, which were characteristic of their Holland ancestors. Their character was made of strong material and it has worn well.

As in every country town there have been feuds between separate families, and party feeling has at times raged to an extent altogether disproportionate to its cause, yet it has never culminated in violence, and by those not immediately interested it has been the subject for a smile rather than for reproof.

In this emphatic statement of the morality of this people, and of their freedom from the commission of any crime for more than a hundred years, we have reference solely to the descendants of the Dutch settlers.

The old Dutch Church has reason to rejoice over the impression she has made upon the religious sentiment of the community, and the training which has led her children into the ways of honor and virtue through so many generations.

If there are those who think that this assertion of the morality of the Dutch is from one who is strongly biased in their favor, we would say in reply that it is substantiated by the characteristics accorded to this nation for two hundred years.

Says Brodhead, speaking of the Dutch in the Netherlands in 1648 : "The purity of morals and decorum of manners for which the Dutch have always been conspicuous may, perhaps, be most justly ascribed to the happy influence of their women.

". . . With all their economy and thrift, the Dutch were neither mean nor sordid. . . . The wealth which their industry gained was liberally expended in acts of humanity and charity. . . . Of all the moral qualities which distinguished the Dutch, the most remarkable was their honesty," etc.

We take pleasure in recording the statement of this historian as to the character of the Dutch as a race, for it corroborates what we have said of them as a community.

CHAPTER XX.

NEARLY all the landed proprietors in Flatbush are those to whom the titles of their farms have been transmitted for several generations, dating in many cases from the settlement of the Dutch on Long Island.

Now the land is passing out of the hands of its former owners, the old names are disappearing, and the descendants of the first settlers are comparatively few. As long as it was possible to do so, the landowners retained their farms as such ; they were not anxious to cut up their beautiful fields into city lots, or to widen the green lanes and country roads into dusty avenues and wide boulevards.

The southern borders of Flatbush bound the towns on which the ocean waves measure the rise and fall of the tides ; toward the north lies the ridge of hills that long kept back the ebb and flow of the tide of human life in the adjoining city. In past years Flatbush slept as quietly between the two as if the waves of the one could no more reach it than could the waves of the other. But the separating hills have been leveled, and the village has been awakened by the noise of approaching voices. The tide of increasing population within the city boundary has risen higher and higher, and has swept hitherward in larger and ever-increasing circles. The first ripple of this rising tide has touched our borders, and before long the sudden rush of some great wave will sweep away every trace of village life.

Anticipating these changes, we propose to show what the size and appearance of the village are at this present time, and to measure its growth since 1842, the time at which Dr. Strong's history was written. The map attached to that history gives us the streets and houses at that date ; following down the course of the main street through its whole extent, we shall be enabled to note the changes which have taken place.

We will also give such information as we have been enabled to obtain relative to the original ownership of the farms.

Beginning at the southern boundary of Flatbush, the first change we meet is that in the highway itself. In 1877 the road at the boundary between Flatlands and Flatbush was straightened, and the avenue was extended down to the bay.

The irregular curves upon an old road may not be convenient for business purposes, but its picturesqueness as it winds among grain-fields and orchards is entirely lost when it is converted into a straight, broad avenue, with nothing to relieve the monotony of its barren, dusty expanse. The level extension of the fields in southern Flatbush and Flatlands is very favorable to agriculture ; when these highly cultivated farms were seen through the trees by the wayside, they formed a pleasant rural landscape. This effect is almost lost in the change recently made ; it may have been necessary, but, remembering the quiet beauty of the old road, we hesitate to call the change an improvement. The straightening of the road also changed the door-yards of those living near it. At present both the old road and the new are open to travel ; sometimes the two run parallel, sometimes they blend, and sometimes they cross each other or are separated by the rough and unsightly hummocks left by the removal of the dividing fences.

The land called on Dr. Strong's map " The Little Flat" contained two dwelling houses ; that on the east side of the road is marked as the residence of J. Antonides : it has since been pulled down to give place to the modern structure which was built by the son of the occupant of the old house. This family are descendants of the Rev. Vincentius Antonides, who was sent out from the classis of Amsterdam, Holland, to preach in the Dutch towns on Long Island in 1704. After this generation this old and respected name will become extinct in Flatbush, as the present Mr. Antonides is the only male representative of the family.

On the west side of the road the old-fashioned farm-house is still standing which was occupied by Mr. Allgeo when Dr. Strong wrote his history. His father, old Mr. Allgeo, was a cabinet-maker by trade. The making of coffins was at that time part of a cabinet-maker's work, and it is said that many years before his death he made his own coffin and placed it in the loft of his workshop. This act was significant of the fact that death had no terror for him, and that he was in every sense prepared for the change which came to him at the end of a long and peaceful life. The long, snow-white hair of Mr. Allgeo, and a certain peacefulness in the expression of his countenance, reminded one of the pictures of Charles Wesley. Mr. Allgeo was born in 1766, of English parentage, in the city of Montreal. He married a daughter of Mr. Antonides, and settled in Flatbush. His grandson, Mr. William Henry Allgeo, still lives in this house and works this farm, which is the property of the heirs of the late Hon. John A. Lott.

On the same side of the road, north of this farm, stands a large house which was built by Mr. David Johnson. After the death of Mr. Johnson, his widow, a lady who was much respected in the village, removed to Brooklyn. She sold the property to Mr. Robert Fox, who afterward purchased Fisher's Island, in Long Island Sound, and the land again changed owners. It is at present the property of Mr. Giroux, president of the Lafayette Insurance Company.

Adjoining the garden of Mr. David Johnson was the residence of his father-in-law, old Mr. Parmalee, after whose death it was sold, and has since had various owners.

Newkirk Avenue was opened in 1868 upon this property, running from Flatbush Avenue westerly to the Coney Island road.

On the corner of this and Flatbush Avenue Mr. Charles Baxter, of Brooklyn, erected a neat dwelling-house in 1870.

North of this is a house upon the farm of Mr. Henry S. Ditmas, which has been through successive years rented to various persons.

Adjoining is the pleasant homestead of Mr. Henry S. Ditmas. It stands with the gable-end to the road, and, judging from its appearance, it must have been built in or before the year 1800, as it had before alteration many of the characteristics of that period. The front door was divided into an upper and a lower section, with the circular glasses known as " bulls'-eyes " in the upper half to light the broad hall. The slope of the roof also marks it as one of the Dutch houses of that period.

The Ditmas family are the descendants of Jan Janson, from Ditmarsum, in the Duchy of Holstein, who came to this country at an early period—about, or previous to, 1647. His wife was Aaltje Douws. This farm, originally the property of Douwe Ditmas, extended southward, embracing the land on which Mr. David Johnson built his house, before referred to ; northward it extended to the farm of the Suydam family. We have been informed that the former homestead of the Ditmas family was an old stone house, south of the present residence of Mr. Henry S. Ditmas.

The antiquated appearance of the house on the next farm north, the home of Mr. John Ditmas, proclaims at once its age. There are very few dwellings of this style still remaining in this county. This is a long, low house with a heavy roof and no front windows in the second story.

We look upon these venerable houses with respect akin to that which we entertain for old friends, particularly when, as in this case, and the residence of Mr. Henry S. Ditmas, these have been the homes of those who, through many generations, have been prominent in the church and respected in the town.

This house was formerly the homestead of the Suydam family. The farm, after the death of Jacobus Lott, an early settler, was purchased by Hendrick Suydam. The late Mrs. John Ditmas was the daughter of Mr. Andrew Suydam. Hendrick Rycke, the ancestor of the Suydam family, emigrated in 1663 from Suytdam, or Zuytdam, in Holland. He married Ida Jacobs, and set-

tled in Flatbush. Mr. John Ditmas built houses for
two of his sons adjoining his own : that at the south for
Mr. Abraham Ditmas, that at the north for Mr. Henry
Ditmas.

Returning to the southerly extremity of the village,
on the east side of the old Flatbush road, we find upon
Dr. Strong's map the large adjoining farms of Mr. Gerret and Mr. John C. Vanderveer. These were both
elderly gentlemen when Dr. Strong wrote his history,
and they furnished him with much information in regard to the War of the Revolution. They were brothers, and were wealthy and prominent men in this town,
and both reached an advanced age. Mr. Gerret Vanderveer had no sons. His daughter was the wife of Mr.
Simon Cortelyou. The old farm and homestead have
been sold for division among the heirs, and none of the
descendants of this family now live upon the place.

The Vanderveer family still occupy the house of Mr.
John C. Vanderveer, and cultivate the farm upon which
their ancestors settled. The present head of the family is the son of the old gentleman mentioned in Dr.
Strong's history. In May, 1878, he celebrated his gold-
en wedding, and is still happy in being able to say that
not a death has ever occurred in his family of children
and grandchildren.

Adjoining this venerable homestead, on the south,
is the house built for his son ; on the north is the house
built by Mr. Henry Vernon Vanderveer, also a grandson of old Mr. John C. Vanderveer, and son of Dr.
Adrian Vanderveer.

The Vanderveer property extended over a large tract
of land, and the family were among the oldest settlers
in Flatbush. They are the descendants of Cornelis

Janse Vanderveer, who emigrated to this country from Alkmaar, a free city on the North Holland Canal, in 1659. He bought a farm of Jan Janse in Flatbush, and settled there.

An old mill formerly stood on this farm in sight of the road. It was recently destroyed by fire. We give the history of it from the newspaper account published at that time.

"VANDERVEER'S MILL.

"Last Tuesday night [March 4, 1879], about a quarter before seven o'clock, a fire broke out in the 'Vanderveer Mill,' on the farm of Messrs. John Vanderveer & Sons, between Canarsie Lane and Pardaegat Pond. The spectacle of its destruction was such as has rarely been witnessed, and, mingled with the many people of the town who had gathered, were those who had been attracted for miles by the flames which lit the sky. The strong oak timbers stood up until the very last, while the shingles which covered it fell away, sending up showers of sparks, which, against the sky, looked like gold-dust sprinkled on a cloth of blue. Still the flames burned on till nothing remained but the bare timbers raising gaunt arms appealingly against destruction ; but the element did its work, and after a couple of hours had passed, that which it had taken years to build, and which had stood time's ravages for three quarters of a century, was laid in ruins.

"It was the first windmill erected on Long Island. It was completed in 1804, having been begun about three years before by John C. Vanderveer, father of the present owner. It was of immense strength, the main timbers being twenty-eight feet high and two and a half thick, hewn from trees grown on the farm. The carpenter was Abijah Baldwin, Joseph Mead being the millwright. John Oakey, Sr., father of the present Assisttant District Attorney, worked on it as an apprentice. It was four stories high, with a stone foundation of about three feet.

The arms and sails were twenty-six feet long, and it had three run of stone. The sails were first blown off in the famous September gale of 1821, and repaired by Baldwin. About ten years after the sails were again blown off, since which time they have not been repaired, the building being used as a storehouse for hay, etc. It was full at the time of the fire. When it was working, farmers came from the adjoining counties with their grist for the famous mill. The view from the upper windows was very fine, including Coney Island, the Narrows, Jersey, and Rockaway, and all places within a radius of twenty miles. During the draft riots of 1863 it was a refuge for the colored people of the village, and they will hold it in grateful remembrance."

Opposite to the road leading eastward to Canarsie is the road leading to New Utrecht called "the little lane."

The property between this "little lane" and the farm of Mr. John Ditmas was the property of the late Mr. Jeremiah Lott. This gentleman was for many years the leading, if not the only, surveyor in Kings County. He is spoken of as such as early as 1816.

We here give the copy of a manuscript written by Mr. Jeremiah Lott in 1858 by request. It is the genealogy of the large and influential family of which he was a member :

" Peter Lott, from whom all the families of that name in this country have descended, emigrated from Europe in the year 1652, and settled in Flatbush on Long Island. He was one of the patentees named in the patent granted by Lieutenant-Governor Dongan in 1685 to the inhabitants of Flatbush. It is the generally received opinion that the family came originally from England, but by subsequent intermarriages soon became fully identified with the Dutch. His wife's name was Gertrude:

neither the date of their birth nor their marriage is known. They both died in Flatbush, and the death of the wife occurred in 1704.

"Engelbert Lott, their eldest son—my great-grandfather— was born in December, 1654, in this country, and was settled at New Castel, on the west bank of the Delaware River, about thirty-five miles below Philadelphia. He was united in marriage with Cornelia De la Noy, the daughter of Abraham De la Noy, who was of French extraction and a resident of the city of New York. At the time of his marriage he owned a considerable tract of land and marsh on Christiana Creek, in New Castel County, and two lots in the town of New Castel. This property he continued to hold for several years subsequent to his removal to Long Island, but he eventually disposed of it by deed, September 1, 1707, to Abraham Santford, John Harbadink, and Jane Tuttle. Toward the close of the year 1682, New Castel, with the adjacent territory, became united with the province of Pennsylvania, under William Penn. Shortly after this union was effected, he took the oath of allegiance and promising fidelity and lawful obedience to William Penn, the Proprietor and Governor of that province, in compliance with an act passed at Chester by the Colonial Legislature of Pennsylvania. He was on terms of intimacy and friendship with Governor Penn, who held out strong inducements for him to remain at New Castel; but the unhealthiness of the place and surrounding country, together with an ejectment suit which had been several years depending before the Court of Sessions, then held at Gravesend, in the West Riding of Yorkshire, on Long Island, in which Derick Jansen Hoghlant was plaintiff, and his father, Peter Lott, defendant, caused him to remove. In 1682, with his wife Cornelia, he came to Flatbush, on Long Island, with a view to make it his permanent residence, and purchased a house and about two acres of land situated on the easterly side of the road and a short distance south of the Erasmus Hall Academy, near the property of Tunis J. Bergen. In the month of December, in the same year of his removal, he and his wife Cornelia were admitted on certificate as members in full communion of the Reformed Dutch Church of Flatbush, then under the pastoral charge of the Rev. Casparus Van Zuren. In 1688 he hired for farming purposes from the church of Flatbush a tract of land situated on the south side of the road leading to New Lots, and north of the land of John Stryker, with the salt meadows thereto appertaining, for the term of seven years, at the yearly rent of two hundred and twenty-five guilders, payable in sewant, or in wheat, to be delivered at Brooklyn Ferry at the current price. In 1709 he disposed of his house and two acres of land, and purchased from Daniel Polhemus and Neltje, his wife, the southerly one third part of the farm of the Rev. Johannes Theodorus Polhemus, the first minister of the Reformed Dutch churches in Kings County. In 1698 he was appointed high sheriff of the County of Kings by Richard, Earl of Bellamont, Governor of the Province of New York. He lived on his farm until the time of his death, which I am inclined to think occurred in the year 1728, at the age of seventy-four years. Engelbert Lott left two sons, Abraham and Johannes.

"Abraham was born in Flatbush, September, 1684. In the early part of his life he went several voyages on board of a trading vessel to the West Indies as supercargo, and probably part owner. In 1709 he was united in marriage to Catherina Hegeman, daughter of Elbert Hegeman, of New Lots, and from that time lived with and cultivated the farm of his father, Engelbert Lott, in Flatbush. Catharina, his wife, was born November 11, 1691, and died November 19, 1741.

"At his father's death he became the owner of his father's farm, which he had previously cultivated. This farm was by him afterward devised to his son, Jacobus Lott, who held it during his lifetime, and upon his death it was sold to Hendrick Suydam, and is now in possession of Sarah Suydam, the wife of John Ditmas. In May, 1730, Abraham Lott obtained by purchase from the widow and children of Daniel Polhemus, then deceased, the northerly two thirds parts of the Polhemus farm, and by this purchase, with the previous devise to him of his father's farm, he became possessed of all the land, woodland, and meadows originally patented by Governor Stuyvesant to the Rev. Johannes Theodorus Polhemus.

"In the year 1743 he was elected a representative from the County of Kings in the Colonial Legislature of New York, and served in that capacity one legislative term of seven years, and upon his reëlection commenced another term, but did not live to see its termination. He died July 29, 1754. He left three sons, Jacobus, Engelbert, and Abraham, and one daughter, named Cornelia, who was married to John Vanderveer, of Kenter's Hook.

"Jacobus Lott, his eldest son, married Teuntie De Harte, the daughter of Simon De Harte, and lived in Flatbush on the farm purchased by his grandfather, Engelbert Lott, of Daniel Polhemus, and died in possession of the same, leaving several sons and daughters.

"Engelbert Lott, his second son and my grandfather, married Maritje Ditmas, daughter of Johannes and Helena Ditmas, and lived on the farm purchased by his father, Abraham Lott, of the widow and children of Daniel Polhemus, deceased, leaving children as hereinafter mentioned.

"Abraham Lott, his youngest son, married Gertrude Coeyman, daughter of Andrew Coeyman, and commenced mercantile business in the city of New York, which he carried on for many years. He occasionally officiated as Clerk of the Colonial Assembly, and was subsequently appointed Treasurer of the Colony of New York, which office he held until the year 1776. He died in New York at an advanced age, leaving one son, named Andrew, and four daughters. Andrew married a daughter of Peter Goelett; Catharine was married to Colonel William Livingston, and Cornelia to Comfort Sands. The two other daughters died unmarried.

"Engelbert Lott, the son of Abraham Lott, my grandfather, was born in Flatbush, May 17, 1719, and lived with his father, who, when he purchased the northerly part of the Polhemus farm, removed with him thereon and continued to cultivate it during his father's lifetime, and upon the death of his father he became the owner thereof. December 4, 1742, he

was united in marriage with Maritje Ditmas, daughter of
Johannes and Helena Ditmas, who was born January 8, 1723,
and died April 27, 1797. He was at one time the principal
land surveyor in the County of Kings, and also held the office
of one of the Judges of the Court of Common Pleas in the
county. During his lifetime he conveyed to his son, Johannes
E. Lott—my father—his farm in Flatlands, which he, with his
father, had purchased of Aert Willemse, and by his last will and
testament devised to my father the residue of his real estate.
He died in Flatbush, November 17, 1779. He left three sons,
Johannes, Abraham, and Engelbert. His son Johannes E. Lott,
my father, upon his first marriage removed to the farm in Flatlands purchased of his father, Engelbert Lott, leaving children
as hereinafter mentioned. Abraham E. Lott and Engelbert
Lott, his two remaining sons, were merchants in New York,
and continued the mercantile business until the commencement
of hostilities between this country and Great Britain in 1776,
and returned to Flatbush a few months previous to the landing
of the British army in that year. Upon the capture of Long
Island by the British forces under General Howe, the greater
part of the inhabitants of Flatbush left their homes and went
into Queens County. In this flight Abraham E. Lott and Engelbert Lott were pursued and overtaken in Flushing. Engelbert was taken prisoner and brought back to Flatbush, then in
possession of the British army, and confined in Flatbush church,
but was soon set at liberty on his parole. He remained in Flatbush and attended to the public business of the town and
county, and was occasionally engaged in surveying and conveyancing. While engaged on public business at the tavern of
Dr. Hendrick Van Beuren, he was suddenly attacked with
apoplexy, and died there, November 29, 1779, in the twenty-
sixth year of his age, and only twelve days after the death of
his father, Engelbert Lott.

"Abraham E. Lott, the remaining brother, escaped from his
pursuers by secreting himself in a cornfield, and when they
had abandoned their search he went to the shore and crossed
Long Island Sound to the Westchester side. Thence he pro-

ceeded through the city of New York, and, on his journey meeting with the late Elkanah Watson, they both went south to Edenton, North Carolina. At that place he carried on the mercantile business under the firm of Lott & Payne. After the termination of the war he was about making preparations to leave Edenton for New York, but was suddenly cut off by death before his designs were accomplished. He died in Edenton, at the house of Mr. John Green, March 4, 1785, in the thirty-seventh year of his age.

"Johannes E. Lott, the eldest son of Engelbert Lott, my father, was born in Flatbush, September 1, 1746. During his minority he lived with his father and assisted in the cultivation of his farm, having previously received such education as the country schools at that time afforded. May 3, 1766, he was united in marriage with his first wife, Adriantje Voorhees, daughter of Adrian Voorhees, and moved on the farm in Flatlands which he then purchased of his father. Adriantje Voorhees was born September 4, 1746, and died October 21, 1773. By this first marriage he had one son, named Engelbert, and a daughter named Phebe. His son Engelbert on his marriage was settled on a farm in New Utrecht, near the Bath House, where he died, leaving a widow, four sons, and three daughters. His daughter Phebe died unmarried. After the death of his first wife, Adriantje, he was again united in marriage, January 12, 1775, to Catharine Vanderbilt, daughter of Jeremiah and Sarah Vanderbilt. Catharine was born February 13, 1757, and died October 23, 1840, aged eighty-three years.

"He lived in Flatlands, on his farm there, until the death of his father, Engelbert Lott, in 1779, when he removed to the farm of his father in Flatbush, which his father had devised to him by will. He was chosen one of the six delegates from the county of Kings to attend the Provincial Congress held in the city of New York in the year 1776. In the year 1784 he was chosen a member of Assembly from this county. He was appointed the first Surrogate of the County of Kings under the Constitution of the State of New York, which he held with that of the office of one of the Judges of the Court of Common

Pleas, until his appointment to the office of First Judge of the Court. He held the office of First Judge from the year 1793 until his resignation in 1801. From that time he attended to his domestic duties, and died August 13, 1811. By his wife Catharine he left three sons, Jeremiah, John, and Abraham, and two daughters, Maretje and Sarah. Jeremiah Lott and his wife and children are hereinafter mentioned.

"John Lott, the second son, after receiving his education at Erasmus Hall Academy, was brought up as a farmer, and, on his marriage with Elizabeth Garretson, the daughter of Samuel Garretson, of Gravesend, in 1799, settled on the farm in Flatbush purchased by his father of the heirs of Philip Nagel, deceased, and of which he became fully possessed on his father's death. John Lott died in February, 1858, in the eightieth year of his age. He had two sons, John I. Lott and Samuel G. Lott. John I. Lott died previous to his father. The other son, Samuel G. Lott, is still living, and resides on his farm in Flatbush, purchased of Abraham Vanderveer.

"Abraham Lott, the third son, was also brought up and educated like his brother John, and on his first marriage, with Maria Lott, the daughter of Jeromus Lott, of Flatlands, in 1805, settled on the farm in Flatlands, of which he became the owner on his father's death.

"By this marriage he had one son, John A. Lott, who, after receiving a collegiate education, was bred to the law, and which profession he diligently followed until he was elected one of the Justices of the Supreme Court.

"Upon the death of his first wife, Maria, Abraham Lott married a second time, Jane Voorhees, the widow of Lawrence Voorhees, deceased, and daughter of Samuel Garretson, and then purchased the farm on which she lived of Van Brunt Magaw and Adriana Voorhees, his wife, and on which he then moved.

"Upon the death of his second wife he was again married to Lavinia Betts. He died November, 1840.

"Maretje (oldest daughter of Johannes E. Lott) was born October 10, 1781, and was married to Jacob Van Pelt, of New

Utrecht, August 19, 1802. She died in 1852, leaving one son, John L. Van Pelt, and a daughter, Gertrude Van Pelt.

"Sarah (youngest daughter of Johannes E. Lott) was born October 10, 1795. She was married February 10, 1817, to John Vanderbilt, and lived on the place in Flatbush where her mother, Catharine Lott, was born. Her husband, John Vanderbilt, died in 1842, leaving her a widow with three sons and two daughters: John, Jeremiah Lott, Abraham L., Catharine, and Sarah.

"Jeremiah Lott, eldest son of Johannes E. Lott by his second marriage, was born October 14, 1776. At the age of twenty years he commenced the business of land surveying and conveyancing, which he followed for about thirty-five years, and was at one time the only county surveyor. In 1801 he was appointed Clerk of the Board of Supervisors of the County of Kings, and held that appointment uninterruptedly for a period of forty-two years. In the year 1814 he was the member of Assembly representing this county in the State Legislature. In the years 1821, 1822, and 1839 he served in the same capacity. He held the office of surrogate, to which he was appointed in the year 1814, successively for the period of nineteen years. In the War of 1812 with Great Britain, he held a captain's commission in the Flatbush company of militia. In September, 1814, he was called with his company into the United States service under Brigadier-General Johnson, and stationed at Fort Greene, in Brooklyn. During this time he lived on and cultivated the farm in Flatbush on which he now lives, and which was devised to him by his father, Johannes E. Lott, and which is the same farm which his great-grandfather, Abraham Lott, obtained by purchase from the widow and children of Daniel Polhemus in 1730, having been owned and occupied by four successive generations in direct lineal descent.

"January 17, 1805, he was united in marriage with Lydia Lloyd, the daughter of Bateman Lloyd, formerly of Woodstown, Salem County, West New Jersey.

"His eldest daughter, Catharine L. Lott, was born October 17, 1807, and was married February 16, 1829, to her cousin

John A. Lott, the son of Abraham Lott, deceased. Their children are Abraham, John Z., Jeremiah, Abby, and Maria.

"Abby Lefferts Lott, the second daughter, was born April 12, 1811, and was married October 13, 1830, to John B. Zabriskie, son of the late Rev. John L. Zabriskie, of Millstone, New Jersey. Her husband, Dr. John B. Zabriskie, died February 8, 1848, leaving her a widow with five children, John Lloyd Zabriskie, Jeremiah L., Nicholas Lansing, Harriet Lydia, and Sarah Berrica.

" JEREMIAH LOTT.

" FLATBUSH, *June* 1, 1858."

Mr. Lott lived to be eighty-five years of age, and to the time of his death he was active and vigorous.

On the east side of the road, north of the road leading to Canarsie, is the house in which Mr. Cornelius Duryee lived at the time Mr. Strong's history was published. Mr. Duryee was in the New York Customhouse for many years, and so punctual was he in his movements that, as his gig was seen driving leisurely homeward in the afternoon, it was considered as surely the signal for the hour of four as if the clock had struck. This house is said to have been at one time the residence of Lord Stirling; portions of it are very old, but the additions of after-years have taken from its exterior appearance the characteristics of an old Dutch house.

The house of Mr. Jacob Duryee was next to that of his brother Mr. Cornelius Duryee, toward the north. It was sold for division of property, and passed into possession of the Brooklyn City Railroad Company. The car stables of the Flatbush Avenue line are built here at the terminus of the road. This house is very old, and fast falling to decay. It was the old homestead of the Van Beuren family, none of whom are left to represent the name in this town.

Dr. Strong in his history tells us that north of the house of Mr. Jacob Duryee once stood a public brewery. This brewery was divided into shares which were apportioned to the several farms, and gave the possessor the right of brewing in the establishment.

Upon the southerly corner of Vernon Avenue and Flatbush Avenue stands the Willink House, a hotel built by two ladies, Mrs. Willink and her sister Miss Ludlow. They proposed to make this an agreeable summer residence, but it was never an attractive place; pecuniarily and in every way it proved a failure.

Retracing our steps to the "little lane" on the west side of the road, we find upon this corner a house formerly occupied by Mr. Teunis Bergen; at his death it was purchased by Mr. Jeremiah Lott.

Next northward is the comfortable, old-fashioned dwelling-house of the late Mr. Jacobus Schoonmaker, who died in 1877 at an advanced age; his widow survived him but two years. Their three sons still occupy the old homestead in happy demonstration that the old adage which says that "no house is large enough for two families" is not always true. This is a pleasant, home-like Dutch house, with the gable-end to the road. Dr. Strong says that the timber with which this house was built was that taken from the court-house which was pulled down in 1792. The house was moved a short distance southward in 1879 to allow for the opening of a street north of it.

The Schoonmaker family on Long Island are descendants of Rev. Martinus Schoonmaker, who was in 1785 placed over the united congregations of Kings County.

Joachim Schoonmaker and Antje Hussey, his wife, of Kingston, New York, were the parents of Joachim, father of Martinus Schoonmaker, who was born March 1, 1737. He married Mary Basset, 1761, and died in Flatbush at an advanced age.

Next northward is the property at present owned by Mr. William Matthews; the house is rented and occupied by Dr. T. Ingraham. This was formerly the farm of Mr. Samuel G. Lott. Mrs. Lott was the daughter of Mr. Theodorus Bergen; she died of yellow fever, caught while unselfishly devoting herself to the care of her brothers and sisters at Gowanus during the prevalence of that fearful epidemic in the autumn of 1856. Mr. Lott died some few years after. An old stone house stood upon this spot in earlier times; it was pulled down to give place to the modern house at present standing, which was built for Mr. Lott; the stone house and farm belonged to Mr. Abraham Vanderveer, and extended southward toward the little lane leading to New Utrecht, the southern portion of the farm being the share of the sister of Abraham Vanderveer, Charity, wife of Stephen, and mother of the late Jacobus Schoonmaker.

Mr. Theodore Lott, son of Mr. Samuel G. Lott, resides in the pleasant dwelling-house south of what was formerly his father's place. The extreme neatness of the house and grounds makes this a cheerful and attractive spot.

Waverly Avenue runs westward from this point, separating the land which once formed the farms of Mr. Samuel G. Lott and Dr. A. Vanderveer.

The house indicated on the map as belonging to Dr. Vanderveer was an old-style, cozy-looking house, and stood so close upon the road that the front door yard formed an ellipse upon the sidewalk.

This house was standing during the Revolutionary War, and was one of the oldest in the village. It was formerly the property of Dr. Schoonmaker, a son of old Domine Schoonmaker, from whom the house, with about five acres of land, was purchased for Dr. Vanderveer by his father.

Rev. Dr. Livingston, at some period previous to 1794, either owned or rented the house, and lived here for many years.

Dr. Adrian Vanderveer, one of the sons of Mr. John C. Vanderveer, before alluded to, sold this property on the west side of the Flatbush road to Mr. Henry Lyles, and built for himself a large house on Vernon Avenue, with greenhouses and graperies attached. Being very fond of arboriculture and horticulture, he devoted much time to the cultivation of his grounds. He planted a great variety of trees, and the shrubbery about the house was selected with great care.

Two of the sons of the Doctor, Mr. John and Mr. Adrian Vanderveer, have erected neat and tasteful houses upon Vernon Avenue, which they at present occupy.

Near the site of the old house last occupied by Dr. Vanderveer, Mr. Henry Lyles, Jr., built a large and comfortable house. After this the old landmark, which had antedated Revolutionary times, was pulled down.

The well-kept lawn in front of Mr. Lyles's house has been planted with fine trees, and it presents a pleasant appearance.

Mrs. M. C. Lyles was the only daughter of Mr. Samuel G. Lott. Mr. Lyles recently held the responsible

9

position of president of one of the largest savings banks in New York.

The house on the north side of Vernon Avenue and on the east of the Flatbush road is the property of Mr. Edwin Garvin. This house, which was built by Mr. David Johnson, has been greatly enlarged and improved, so much so that it could scarcely be recognized as the same building. Like the march of improvement in other directions, the old has given place to the new, with comforts, conveniences, and appliances which were unknown in earlier days.

Before Vernon Avenue was opened this was a Vandeventer farm. It ran back eastward a long distance to the farms of Mr. Michael Stryker and Mr. Suydam.

The old house of Mr. Jacobus Vandeventer stood close upon the roadside. South of it was a large pond. There were formerly many of the name of Vandeventer in Flatbush, but it has now entirely died out.

North of and next to Mr. Garvin's place is the old house marked "R. Crommelin" on the map of Dr. Strong. This house is now rapidly going to decay. It was owned by Mr. John Hess through his wife, who was a Miss Van Beuren.

It was purchased for a parsonage in 1711, and used for that purpose when there were two ministers, Rev. Mr. Freeman and Rev. Mr. Antonides, preaching in the Dutch towns on Long Island. For a long time it was in possession of Domine Lowe. This house was built on a portion of the front of the Vandeventer farm.

The late Mr. Teunis J. Bergen erected a large house on his property, adjoining that in which his family had formerly lived for many years. That house he then sold to Dr. H. L. Bartlett. Afterward it passed into the possession of Mr. Joseph Gray, who is still its owner.

This land, formerly owned by Mr. Tunis Bergen, also that on which the new house still owned by his heirs now stands, was at an early period the property of Mr. Adrian Hegeman, for many years schoolmaster in Flatbush, and afterward County Clerk in Brooklyn.

Grant Street is a new street, opened 1876, leading easterly to that portion of the village called the "English Neighborhood." This locality was thus named because the land was purchased and cut up into lots by some English mechanics, who built small houses and settled there with their families.

On the westerly side of the road next adjoining the grounds of Mr. Lyles is the old house marked "J. C. Bergen" on Dr. Strong's map. There is every reason to believe that this house was built by Domine Freeman.

Stiles, in his "History of Brooklyn," says : "In 1735 he (Domine Freeman) purchased seven acres of land in Flatbush, and built a house which is still standing, although altered. . . . His only child, Anna Margaretta, married her cousin David Clarkson."

The Clarkson family, during and before the War of 1776, lived in this house, and it is probable that it came into their possession through their mother, the daughter of Rev. Mr. Freeman.

This house is referred to on page 144 of Dr. Strong's history. It was here that during the War of the Revolution the British soldiers found the costly wine which had been stored under the eaves by Mr. Clarkson.

This, which is one of the oldest houses in Flatbush,

has the low ceilings and the heavy cross-beams characteristic of the houses built by the early settlers, and probably few have been left so entirely free from modern improvement.

The heirs of Mr. J. C. Bergen have had the good taste to leave the house as it was built, without attempting to modernize it.

Although this was the homestead of the Clarkson family, the name was subsequently transferred to the land north of the church, on which they (the heirs of the Clarkson family) at present reside, by the marriage of one of the sons to the daughter of Hon. John Vanderbilt, so frequently mentioned in Dr. Strong's history.

The ancestor of the Bergen family on Long Island was Hans Hansen Bergen. He was a native of Bergen, in Norway; he went to Holland, and from thence to America in 1633.

The ancestor of this family was Cornelius, born 1761; married April, 1785, Gertrude, daughter of Hendrick Suydam of Flatbush, and resided on the farm his wife inherited from her father.

The handsome new house next adjoining this old time-honored place was built by the heirs of Mr. John C. Bergen; it is at present occupied by his son-in-law and daughter, Mr. and Mrs. William Story.

The house marked on the map "D. Wiggins" was at that time a public-house. At the death of Duryee Wiggins, the property was purchased by the late Hon. John A. Lott, and the house was remodeled for his eldest son, Mr. Abraham Lott, to whom it at present belongs. Mr. Abraham Lott married the second daughter of Mr. Bergen, whose land adjoined his own.

This property was formerly known as "the court-house lot." Here stood the county court-house and jail, which was burned down in November, 1832.

In November, 1692, the Court of Sessions for Kings County ordered that each town in the county should have "a good pair of stocks and a good pound," and that "the clerk of the court should issue a warrant to the constable of every town, requiring them to see this order complied with at their peril."

On this lot, in front of the jail, stood the stocks and whipping-post. It is thus described by a gentleman who still remembers it:

"The tall post on one end was the whipping-post; from this extended a horizontal beam in which were semicircular excavations graded from larger to smaller circumferences, to fit larger or smaller limbs; the other half of this horizontal beam, rising upon a hinge when lowered in its place, fitted exactly over the lower half, and, when fastened down, secured the prisoners' legs in the rings thus formed."

It is probable that the stocks and whipping-post were destroyed when the jail was burned; there is no record made of it.

The first county court-house was built in Gravesend in 1668. In 1686 the courts were removed to Flatbush, where a court-house was erected, which was in 1758 replaced by one which was burned down in 1832. The county court-house after this was removed to Brooklyn. This had been long desired by the inhabitants of that place, and there had been for some time previous much dissatisfaction at the location of the court-house.

In an old newspaper called the "Long Island Patriot," "published every Thursday at 99 Fulton Street, near Sand Street," we find, in a number issued March 3, 1825, a memorial to the Legislature, "showing the propriety of erecting a new court-house, and naming Brooklyn as the only desirable location." The arguments for the removal occupy two columns of the newspaper, and it is probable that there was much excitement occasioned. We copy a few lines from the "Memorial to the Legislature" in favor of the removal :

"A remonstrance against the removal of the court-house has been circulated in the county, in which it is stated that Flatbush is nearer the center of the county. The fact we admit; but we think the center of population of infinitely more importance than the center of territory—it being the people who attend court, and not the acres of land; and that in a county extending but eleven miles the center can be of little importance."

In 1826 a law was passed by the Legislature that henceforth the Courts of Common Pleas and General Sessions of the Peace should be held alternately at the Court-house at Flatbush and at the Apprentices' Library, Brooklyn.

In 1829–30 a law was passed empowering the Board of Supervisors to raise by tax a sum of money to devote to the purchase of lots in the village of Brooklyn, to erect a suitable building thereon for the accommodation of the courts of the said county.

But in 1832, the old jail being burned, an end was put to any complication which might have arisen from conflicting interests. In the next year another law was passed to the effect that the court-house and jail in and for the County of Kings should be erected in the village of Brooklyn.

After this, as we have stated, the land was sold, and "the court-house lot" finally came by purchase into possession of Judge Lott.

Near this spot is where the old Van Beuren tavern stood, kept as such afterward by Mr. Simon Voorhees for many years. All these inns have now given place to family homes. The residences of Mr. Abraham Lott and of Mr. John Z. Lott, with neat gardens and adjoining lawn, kept with so much taste and care, present a delightful contrast in their present aspect as compared to that which they presented when Dr. Strong wrote his history.

On the easterly side of Flatbush Avenue, corner of Grant Street, stands the new and beautiful chapel of the Reformed Church, completed in 1871. It occupies nearly the site of the old house marked "J. Vander-veer" on Dr. Strong's map, near the blacksmith-shop; both the house and the shop were pulled down some years ago. The property at that time belonged to the Antonides family.

The chapel is used as a Sunday-school room and also for prayer-meetings. It was a costly building, and has been much admired. A large and graceful elm shaded it when first built; unfortunately, this tree died and was cut down in 1877.

Erasmus Hall Academy stands next north of the chapel. It is the third oldest academy in this State. It was built in 1786, and was incorporated by the Regents of the University in 1787.

We here copy the subscription list for the building of Erasmus Hall as it is given by Dr. Strong; it shows that many well-known persons, non-residents of Flatbush, were interested in it:

John Vanderbilt	£100	Adriantie Vorhies	£30 ·
Peter Lefferts	60	Hendrick Suydam	25
John Vanderbilt	50	William B. Gifford	20
Gerret Martense	50	Philip Nagle	15
M. Clarkson	50	Peter Cornell	15
Joris Martense	50	Johannes Waldron	5
Aa Giles	50	George Clinton, for any	
Jacob Lefferts	50	place in Kings County	15
Johannes E. Lott	50	John Jay	15
Cornelius Vanderveer	50	Robert R. Livingston	15
James Duane	15	John Sloss Hobart	5
Richard Varick	10	James Giles	5
Brockholst Livingston	10	John H. Livingston	5
Alexander Hamilton	10	Comfort Sands	20
William Duer	15	Samuel Franklin	10
Walter Rutherford	10	Francis Childs	5
Carey Ludlow	10	Richard Platt	10
Edward Livingston	10	W. Edgar	5
William Wilcocks	10	Sampson Fleming	5
D. C. Verplank	10	Aaron Burr	10
—— McCombe	10		

The money thus raised was not sufficient to defray all the expenditure, and the following plan was adopted to increase the fund.

There was at that time a tract of land called Twillers and Corlear Flats, held by the inhabitants of Flatbush in common. Consent was obtained for the sale of this land. The founders of the Academy agreed that their respective proportions should be applied toward paying the debt. The land sold at sixteen dollars per acre. Fifteen hundred dollars were given toward the Academy. The remainder was divided among the property owners who would not relinquish their claim in behalf of Erasmus Hall. Subsequently the remaining part of the commons was sold, and the money applied to liquidate the debt, but it was not fully accomplished until 1825.

The above account is taken from Dr. Strong; he says, also, that at this time it was proposed to locate here the theological seminary of the Reformed Church. It is much to be regretted that Flatbush was not selected, instead of New Brunswick, as the site of the college and seminary buildings.

In an old leather-bound book, published in Boston in 1791, we find the following allusion to this Academy : "In this state [New York] there are *several academies.* One of them, Erasmus Hall, is in the delightful and flourishing village of Flatbush." Coming from the source whence it does, the recognition of this venerable seat of learning, without mention made of the rest, implies some degree of celebrity.

North of Erasmus Hall is the house formerly used as the parsonage of the Dutch Church ; this was built for Dr. Strong. He lived here when he wrote his history of Flatbush.

The land on which this house stood, however, belonged to the public school. It was sold, and when the old parsonage next to the church was pulled down, a new building, the present parsonage, was erected upon that land ; then this lot was purchased from the trustees of the public school by Mr. Richard L. Schoonmaker, youngest son of Mr. Michael Schoonmaker. He died in 1876. Miss S. Ella Schoonmaker, his daughter, now owns the house and land.

This lot of ground is referred to in Dr. Strong's history. He says it was a triangular piece of ground, on which stood three distinct buildings, joined together, but evidently erected at different times. In this building the village school was held until the year 1803. Dr. Strong says that the oldest portion of this building was of stone, the subsequent additions being of wood. We infer, from his description of this building, that this was the first village school-house erected by our ancestors in Flatbush. As Dr. Strong gives the list of schoolmasters from the year 1659, we are also led to believe that this old stone school-house may have dated back to that time.

When this school-house was pulled down, the lot of ground remained vacant until, during the last war with Great Britain, the Government erected a gun-house upon it.

About the same time, the old store, still standing, was built by Mr. Michael Schoonmaker, and in the year 1823 the house was built which, during the early portion of Dr. Strong's ministry, was the parsonage.

Next adjoining the old store, a new building was erected by Mr. Richard L. Schoonmaker, the second story of which was intended for use as a public hall. Until the erection of the town hall, this room was used for purposes of entertainment, business assemblages, etc., and was found very useful for any public gathering. It was known as Schoonmaker's Hall.

The upper story of this building has for many years been rented as a Masonic lodge to the large and highly respected body of Freemasons in Flatbush.

On the east side of the road, near the corner of what is now called East Broadway, formerly stood one of those long, low, old-time houses such as we have already alluded to as being in the Dutch style of architecture of the past century.

There were half-doors, with round glasses in the upper half to light the room into which the front door opened. A large linden-tree stood upon the sidewalk before the door, shading the long stoop. A side view of this house may be had in the picture of the Dutch Church taken for Dr. Strong's history.

This house, soon after the settlement of Flatbush, belonged to the Waldron family. The last of the name, being an old bachelor, left it to his nephew, John Fish, who married a daughter of Peter Strycker, from New Jersey.

Mrs. Fish's sister, another of the Strycker family, took her niece to live with her. This niece, to whom she left this property, married Mr. Michael Nefus. The descendants of this family have left the village, and the house has since been partly taken down and partly converted into an addition to the large store built upon the corner of this street by Mr. Randolph, who at one time held it as a large grocery store. It has now been rented as an apothecary shop. There are one or two smaller shops between this and the building known as "Schoonmaker's Hall," so that this corner of the street does not present a vestige of its former appearance.

The liberty-pole, near the site of a former one which was erected at the close of the war, may also be seen in the picture of the old Dutch Church, where the two roads cross each other.

This liberty-pole was raised when Henry Clay ran for President. It was taken down some years after, to prevent accident in case of its falling, as it was in a decayed state.

To return to the west side of the street : next, south of the two houses built for his sons, stands the late residence of Judge John A. Lott, in which his widow still resides. It is spoken of in Dr. Strong's history as being at that time (1842) a new house, built on the spot where once stood the "long, gloomy, but time-honored house of Barent Van Deventer."

On this same lot at one period was a building erected by Abraham Vanderveer, and used as a grocery store and post-office.

Judge Lott died here in the summer of 1878. We here insert a sketch of his life, taken from the "Christian Intelligencer" of July 25, 1878 :

"John A. Lott was born February 11, 1806. His preparatory education was obtained at Erasmus Hall Academy, in Flatbush, and when about twenty years of age he entered Union College, from which he graduated with high honor. He studied law with Henry E. Warner, Esq., of this city, at the time a distinguished member of the bar. After practicing a short time in this city he formed a partnership with the Hon. Henry C. Murphy, and transferred his office to Brooklyn. Judge John Vanderbilt was afterward admitted to the firm, which became the leading one in the city and county. The firm, Lott, Murphy & Vanderbilt, was well known throughout the country among the profession, and was held in the highest esteem. It was for many years a famous office, and one of the chief centers of local political movements, and also influential in State affairs. In those days, when there was not, as at present, a body of irresponsible, vicious voters, who could be bought, sold, and delivered, the political conflicts in the State were campaigns in a war of giants. In those conflicts this powerful firm was often conspicuous, and for many years the chief combatants. Their legal business was very large, and included cases of the highest importance. Judge Lott applied himself with untiring energy and devotion to the business of his profession, and soon took his place among the foremost lawyers of the State. His great knowledge of the law and his strict integrity led to his election as County Judge in 1838, an office which was held for four years,

during a part of which time, in 1841, he was also a member of
the Assembly. In 1842 he was elected to the State Senate, in
which he served for four years with great ability. He then returned to the practice of his profession, to which he devoted
himself with great earnestness and assiduity, and became one of
the leaders of the bar, especially in cases involving large interests and requiring the most profound and accurate knowledge of
the law. He was a great lawyer. In 1857 he was elected a
Judge of the Supreme Court, to fill the unexpired term of Judge
Rockwell, and when the four years of the term had passed, so
general was the confidence of men of all parties in his integrity
and ability, that he was reëlected without opposition for a full
term of eight years. In 1869 he was elected a Judge of the
Court of Appeals, the highest court of the State, to fill an unexpired term, and not long after, when a Commission of Appeals
had been authorized to clear away the enormous accumulation
of cases in this court, he was made the Chief Commissioner, an
office which was held until 1874 or '75, when the commission
expired by limitation. In the election of 1869 signal proof of
the popular confidence was afforded in the remarkable fact that
he ran ahead of his ticket, when usually the vote for a judge is
smaller than that for other candidates, the interest in such appointments being less general.

" Within a short time Judge Lott resigned as a director of
the Atlantic Bank, Brooklyn, and at the time of his death was
President of the Long Island Bible Society, a trustee of Rutgers
College, a member of the Board of Domestic Missions of the
Reformed Church, the president of the Long Island Safe Deposit
Company, the president of the Flatbush Gas Company, president of the Village Board of Improvement, director of the Nassau Insurance Company and of the Long Island Insurance Company, a director in the Flatbush and Coney Island Railroad, of
which he was president during its construction, a work that
was completed without a single lawsuit in connection with the
purchase of the right of way, all concerned accepting his judgment and relying upon his integrity. He was also a trustee and
the treasurer of the venerable Erasmus Hall Academy. Although

beyond three score and ten years, the duties of these various responsible positions were performed by him regularly, promptly, and vigorously. Indeed, at every meeting he was a source of life and movement.

"During this long and eventful career Judge Lott was distinguished for intellectual power, thoroughness, decision, but especially for integrity and industry. His application was wonderful; it was a devotion to the work in hand, prompted and maintained by a conscientiousness of remarkable strength and constancy. Judge Lott was a great man, a great lawyer, a great judge, whose decisions will stand unchallenged, but he was especially great as a man of the highest integrity in thought, purpose, and action. His was the greatness of goodness. This led him to put his whole strength upon any work intrusted to him. A sense of duty, a consciousness of the responsibility resting upon him, impelled him to master all the facts and all the law of any case, however trivial, committed to his care. As a judge, though sometimes brusque and even harsh, he was noted for the dispatch of business. He made the attorneys work hard, but he worked harder than any of them. So strictly upright himself, he had no patience with those who were untrue, or unfair, or given to tricks, and sometimes on the bench manifested his contempt for lawyers guilty of such faults. But to men of character and sincerity, though sometimes abrupt, he was always fair and respectful, and often helpful. About twenty-five years ago Judge Lott became a member of the Reformed Dutch Church of Flatbush, by a profession of his faith in our Lord Jesus Christ. He was at the time in the height of his ability, having a vigorous mind sustained by an equally vigorous body. The conviction of such a legal mind is a proof of the power of the truth. Before that one of the best of men, he had since been becoming more and more estimable in character. The Gospel softened asperities, set free more and more the large and generous heart which had been in a degree repressed. He became active in the service of the Church, and in various capacities and gratuitously gave her work the benefit of his ability and experience. His generosity is too well known to need repetition here. All the charities and all the institutions of the Church received liberal gifts again and again from his hand. He loved the Church with an intelligent, hearty, and self-denying love, and was keenly alive to her successes or disasters."

North of and adjoining the garden of Judge Lott once stood a little country inn, which was a favorite resort for families driving out from New York and Brooklyn during the summer, at a period when an afternoon's drive and a country tea took the place of the present excursion by steam or by rail. The house is still standing, although it is no longer an inn as formerly.

The sign, which swung between two high poles in front of the door as late as 1842, bore the English coat of arms, the same which had been there since the old colonial times. Although so blackened by time and dimmed by age as to be scarcely distinguishable, yet there the lion and the unicorn were fighting for the crown until Time, the conqueror of all things, impartially reduced them both to indistinctness.

Where the present parsonage of the Dutch church now stands, there was previously an old house which probably from about 1711 had been the parsonage for all the Dutch towns; subsequently Flatbush, by purchase, came into the sole possession of the property.

It was a long, low building, without front windows on the second story, and with a steep, heavy roof, after the pattern of the first Dutch houses.

Dr. Strong says of this old house : "It is probable that about the year 1698, when the first church was pulled down, in which there was accommodation for the minister and his family, the first parsonage was built.   This is the south part of the present building."

The "present building" of that period has given place to the large and roomy parsonage where Dr. Strong lived at the time of his death, and where his successor, the present pastor, Dr. Wells, resides.

Dr. Strong was the pastor of this church for a period of thirty-nine years.   As a minister he had the respect of the church ; as a true and firm friend he was beloved by his people ; as a Christian gentleman he was remarked for his courteous manners and the quiet dignity of his deportment.   In time of trouble he was ever ready with sympathy, and the cordiality with which he met those who sought him for pastoral instruction served to bind him to them in affectionate regard.

After the death of Dr. Strong the pulpit of the Dutch Reformed Church was temporarily filled by Rev. Mr. Howard, an English clergyman, who was at that time principal of Erasmus Hall Academy.

Rev. C. L. Wells, D. D., soon after accepted the call to the place left vacant by the death of Dr. Strong, and has since 1862 been the occupant of the parsonage.

Rev. Dr. Wells was preaching in Jersey City at the time of receiving the call, and from that to the present time he has been the stated preacher of the Reformed Church in Flatbush and a zealous guardian of its interests.   In 1878 the title of Doctor of Divinity was conferred on him by Rutgers College.

The old consistory room, standing between the church and the parsonage, was built in 1830.   It was formerly used for the Sunday-school, for prayer meetings, and lectures.

After the chapel was built, on the corner of Flatbush Avenue and Grant Street, the use of the consistory room for such purposes was abandoned, and it is now only occasionally required, and is beginning to show signs of falling into decay.

The street running east and west, and crossing Flatbush Avenue here at right angles, is known on the east as East Broadway and on the west as Church Lane.

At the easterly extension of this street, and of those parallel to it, lie some large and finely cultivated farms belonging to the old Dutch families of Schencks, Suydams, Williamsons, Remsens, and Kouenhovens ; some of these farms extend into Flatlands. The ancestors of the Kouenhoven family (variously spelled by the different branches) came from Amersfoort in the Netherlands in 1630.

The Suydams were descendants of Hendrick Rycken, from Suytdam, who settled in Flatbush about 1663.

The Schenck family were descendants of Johannes Schenck, who settled here in 1683. The family history has been published recently by Dr. P. L. Schenck ; it is a work of much interest, and contains facts of importance relating to the early settlement.

Fronting southward on the corner of Flatbush Avenue and Church Lane formerly stood the house of Dr. Zabriskie, which was pulled down in November, 1877. This was one of the old landmarks ; there were none who could furnish a record of the time when, or by whom, it was built. In its heavy, sloping roof, its long, narrow front stoop, and the low ceilings of its roomy first floor, it showed the characteristics of the houses which were built at an early period.

It was almost with a feeling of pain that we saw

this old homestead pulled down ; this, that had been the happy home of generations dead and gone. With every other sign of age, even yet its hospitable roof showed no visible mark of decay, as if, stanch and firm, it would fain show itself to be faithful to the end.

The old tree referred to in Dr. Strong's history as the one under which Major Lenox parted from his brothers stood on this corner, opposite the gable-end of Dr. Zabriskie's house. " When asked by his brothers to abandon the American cause, although the tears were in his eyes, he replied with Roman firmness, 'I will never do it.' "

It is quite remarkable that this old tree, an English linden, stood erect until the centennial celebration of the freedom of which it had witnessed the dawn. A dead or dying branch was the only sign it gave of capitulation to Time, the great conqueror, until the full century of freedom was completed ; then, upon a quiet day when there was scarcely a breeze to account for its fall, it slowly yielded to the power of decay, and, as if of its own consent, without the compulsory power of the external elements, it gave up its life and fell to the ground.

When Dr. Strong's history was written, Dr. John Zabriskie, father of the present Dr. John Lloyd Zabriskie, was the head of the family in this venerable house. He was a man of fine physique and noble appearance. His tastes indicated refinement and intelligence, for he devoted his leisure from professional duties to the cultivation of music and to books. Fond of reading himself, he was ever anxious to encourage young people to study, and he endeavored to promote a love of learning in the village. He was in the habit of lending out books from his private library, and was ever willing to direct the course of reading among his young friends and the children of his neighbors.

At one of the windows in the easterly gable-end of the old house of Dr. Zabriskie, we distinctly remember seeing the grandmother of Mrs. Zabriskie, old Mrs. Lloyd. This was her favorite seat. She lived to a great age, and used to vary her daily reading and knitting by cutting pictures of fruit and foliage, which she frequently handed out to the school children as they, passing her window, stopped to say "Good morning." We have still in our possession a specimen of the old lady's skill. It was cut in her eighty-third year, and represents a neatly outlined tracery of twining leaves and branches, and is pasted upon one of the leaves of the old linden-tree which shaded her window. The motto upon it and the date—" We all do fade as a leaf, 1839 "—is the more impressive as the passing years have in their changes seen the old lady borne to her grave, the tree fall from age, and the house in which she lived leveled to the ground.

Next to the old house, on this corner, was the store which was built by Mr. Bateman Lloyd in 1805 from the timber of the first school-house.

We can not say if the school was held continuously in the same building, but it is probable that it was, and if so, then this timber must have been felled somewhere about 1660. The first school building was removed in 1803, Erasmus Hall Academy being then the school which the village children attended.

The store built from the timber of the old school-house was pulled down in 1825, and was converted by Dr. Zabriskie into a barn.

A large and handsome house was erected by Dr. John L. Zabriskie, in 1876, northwest of the old homestead pulled down in 1877.

Adjoining this, and within the inclosure of the same lawn, is the tasteful and comfortable residence of his mother, Mrs. A. L. Zabriskie, widow of the late Dr. J. Zabriskie. This house was built in 1865.

The property on the west side of the road, from the Dutch church on the south to what is now East New York Avenue on the north, was once held entirely in the names of the Lefferts, Martense, and Vanderbilt families. Beginning at Church Lane, the present property of Dr. Zabriskie, as far as Mr. Clarkson's lawn, was in the Lefferts family. Mr. Clarkson's was the Vanderbilt place. From Caton Avenue to the boundary line north of the residence of Dr. and Mrs. J. M. Ferris was the Martense farm, one of the largest, if not the largest, in the village. Next was another Lefferts farm, and adjoining that the Vanderbilt farm extended as far north as the present residence of Mr. J. Lott Vanderbilt. The property adjoining, north of the Vanderbilt farm, was owned by a Lefferts family.

No male representatives of these families at present hold this property, except in the case of Mr. John J. Vanderbilt and Mr. J. Lott Vanderbilt. The Zabriskie family, through Miss Abby L. Zabriskie, are the lineal descendants of the Lefferts family who once held that place. The Clarkson family, through Mrs. Clarkson, represent the former owner of the Vanderbilt property. The children of General Crooke, through their grandmother, and the heirs of Judge Martense, Mrs. Ferris and Mrs. Wilbur, represent the Martense farm.

The handsome lawn and grounds of Mr. Matthew

Clarkson were, in the early settlement, the property of Senator John Vanderbilt. Dr. Strong says of him that he was a man of "great nobleness of mind, of liberal views, and of enlarged public spirit." He was among the deputies from Kings County who met in New York in convention, April 10, 1775, for the purpose of choosing delegates to the first Continental Congress.

The large and showy mansion in which Mr. Matthew Clarkson and his family reside was built about 1836. The beautiful lawn surrounding it was carefully planted under the supervision of the late Mrs. Matthew Clarkson.

For the extent of its grounds, the handsome trees, and the situation and size of the house, this is considered the finest place in Flatbush.

When the house was completed in which the family of Mr. Clarkson still reside, the old house was sold and moved by Captain Story across the street. It has undergone so many alterations and improvements as to be scarcely recognized by those who remember its former appearance. A printing-office, owned by Mr. Riley, formerly stood on the north side of what is now Mr. Clarkson's lawn.

It was occupied by soldiers in the War of 1812. It was subsequently pulled down and carried to Brooklyn, where it still forms a part of the present "Mansion House," in Hicks Street.

The property of Mr. Clarkson has been separated from that of General Crooke on the north by the opening in 1876 of a street called Caton Avenue, from Flatbush Avenue to Coney Island road.

We now return from the west to the east side of the street, beginning from the cross-road running from east to west beside the church. This road has of late years been called East Broadway, but at an earlier period it was known as Cow Lane, probably from the fact that there was much pasture land in this portion of the town.

The store at this northeast corner still remains very much the same in appearance as it did some twenty years ago, except that toward the east its length has been extended by useful if not ornamental additions.

An old brewery formerly stood near where the corner grocery now stands, upon the Stryker property. The Stryker homestead was a long, low, brick house, close upon the road. The date upon the front was marked in colored brick as 1696. This venerable house was pulled down to give place to the cottage in which Mr. Garret Stryker now lives.

Mr. Peter Stryker and his wife Mrs. Maria Cornell Stryker, who lived in this old house, had no children. They perpetuated their name by giving the Stryker and Cornell scholarships to Rutgers College, New Brunswick, New Jersey.

The Stryker family were among the earliest settlers in Flatbush. Their ancestor, Jan Stryker, came from a province of Drenthe, in the Netherlands, in 1652. His son Peter resided in Flatbush, and was one of the patentees named on Dongan's patent.

Old Mr. Garret and Mrs. Anne P. Stryker formerly lived in the house next to this, which was also at one time the property of the Stryker family, and stood upon the large tract of land formerly in their possession.

It was sold in 1840 to Mrs. Helen Martense, who occupied the house for some time, and then gave it up to her son, Mr. Jacob V. B. Martense.

Mrs. Helen Martense and her daughter, Miss Esther Martense, removed to the residence of her son-in-law, Mr. J. D. Prince, where they lived until the death of Mrs. Martense, which occurred in 1875.

Mr. J. V. B. Martense still resides with his family in this house. His wife was a daughter of Dr. Adrian Vanderveer.

The Martense family in Flatbush are the descendants of "Martin de Boer," or Martin the Farmer, so called because he owned so large a tract of land in the town.

This farm extended somewhat as follows: From Caton Avenue as the southern boundary to the northern boundary on the limits of the property of Mrs. L. Wilbur and Mrs. J. M. Ferris, heirs of Judge Martense, deceased; and from Flatbush Avenue westward to an irregular line extending as far as the boundary of the town of New Utrecht.

The homestead of "Martin de Boer" was situated on what is now the Parade Ground.

A small dwelling also stood on this farm, near where General Crooke's house now stands, which was pulled down when that house was completed in 1800.

The division of this large farm to the sons was as follows: Rem, the father of George Martense, inherited the farm on which General Crooke's house now stands, extending from Caton Avenue on the south to Franklin Avenue on the north. Gerret inherited the farm from Franklin Avenue to a point where the toll-gate now stands, or nearly opposite Hawthorn Street. The westerly division descended through Adrian Martense to the heirs of the late George and Helen Martense. The remainder descended to the family at present represented by the heirs of Mrs. Story, a daughter of Mrs. Deborah Martense.

The birth of the three sons of Martin Adrianse, who, according to the custom of the age, reversed the name of their father and were called Martin's sons, or, as it has now become, Martense, is thus recorded in the Dutch Bible, still in possession of the family of General P. S. Crooke :

Rem Martense es geboren en et jaar 1695 der 12 Dec.
Gerret Martense es geboren en et yaer 1698 der 24 Oct.
Adrien Martense . . . . 24 Oct 1707.

Then appears the record of the death of their parents as follows :

1723 den dertigste April es overleden Sara, huysvrouw von Marten Adrianse en es begraaven den tweede dagh von Mey.

1754, Oct 30 es onze vader Marten Adrianse overleden ende begraaven de erst dagh von November.

The house adjoining that of Mr. J. V. B. Martense, and also the one next to that, are the property of the heirs of Mrs. Deborah Martense, deceased.

The house owned and occupied by Mrs. Story, widow of the late Captain Story, formerly stood on the opposite side of the road, and is the house to which allusion has already been made as having formerly belonged to Mr. Clarkson.

A small farmhouse, owned by Judge Gerret L. Martense, stood near the street on this property ; this was sawed into two and moved to the rear, forming barns for each of the two houses. It is said that Lord Stirling lived for a short time in this house during the Revolutionary War.

A wide street called Linden Boulevard has been opened north of this property, running eastward from Flatbush Avenue.

North of this street, on the property adjoining, stood the house once occupied by Mrs. Anne Stryker, widow of Gerret Stryker.

This house at one time stood close upon the road, and was used as a hotel by Duryea Wiggins. Afterward it was moved back from the road by Mrs. Stryker, and occupied for a time by herself and her daughter.

It has passed through various hands, and at present it is owned by Mr. Voit, a German gentleman.

The small house opposite Caton Avenue was for many years the property of Wilhelmus Stoothoff. Passing successively into the ownership of various persons, it at present belongs to Miss S. Ella Schoonmaker.

The printing-office of the "Rural Gazette" is upon what was formerly the farm of Mr. John Lott. The building itself was at one time an inclosed summer-house, built by Mr. Willink within his grounds at the north end of the village. After the Willink place was sold, the editor of the "Rural Gazette" purchased and removed this summer-house to its present locality, where it has formed the nucleus of several additions which have since been made to it.

The first number of the "Rural Gazette" was issued in April, 1872. It has the largest circulation in the rural towns of any newspaper except the "Brooklyn Eagle." The editor is Mr. Egleston ; the assistant editor is Mr. Green.

Diamond Street, a fine, wide street, with an asphalt pavement, was opened eastward from this point in 1868.

10

218 *THE SOCIAL HISTORY OF FLATBUSH.*

Mr. Westfall has erected a large and showy dwelling upon this street, near the corner of Flatbush Avenue, and east of the Methodist church Mr. Rust has also built for himself a neat and tasteful residence.

The Methodist church was built upon this street after the congregation had outgrown the small church in East Broadway in which they first worshiped.

The first dwelling-house erected upon this street was that of Mr. Furman Nefus, son of Mr. Peter Nefus, of New York.

Opposite the junction of Diamond Street and Flatbush Avenue is the residence of General Philip S. Crooke. It is marked on the map as the house of Mrs. Caton. This was originally part of the large Martense farm. Mrs. Caton was a daughter of Mr. George Martense, mentioned in Dr. Strong's history. This house was built about the year 1800 ; it has undergone some alterations, but not such as to materially alter its style.

The large tree in front of the door is the last one of the four English lindens of which Mr. Strong speaks in his history as being venerable trees at that time. He says of these : "One stood in front of the house which was taken down to make room for the present dwelling of Judge John A. Lott. About the period of the American Revolution a limb of this tree became broken, and Colonel Matthews, Mayor of New York, who then lived on the premises, had it leaded up, and it grew again. But after a while it was split by the wind, and he then sent to New York for riggers, who bound it up with ropes and so preserved it."

The second linden stood opposite the Dutch church, on what is now the corner of Flatbush Avenue and East Broadway. The third was the one we have referred to as standing at the eastern gable of Dr. Zabriskie's house which fell in the summer of 1876. This, in front of General Crooke's house, is the last of these four venerable trees. It has been hooped and banded with iron in various places to strengthen and preserve it, but it begins to show signs of age.

Clarkson Street and Franklin Street have been opened westward from Flatbush Avenue, through the farm formerly owned by Mrs. Caton, which extended at that time in unbroken length to what is now Franklin Street.

Several fine houses have been erected in this vicinity, in the western part of Flatbush. One of these was built by Mr. William Matthews, who was born in Scotland. It presents an imposing appearance at the approach from Ocean Avenue, and is a picturesque feature in the landscape, as seen, inclosed in trees, from the south side of Prospect Park. Mr. Matthews's eldest son married Miss Gertrude Prince, a descendant of the first settler, Marten, the large landed proprietor who, in 1646, owned the farm upon which Mr. Matthews's house now stands. A cottage was also built on Irving Place by Mr. Matthews for his daughter, Mrs. Mackenzie.

Mr. Wall, Mr. John H. Bergen, and other gentlemen have built cottages in this part of Flatbush which are now pleasantly shaded by elms and maples, so that for the quiet and seclusion of summer residences this is the most desirable part of the town.

Mrs. John H. Bergen is a daughter of General Crooke, and through her mother a descendant of the Martense family who originally owned this farm.

Mr. Longmire, living upon Irving Place, married a granddaughter of Mr. Henry S. Ditmas, to whose old homestead reference has been made.

Mrs. William Robinson, on Franklin Street, was a member of the Duryee family, settlers in the southerly side of Flatbush.

The rectory of St. Paul's Protestant Episcopal church is situated pleasantly in this portion of the town.

The land on the east side of the road, from opposite Caton Avenue to Clarkson Street, was the farm purchased by Johannes E. Lott, in 1799, from the heirs of Philip Nagle. There are no longer any of the Nagle family living in Flatbush. The long, old-fashioned house, still standing, has all the characteristics of the houses built in or about the year 1800.

The genealogy of Mr. John Lott, for whom this house was built, is included in that of the Lott family given by his brother, Mr. Jeremiah Lott.

This farm was sold for division of the property about 1865. It was afterward cut up into lots, some of which were sold, and the pleasant rural appearance of this part of the town was in consequence lost. Heavy brick stores, red and warm-looking in summer and scarcely more attractive in midwinter, loom up upon the corner lots. They are the harbingers of the changes which in time must come, but which might have been for some years deferred. The owners of these stores have anticipated a future in which they may be needed rather than a present in which they are.

A large brick building stands at the south corner of Diamond Street, and other stores, including the post-office, stand at the southeast corner of Clarkson Street, upon what was once this beautiful stretch of level farming land.

From the south corner of Clarkson Street to the

south corner of Winthrop Street was a farm owned, probably, by Jan Aertsen Vanderbilt, about the year 1720. The old house stood near the spot where Mr. Prince's house now stands. The first portion of this sold was the twenty-five acres at the north corner of Flatbush Avenue and Winthrop Street, on which was built the old house recently occupied by Dr. Robertson. The remainder of the land fronting on Flatbush Avenue was first sold to William Gifford, and by him to Charles Clarkson, father of Mrs. Matthew Clarkson, and, passing through various owners, has at length come into possession of its present proprietors. The southern half now belongs to Mr. J. D. Prince, the remainder to Mr. William Brown. The house owned and occupied by Mr. Prince was built by Mr. Peter Nefus, and the house owned and occupied by Mr. Brown was built by Mr. Robert Crommelin.

On the corner where Mr. Prince's house now stands was formerly an old house kept as a tavern or stage house. In the rear of it was Crommelin's mustard factory.

Frederic and Richard Crommelin married the daughters of Teunis Bergen, who lived in a house (since burned down) corner of Flatbush Avenue and the "little lane" leading to New Utrecht.

Mr. J. D. Prince is a grandson of Dr. John Duffield and Margaret Debevoise, a descendant of Carel Debevoise, first settler of that name in Brooklyn.

Mrs. Prince was a daughter of Mr. George Martense, a descendant of "Martin de Boer," or the farmer, of whom mention has been made ; Mrs. Helen Martense was a descendant of Rutger Joesten Van Brunt, who emigrated from the Netherlands in 1653, and was among the first settlers in New Utrecht in 1657. Mrs. Martense was public-spirited and generous, taking an active part in whatever tended to the public good and to the cause of benevolence.

Mr. William Brown owns and occupies the house adjoining that of Mr. Prince. The grounds of these two gentlemen are exceedingly ornamental to the village. The separating fences have been removed and the gardens thrown into one, an act significant of much friendly feeling and neighborly intercourse.

Upon the land which was sold by the heirs of Mrs. Caton Mr. George Stillwell erected a neat and pleasant house on the northwest corner of Clarkson Street. Mrs. Caroline Stillwell was a daughter of Mr. Jeremiah Vanderbilt.

The small but neatly kept house of Mr. J. Smith adjoins that of Mr. Stillwell.

At the southwest corner of Franklin Street and the Flatbush Road stands a house built by the late Mrs. Jane Rhodes. Mrs. Rhodes was a daughter of Mr. Peter Leake, one of the old inhabitants of Flatbush, who lived for many years on the "church lane."

Her eldest son, Mr. John Rhodes, studied for the ministry, but ill health compelled him to resign his work, and he died soon after.

Upon the completion of Prospect Park, Franklin Avenue, opened, widened, and planted with shade-trees, became one of the handsomest streets running westward from Flatbush Avenue. This street was named after old John Franklin, along whose property it ran. John Franklin and Charity, his wife, were members of the Society of Friends. This property was formerly part of the Martense farm ; the house was built by the grandfather of the late Judge Martense, and was sold to John Franklin ; it remained in possession of his heirs until a comparatively recent date, when it was purchased by Dr. Norfolk, who has made some alterations and improvements in the house ; he still owns it, and has made it for a few years past his place of residence.

Opposite the junction of Franklin Avenue is one of the oldest houses in Flatbush ; it belonged until recently to Dr. John Robinson. It is pleasantly situated some distance from the road, and is approached through a handsome walk overshadowed by pine-trees. These pine-trees are of comparatively recent growth. Before the Revolution it is probable that the house could be seen from the street more plainly than it is at present. This house belonged during the War of the Revolution to Colonel Axtell, and is frequently referred to in Dr. Strong's history as a great resort of the Tories of New York. It was an unusually large and convenient house for one built at that period, and is not in the old Dutch style of architecture. It contained hidden closets and rooms almost inaccessible of approach in ordinary ways. Colonel Axtell himself was obliged to remain secreted in some of these hiding-places, so that there came in time to be an air of romance about the place, and it got to be looked upon as the haunted house of the town.

There is no house in Flatbush which has had so many different owners as this, and none of which so many fanciful stories have been told.

The real history of the place is this : This was the remainder of the twenty-eight acres forming part originally of a Vanderbilt farm to which we have already referred. This portion of it was purchased by an Englishman by the name of Lane.

In 1749 he built what was, for that age, a large and showy house; it had a greenhouse at the rear. The cornices in the drawing-rooms were gilded, the rooms wainscoted, and the halls wide. The grounds were laid out in flower-beds; beyond the garden was a handsome lawn. Mr. Lane was an Englishman of a good family who was banished from his home on account of the wild life he led. He had married a woman of low parentage, and they lived here on an annuity which ceased at his death; after that she could not support the style in which they had lived, and the house was offered for sale, and purchased by Colonel Axtell.

This gentleman was a Tory, and most of the friends whom he entertained—the Mayor of New York was one —were kindred spirits, and drank toasts to the King and success to his army.

It is said that Colonel Axtell built some of these secret closets for the concealment of his Tory friends; they were just the dark corners in which ghost stories take their rise.

Colonel Axtell liked gay and convivial guests, as did the young Englishman who had lived there before him. The ghosts said to have haunted the house gave no sign as to which family they belonged, but long after the War of the Revolution no one liked to venture after dark within the haunted premises. But time quiets even ghosts, and when the old people were all dead who had seen the apparitions that made the mysterious interest of this locality, then the ghosts too began to disappear.

They say that human remains, bones, hair, and mili-

tary buttons have been found on digging upon the
premises, but we spoil the mystery by explaining that
it was known that some English soldiers who died during
the war were buried here.

Mrs. Axtell, who was said to be a very haughty
lady, brought with her to this house a poor, pale,
sickly-looking child ; it was her sister or her niece,
who, they used to say, was always crying with home-
sickness and longing to go back, but was never allowed
to go.

She was taken very ill, and the neighbors came in
to assist in watching at night beside her. Her heavy
masses of beautiful hair were wet from the dew of death
upon her forehead, and she turned her dying eyes upon
Colonel Axtell, they said, and not toward her sister.

Her gravestone was never put up at the head of her
grave ; it lay for years resting against the churchyard
fence, with this inscription : "Sacred to the Memory
of Susannah Shipton, who died Sept. 9th, 1793."

Another sister lived with Mrs. Axtell, and she was
of a different mold. She could bear up against whatever burden may have been placed upon her shoulders.
She was wooed and won by General Giles, of the American troops ; he was forbidden to enter upon the domain
of Colonel Axtell, but the lady met him at the gate,
beyond which, upon the open highway, the Colonel's
rule could not extend, and one day they ran away and
were married.

By strange poetic justice, or by what has been called
by some one the "irony of fate," when the estates of
Colonel Axtell were confiscated at the close of the war,
they became the property of General Giles, and the lady
who had forbidden the young American officer to enter

her doors was now obliged, if she entered at all, to come as his guest. Colonel Axtell died in England, 1795, aged seventy-five.

Mrs. Mowatt, at one time an actress upon the stage, but better remembered in the village as a young and beautiful woman, the daughter of Mr. S. G. Ogden, of New York, lived in this house. She frequently alludes in her autobiography to this village, in which she spent many happy years. She was very graceful and fascinating, and shone like such a bright figure upon the somber background of the old house, that perhaps it was her presence that came, like the sunshine, to dispel the shadowy visitants.

The property has since passed through many owners, but none have held it so long as its recent proprietor, the late Dr. John Robinson, a physician who practiced medicine for many years in New York city. He finished his course of study in Dublin University, and coming to this country settled in 1844 in Flatbush, upon this property, where he lived with his family until his death in 1879.

North of Dr. Robinson's place a street was opened in 1831 which has been recently called Winthrop Street.

The Cortelyou farm lies north of this street. It formerly belonged to the Hegeman family. When, in 1794, John Cortelyou, of New Utrecht, married Catharine Lefferts, her father, Peter Lefferts, purchased this farm for her as a wedding gift. Isaac, only son of John and Catharine, lived on this property with his family until his death. It was at a later period offered for sale, to effect a division of the estate. The house, with a few lots of ground, was retained by Mrs. Cortelyou ; after her death this place was purchased by her oldest daughter, Catharine, wife of Mr. William K. Williamson, of Flatlands.

Mr. Isaac Cortelyou, the father of Mrs. Catharine Williamson, was a descendant of Jacques Cortelyou, a Huguenot, who came to this country in 1652, and settled in New Utrecht in 1657.

Opposite Winthrop Street, on Flatbush Avenue, west side, lies a portion of what was formerly the large Martense farm, of which we have already given the outlines. Mrs. Ferris and Mrs. Wilbur hold this portion of the property, being direct descendants of the rich farmer who first settled here.

The handsome house of Mr. Lionel Wilbur, completed in 1878, is highly ornamental to this section of the village. Mrs. Wilbur is the only grandchild of Judge Martense ; Mrs. Ferris, his daughter, lives in the house built by her father, and is the only one of his children now living.

Judge Martense pulled down the old house of Revolutionary memory, referred to in Dr. Strong's history, after building the present mansion to which his family removed, and where his daughter, Mrs. Ferris, still lives.

"This very ancient house of Leffert Martense," as Dr. Strong called it, stood facing southward, with the gable end to the road. It had two front doors opening upon the long front stoop. The projecting roof extended over the front, but at the rear the steep slant extended to some five or six feet from the ground. The fireplaces were large, and tiled in chocolate and blue.

Had it been possible to preserve this house as a relic of pre-Revolutionary times, it would have been curious and interesting ; but, apart from the gradual decay con-

sequent upon its age, it was much injured in the Battle
of Flatbush, standing as it did upon the very borders
of the fight. Many bullets were picked up upon the
grounds afterward, and were kept as relics.

North of this house stands the cottage which Judge
Martense erected for his eldest son.

Next, southward on the map, is marked the house
of J. Birdsall. This house still stands, although much
out of repair and fast falling to decay. It was built
about the year 1800. This farm, in the early settlement of Flatbush, belonged to Leffert Lefferts. The
old house was burned down during the Battle of Flatbush, and the present building was erected upon the
same site. Passing through the hands of various owners, it has not for many years been occupied by descendants of the family by whom it was first held. The
farm originally comprised the land between the farms
of Judge Martense on the south, and Mr. Jeremiah Vanderbilt on the north. It was owned for some time by
the family of Mr. Murphy.

Next, northward on Dr. Strong's map, is marked
the house of Mr. Jeremiah Vanderbilt. The old Vanderbilt homestead stood where the house next on the
map is marked as that of Mr. John Vanderbilt. This
old homestead was burned down during the battle of
Flatbush, and the family remained in this house of
Mr. Jeremiah Vanderbilt until the new house, built in
its place, was finished, which was about the year 1800.
Upon the marriage of the oldest son, Jeremiah, to Ann,
daughter of Mr. J. C. Vandeveer, he moved to this
house, which bears his name on Dr. Strong's map.
Here he lived with his family until his death ; some years
after, the house and a portion of his farm were sold.

The old house, since it has gone out of the possession of its first owners, has not been kept in repair, and it is at present scarcely habitable.

The oldest son of Mr. Jeremiah Vanderbilt, Mr. John J. Vanderbilt, erected a pleasant dwelling-house next north of what was formerly the residence of his father, where he and his daughter, Miss Charlotte S. Vanderbilt, still continue to reside.

The house and grounds are neatly kept, and glimpses of the garden in the rear give evidence of a taste for flowers on the part of the proprietor. Some fine elms on the sidewalk are ornamental to this place, and give it a pleasant summer shade.

Upon the spot where the old homestead was burned in the Battle of Flatbush the present house was built, which was occupied by Mr. John Vanderbilt, who died in 1842. His widow, Mrs. Sarah L. Vanderbilt, who was a daughter of Mr. Johannes E. Lott and sister of Mr. Jeremiah Lott, died in 1859. Since her death the house has been rented to various persons. It is at present occupied by Rev. Robert G. Strong, son of Dr. Strong.

An old paper, bearing date 1661, conveying the farm on which he lived to Jan vande Bilt, signed by Governor Stuyvesant, is still in possession of the family.

The pleasantest portion of the original Vanderbilt farm is now inclosed within the boundaries of Prospect Park. The highest point there was formerly known as Vanderbilt's Hill. It commands a more extended view than any other spot in the Park. The hill next, on which is the carriage-drive or Concourse, was also a portion of the Vanderbilt farm.

This family are descended from Jan Aertson Vanderbilt, or Jan Aerson from the Bild or Bilt. This, according to Mr. T. G. Bergen, was a manor in the province of Friesland, in the Netherlands. The family tradition, however, is to the effect that this ancestor came from the Baltic—Jan van de Belt having that signification. This is strengthened by the fact that his first wife, Anneken, whom he married February 6, 1650, was from Bergen in Norway.

We now retrace our steps, and return as far back as Winthrop Street.

The large farm of Mr. John Lefferts was unbroken by streets at the time that Dr. Strong's map was made. It then contained three hundred acres, stretching from the Cortelyou farm on the south to the Clove road on the north, and from the Flatbush road on the west beyond the road leading to Canarsie on the east.

Mr. Lefferts sold some lots on the southwest corner of his farm to Mr. Jeromus J. Johnson, who built there the handsome house of Milwaukee brick standing south of Fenimore Street. This property again changed owners, and, passing from one person to another, finally was purchased by Dr. Homer L. Bartlett, in whose possession it still remains.

Dr. Bartlett has a good practice as a physician, and is a gentleman of cultivated taste. Mrs. Margaret S. Bartlett, his wife, was a niece of Dr. Strong. Cooperstown, New York, was her native place, and when the street next to their house was opened, it was she who gave it the name of Fenimore Street, after the great novelist Fenimore Cooper, who was an intimate friend of her father.

Close upon the road in front of where Dr. Bartlett's house now stands, there once stood one of the earliest-built houses in Flatbush. It was burned down during the Battle of Long Island. It would have been a curious relic of the past could it have been preserved, as it was built of brick, and was up to that time in an excellent state of preservation. The surbase in the principal rooms was tiled to match the fireplaces ; the heavy beams above crossed the ceilings. It had two front doors opening upon the long stoop in front ; indeed, all the characteristics of the old Dutch houses were peculiarly brought into prominence. The furniture would have been no less curious than the house itself, as some of it came from Holland. This house is mentioned in Dr. Strong's history. It is also spoken of by Mr. T. W. Fields, in his allusion to the Battle of Flatbush, as "the heavy old Dutch structure built in the ponderous style in fashion among the Dutch colonists."

Had it been still standing, it would have descended, as did the land on which it was built, to Mr. John Lefferts, through his grandmother, Mrs. Femmetia Lefferts, who was born in this house in 1753.

Upon Fenimore Street Mr. Lefferts built a large and convenient house, which he sold, together with a few lots of ground surrounding it, to Mr. Doremus, of New York City, in whose possession it remains, and who occupies the house.

The house next south of Mr. Lefferts's present residence was enlarged from an ordinary farmhouse and altered to its present size for Mrs. Cynthia Lefferts, who resided here until her death.

It is at present occupied by Mrs. Spofford, formerly of New York, widow of Mr. C. N. Spofford. Through her long residence in this village, this lady has formed a large circle of warmly attached friends. Hon. John

Oakey married her eldest daughter, since deceased. Her second daughter is the wife of Mr. Charles Walden, grandson of Mr. John Franklin, from whom Franklin Street, Flatbush, was named. Her third daughter is the wife of Mr. Lefferts Vanderbilt.

Mrs. Maria L. Lefferts, whose name and residence appear next upon the map of Dr. Strong, lived in this old homestead until her death, which occurred in 1865. Her son, the present owner, Mr. John Lefferts, has not modernized the house, although many of the present improvements and conveniences have been introduced. This is one of those long, low, heavy-roofed houses which were built prior to the War of the Revolution. It was burned at the Battle of Flatbush, but not wholly destroyed, and it was rebuilt subsequently upon the old timbers, so that the form of it remains as before.

The Lefferts family are descendants of Leffert Pietersen, who came to this country from North Holland in 1660. The name sometimes appears as Leffert Pietersen van Haughwaut, referring to the town whence he came. The large farm on which this house stands has been in possession of the family since 1661, as is stated upon the parchment deed, which is signed by Governor Peter Stuyvesant. This family, like many others in Flatbush, have lived upon the same estate for more than two hundred years.

On the west side of Flatbush Avenue, opposite the old homestead of Mr. Lefferts, Mr. J. Lott Vanderbilt built a house in 1876, upon his share of the front of his father's farm.

The very neat appearance of the grounds and garden reflects great credit upon the taste and care of their owner.

Mrs. Elizabeth Vanderbilt, wife of Mr. J. L. Vanderbilt, was a granddaughter of Mr. John Lott, who owned the farm corner of Clarkson Street.

Next to the farm of the late Mr. John Vanderbilt, who died in 1842, lay a strip of land belonging to the heirs of Elsie Gerretsen, daughter of Leffert Lefferts. This land was known in old records as the "Compie," and was purchased by the late Judge Vanderbilt about 1840. On this property he built the house in 1847 in which his family now reside. He subsequently added by purchase to the land in the rear, which extended northward and westward some distance into what is now Prospect Park. When this house was built by Judge Vanderbilt, neither Ocean Avenue nor East New York Avenue had been opened, so that on the north the property adjoined the Willink place. Judge Vanderbilt had been paralyzed for some years previous to his decease, which occurred May 16, 1877.

We copy from the "Brooklyn Eagle" the following notice of his life :

"THE LATE JUDGE JOHN VANDERBILT.

"The death is announced to-day of John Vanderbilt, who, twenty years ago, was County Judge of Kings, who was afterward elected to the State Senate, who was then nominated for Lieutenant-Governor with Amasa J. Parker running for the first place, and who, for many years before and after these honors befell him (and during the entire period of the honors as well), was the junior partner in the distinguished and very representative law firm of Lott, Murphy & Vanderbilt. The mention of John Vanderbilt's name would at any time start many thoughts in the mind of any Brooklynite whose memory or whose reading takes hold on the men and methods of this county in the times preceding the war between the States. The announcement of

his death to-day will revive and intensify those memories, and
to a very large number of the younger inhabitants of Brooklyn
be as much a surprise as it is a matter of news, because the
departed gentleman's retirement from affairs and general society
for years was so complete as to render him as little thought of
by the mass of men as if he had long since ceased from the
world, instead of merely ceasing from its activities and observation. He occupied, however, too large and too busy a place
in the life of Brooklyn, and, indeed, in the life of the State, not
to have left a deep mark upon the history of both. The older
readers of the 'Eagle' have hardly required the reminder
which the announcement of ex-Judge Vanderbilt's death is, to
enable them to recall the days and the deeds when he was easily
the most popular and one of the most considerable men at this
end of the Empire State. The time seems long since then, and
by any calculation of the life of men and of the epochs of politics it is not short. Yet the painridden, aged-looking, helpless
gentleman who has just exchanged worlds died at fifty-eight,
and had won more recognition before forty than most men
attain at all, though their days extend beyond the limit of the
Psalmist, and beyond the period when philosophy would rate
'life not worth living for.' Moreover, the suffering, decrepit,
and feeble gentleman who had long preferred solitude to society, and whose movements, voluntarily limited to his grounds,
had been dependent on crutches for years, was in the prime of
his energy certainly the most vigorous and handsome man in
public or private life in this county, if not in the State. His
strong, manly beauty mated with and was the exponent of
qualities of mind and heart as attractive as his gifts and graces
of person. In a time when rings were unknown he was a
Democrat; in a time when sectionalism was hardly an appari-
tion and when the State had its full rights, whether it was
weighed or counted as a factor, he was a patriot, and one who
gloried in his whole country; in a time when shysters had not
been evolved, and when pettifoggers were limited to a satirical
stage or a sarcastic literature, he was a lawyer; in a time when
gentlemen were as dominant in politics and scholars as domi-

nant in council as they now are not, he was a scholar and a gentleman. His rapidity of public development, his activity in affairs, his not surpassed qualities of good-fellowship, the magnetism of his mind and manners, and the impressive appeal which he could address to the people, early made him and long kept him what he was fondly called, ' Kings County's Favorite Son,' when that appellation was forcible by its rarity, significant in its meaning, and when it had not been vulgarized by its application to the politicians by profession and to the place-hunters by occupation.

" It will be well remembered by those familiar with Brooklyn politics and society that in the better led but less 'organized' years of the local Democracy, the law firm of Lott, Murphy & Vanderbilt was as thorough a political as it was an eminent legal power in this county. These three gentlemen named, of whom the youngest has died first, brought into local politics the principles of statesmanship, and to civil service the habits of fidelity, independence, and diligence, and that grade of culture, force, and knowledge which have made their public records a bright part of the history of their country, just as their private careers have been a most honorable part of the social and intellectual history of their city. In the times when Democracy was responsive to itself, and when the measure of his influence on the party was dependent on the character and brain of the individual Democrat, Henry C. Murphy, John A. Lott, and John Vanderbilt became leaders without difficulty, and by the very necessity that made leaders in politics out of the same elements which wrought influence in every other department of society. The people demanded their service as well as their direction. They raised Mr. Lott to the highest judicial positions in their gift. They retained Mr. Vanderbilt in this county, but insisted on his appointment to the judgeship of the county, and they sent Mr. Murphy to represent them in Congress, being afterward themselves honored in the honor the nation conferred on him in sending a scholar and statesman of his ability to represent this republic at the court of the country whose people founded this city, and whose sturdy virtues are, to this day, the best characteristic and bulwark in one of its life. Of the legal eminence of the firm in those days it is not needed to speak at length. That eminence is attested by the high station its members attained when the bar was the school of statesmen and the preserve which yielded fit men for fit functions. At the same time the records of our courts historically show that in every case of magnitude, and for every institution or person of influence, the firm were counsel by a principle of natural selection or conceded leadership."

There was much woodland northwest of the place of Judge Vanderbilt at the time he built his house.

This woodland, north of "the Compie" and adjoining it, was divided into sections among different owners.

Going northward toward Brooklyn, the house of Mr. Lefferts was, as late as 1842, the last in Flatbush, on the east side of the road, with the exception of a small house rented to the tenant who worked part of the farm.

Where now East New York Avenue crosses Flatbush Avenue the old Clove road to Bedford branched off to the northeast, and the Flatbush turnpike curved toward the northwest. The triangle formed by these roads was an inclined plain sloping southward. It was at that date a beautiful pasture-field, crowned at the crest, where now Malbone Street runs, with a dense wood. Here were noble hickories, gum-trees, and oaks, with an undergrowth of dogwood and clumps of hazel. It was surrounded with a mossy post-and-rail fence with a stone foundation, tangled with running blackberry vines.

Here the sheep and cows grazed, resting at noonday under the shade of the row of beautiful locust-trees that formed the southward boundary of this sloping pasture-land. How peaceful and quiet it seemed! the very picture of rural and pastoral life ! This was at the time Dr. Strong closed his history in 1842.

Can anything be in greater contrast than the scene which this locality now presents ? It was then the most secluded and quietest portion of the village, now it is the most noisy.

The cars of the Franklin Avenue and those of the Nostrand Avenue line stand here day and night at the terminus of their route. The Flatbush Avenue cars stop here to gather in the multitudes of pleasure-seekers from Prospect Park, and to the shrieking locomotives of the Brighton Beach troop the still more numerous pleasure-seekers to and from Coney Island. Carriages of funerals to the cemetery of the Holy Cross turn off in long lines toward Ocean Avenue or to Flatbush Avenue, and the heavy cars from Hunter's Point thunder past without stopping at the depot for additions to their long and crowded trains.

Streets and avenues have been opened, and innumerable lines of small houses are dotted all over the once peaceful fields.

At the time in which Dr. Strong's map was made, the quiet of this retreat had only begun to be broken ; but as yet there was no possible sign from which the busy future could have been predicted. Only three small houses had then been built on the curve of the road before reaching the place now called the Battle Pass, in Prospect Park, this side of the bowl-shaped hill where the old toll-gate stood.

Opposite to these, on the west side of the road, there was still the natural and unbroken growth of forest. The woods here were particularly beautiful because clear of undergrowth, and through the tall trees the western sun fell across the quiet country road in oblique lines all through the pleasant summer afternoons.

Washington Avenue now cleaves this once beautiful slope of pasture land through the center. The property, as an undivided whole, had belonged to the estate of Mrs. Elsie Gerretsen, daughter of Leffert Lefferts. When it was offered for sale by her heirs, it was divided into lots, and thus became built up with a class of small, cheap houses.

At the time of sale, Judge Vanderbilt purchased the southern terminus of the property and built a house there, which he afterward sold to Mr. Benjamin S. Nelson, who opened it as a hotel. It was, however, quiet and orderly, and caused no disturbance to the neighborhood. This hotel was moved farther easterly, to give room for Washington Avenue when that street was opened, and it now stands directly upon what was once the old Clove road. · After the death of Mr. Nelson it was closed as a hotel. His widow, Mrs. Nelson, a daughter of Mr. Elsworth, still continues to reside here.

East New York Avenue, Washington Avenue, Lefferts Street, and Malbone Street are the highways already opened on the east side of Flatbush Avenue, where once no open road led eastward after passing the Bedford road until reaching what is now Atlantic Avenue ! This was an unbroken stretch of wood and farming land.

We now return on the west side of the road to East New York Avenue. The opening of this street westward to Ocean Avenue separated the lawn of Judge Vanderbilt from the Willink property, which had previously extended in an unbroken line to what is now called the Willink entrance of Prospect Park.

The house once stood on a hill where the depot of the Brooklyn, Flatbush, and Coney Island Railway now stands. It was built in or about 1835. The lawn sloped down pleasantly toward the south and east, and a high and expensive fence, with gates always locked, kept off those who might be inclined to trespass upon the premises.

Mr. Willink was not one of the early settlers. The mother of Mrs. Willink in her girlhood spent her summers here. The story of their residence in Flatbush is this:

Before the War of the Revolution, Mr. Van Horn, a wealthy gentleman from New York, whose winter residence was opposite the Bowling Green, hired for many summers a small house at the north end of Flatbush, which stood on what is now the farm of Mr. John Lefferts.

Mr. and Mrs. Van Horn were of the old Dutch settlers in this State. They possessed great wealth, and moved in the first circles of New York in those days.

They had a large family of daughters, one of whom married Mr. Ludlow. She seemed to have kept alive pleasant memories of the days she had spent as a child in this little rural retreat, and after her widowhood she was accustomed to drive through the village from time to time on bright spring afternoons, often alighting from her carriage to rest on the smooth, grassy sidewalk, leaning on her gold-headed cane, as the infirmities of age rendered such support necessary.

She may have talked with the daughters who accompanied her of the summers of her happy childhood, when she went skipping through these woods, or rambling to the hilltop that overlooked the village, or of an occasional sleighing party in midwinter when, with the young girls of her own age, she went to the Steenbakkery, on invitation of the American officers, who beguiled the tedium of the days in which they were kept prisoners on parole with sliding, skating, and sledding parties on that pond.

Be that as it may, there were lingering memories that drew the old lady toward Flatbush in her declining years, and induced her family to drive out in that direction. When, therefore, the round-topped hill, the most southerly of those which marked the dividing ridge between Flatbush and Brooklyn, was purchased by her son-in-law, and a house was erected there, the old lady was pleased, and told her neighbors that she should be glad to renew the acquaintances she had made there in her youth.

But old age can not always effect its plans, any more than can impetuous youth ; though it seemed a natural thing that she should desire to visit those whom she had known as young girls in her own youth, her daughters had decided upon a different plan of life. They desired entire seclusion ; except in business relations, they wished for no communication with the outer world. Whether it was merely a freak which became afterward a habit, no one can tell.

The result, from whatever cause, was an entire withdrawal from society. No retreat could have been more closely guarded against the intrusion of visitors ; whether acquaintance, friend, or relative tapped at the door, the rebuff was always given, and no one passed beyond the portal of that stately mansion after once the carpenters had left and the four elderly persons who comprised the family took it as their home.

The windows were never opened. The furniture, great crates of which stood in the parlors, was never unpacked. The silver service on which had been given the hospitable and stylish dinners of earlier times was consigned to a vault in the cellar. In the basement were kept great bull-dogs fed on raw meat, to guard the premises at night, for it was whispered about that they had such stores and hoard of silver.

The old lady did not live very long. She had already reached great age, and from the home in which she thought to spend some happy days she was taken to the better home above.

Her son-in-law, Mr. Willink, was in the decline of life as well as herself, but strong and vigorous despite his gray hairs. He boasted that his father, a wealthy banker in Holland, had reached great age, and that he came of a long-lived race. But neither age nor death can be defied, and there are other means than the wearing out of this mortal frame to cut short life.

The old gentleman, as the one pleasure he allowed himself, was fond of gay horses. They ran away with him one day. The vehicle in which he rode was entirely inclosed with glass in front, as if even when out on the street he would have something between himself and the outer world. He could not control his horses under this disadvantage. He was thrown out of his carriage and picked up dead on the road just before the house of his overseer.

After this the two remaining members of the household, Mrs. Willink and Miss Ludlow, secluded themselves from society more than ever, if that were possible. They went from time to time to Trinity Church, New York, where they occupied their old family pew. Miss Ludlow herself attended to the management of their large estates or gave instructions to her lawyer.

She was a tall, gaunt woman. She must have been

11

fine-looking in younger days. She would have been a stately-looking lady still, had she not rejected everything that was tasteful in dress, and assumed the most austere and rigidly plain style of garments.

She had almost an attorney's knowledge of the law, and a shrewd, keen business tact, that enabled her to keep as sharp a lookout over her property as if she had had a fortune to earn instead of to spend.

What they did spend indeed was very little, except in cases where unbounded generosity seemed at sudden times to burst its ordinary bounds and flood some special object. Many a time some peddler was surprised by the purchase of his entire stock ; a church charity would have a gift of some thousands, or a munificent sum would be expended for some favored individual. But this overflow was like the spring torrent of some mountain stream that all the rest of the year leaves its stony bed parched and dry.

One would expect even the employment, the amusements, and the recreations of two beings so unlike the world around them to be different from those of other people ; we know not under which of these heads, if under either, to class the building of a hotel at the south end of the village. They had purchased some property there ; it was unremunerative ; then they undertook the building of the Willink House upon it. They built, furnished, and gave a public reception at the opening. The landlord found that in keeping the hotel he was constantly restricted by the old ladies.

The terms were very liberal on which he rented the house, but even on such terms the hotel could not be a success, from their constant interference.

So it was locked up, and they kept the key in their pocket. Feebler and more feeble grew the elder sister, Mrs. Willink, until at last she also died, and the family vault in Trinity churchyard was opened again.

Now Miss Ludlow was left alone. One would almost irreverently like to draw aside the veil and see if there were ever tears on that stern face. Was she ever sorrowing and mourning and crying, like weaker women? Now that she stood alone in the world, did her heart yearn for the love which even the poor share with each other? She gave no sign if it did.

Now she went again regularly, Sabbath after Sabbath, to the family pew in Trinity Church. That tall woman in a poke-bonnet and waterproof cloak moved among the velvet-draped ladies of that wealthy church like a ghost of the former century. They may have mistaken her for a beggar, or perhaps the story of her eccentricity was whispered to them : or those who were left of the old families there may have known she was one of their number, "so eccentric, you know, and so rich." What attentions she accepted she paid well for, and her liberality to the rector was unbounded. But the doors of her house were not opened ; and no one seemed to find the key of her heart any more than of her house. There may have been painful memories associated with that great bleak house on the hilltop, with its windows boarded up, and the watch-dog's bark echoing through the empty rooms : for she did not remain there so constantly as before. Now she spent much time at the hotel, taking possession of a suite of handsomely furnished rooms.

She may have felt a coming shadow, and if she did not long for human sympathy, at least it seemed more like living as other women did to have a cheerful room furnished and carpeted.

One day an employee spent the evening with her, making up accounts and handing in bills. They could not finish the work. "Come to-morrow morning," she said to him, as she closed the door upon him. "I will come early," he replied ; but Death came earlier, and was there before him.

In the morning she was found dead in her bed. As she had lived, so she had died—alone.

That was a strange funeral in Trinity Church the day she was buried : a velvet-covered coffin, beautiful music, an impressive service, but no mourners—not one even to simulate grief. It seemed a cause for tears that there were none shed. It was depressing that there was no one even to counterfeit sorrow ! Had this woman, gifted with such intellectual power, and holding such wealth in her hand, no capacity to draw any heart to hers ?

The vault in Trinity churchyard was opened now for the last of the family, and the passing crowds in the street paused a moment to peer through the iron railings that separate that graveyard from Broadway, as the coffin was lowered to its place among her kindred dead.

The house that had been so jealously closed was now thrown open to the inspection of the world. As if it had been a vault, the long festoons of dust-covered cobwebs depended from all the ceilings.

There were hoarded things of no possible value, with others of great cost. There were wardrobes stocked with antiquated clothing, crates of furniture which had never been unpacked, boxes of books, new baskets purchased by the dozen from traveling venders, new brooms—dozens of them—none of which had ever been used upon those dusty walls. There were bottles of wine so old that the decaying boxes fell to pieces as they were carried from the wine-room.

As they had hoarded, so it seemed almost as if Time, so long defied, was now avenging itself in the scattering.

No one had been allowed by them to enter yonder door; now every stranger foot had the right to climb the staircase. No one should see the treasures, whether valuable or otherwise, they guarded; now there was no secret drawer, no closet, that was not opened, for the house was now to be sold. Perhaps no gates were ever kept more sedulously locked against the public, and no lawn had ever been more strictly kept free from trespassing feet than the beautiful lawn about this house, and never has one been more entirely free to the public than that spot is now.

The very earth that formed the sloping hill has been carted away; the hill has been leveled, and thousands of footsteps now pour daily through what was once the locked entrance to the Willink place; for here on this now level plain stands the depot of the Brighton Beach Railroad, and the great, white, ghastly-looking house that stands where Ocean Avenue is lost in Flatbush Avenue is the remodeled frame of the house which once stood proudly perched upon the hill, seeming to have no more sympathy than did its reserved inmates with the village at its feet; but leveling years have done their work; Death in his turn took the key and, turning it upon them, has opened to the world the gates of what was once their guarded possessions.

We make no apology for dwelling so long on this, one of the few romantic histories of our village, for has not every old town its bit of romance? And why should not such be recorded along with other annals?

Every word of this is veritable history, and it needs not the adornment of fiction to give it interest.

Northward from the Willink property great changes have been made in the road, and in consequence the course of the old turnpike has become entirely obliterated. Formerly this road curved slightly westward, and, passing through a toll-gate which stood at the city limit, it followed circuitously the line of the little bowl-shaped hill, possibly called for that reason China Hill, through the Battle Pass; on the westward side was a sandpit; the denser shade of the valley caused this spot to be called the Valley Grove; a secluded little inn stood at the junction of the Flatbush turnpike and a narrow, stony road leading to Gowanus, called the Port road. The Port road * turned westward and the turnpike turned eastward, winding around between the hills.

This Valley Grove House was an old, topple-down inn, and stood in the lowest part of the road; in a damp evening one seemed to feel the chill of the heavy air in turning toward it on the way from Brooklyn to Flatbush.

Ascending the hill, there was a house to the right that had never been finished. It had a lonely, dreary look; the willow that stood in the dooryard still remains on the same spot in the Park, and serves to mark the locality of the house as well as to help us recall the line of the old road.

* The name "Port road" is said to be derived from an expression in the old deed or agreement between Governor Lovelace and five Indian chiefs for extinguishing the Indian claim in 1670; it is spoken of as a boundary to a certain parcel of land to which this cleft through the hills was "the port or entrance thereof."

There were some pleasant rolling hills to the left on which horses and cattle were generally grazing—those on the brow of the hill outlined against the sky, for there were no woods or shrubbery upon these pasture fields. This was the southerly boundary of the Polhemus farm.

The next curve in the road brought in view beautiful glimpses of the bay of New York with the wooded heights of the opposite shore. Here was a cluster of pleasant country residences. Mr. Anthony Kerr's house is still standing, also two houses built by Mr. Van Antwerp, and, still farther on, the place of Mr. Levi Hart. At the highest point were two hotels ; the most prominent was kept by Mr. Vonk, and was a great resort for men with racehorses and the owners of '' fancy teams.''

Only a few families lived here permanently, as this locality was subject to malarial fevers, although one of the highest points in the county. There were numerous ponds in the hollows of the hills, and from these arose miasmatic damps, poisoning the air of this beautiful spot, which would otherwise have been so desirable for private residences.

The view from this height was more beautiful then than that from the plaza of Prospect Park is now, for the city of Brooklyn was farther off, and was separated by intervening meadows and shrubbery ; it was thus softened by distance and framed in by woods.

This old road to Brooklyn was at an early period known as "the King's Highway" from Flatbush to New York Ferry ; it is called so in an old release dated 1748, quoted by Stiles in his " History of Brooklyn." It is strange that a portion of the Gravesend road should be, even at this present time, known still as " the King's Highway."

With the assistance of those now living whose memory reaches farther than we can recall, we might continue a description of this while it was yet a *country road* almost to Fulton Ferry. But, as we desire to confine ourselves to matters pertaining to Flatbush, we will not attempt to trace the changes which time has made beyond.

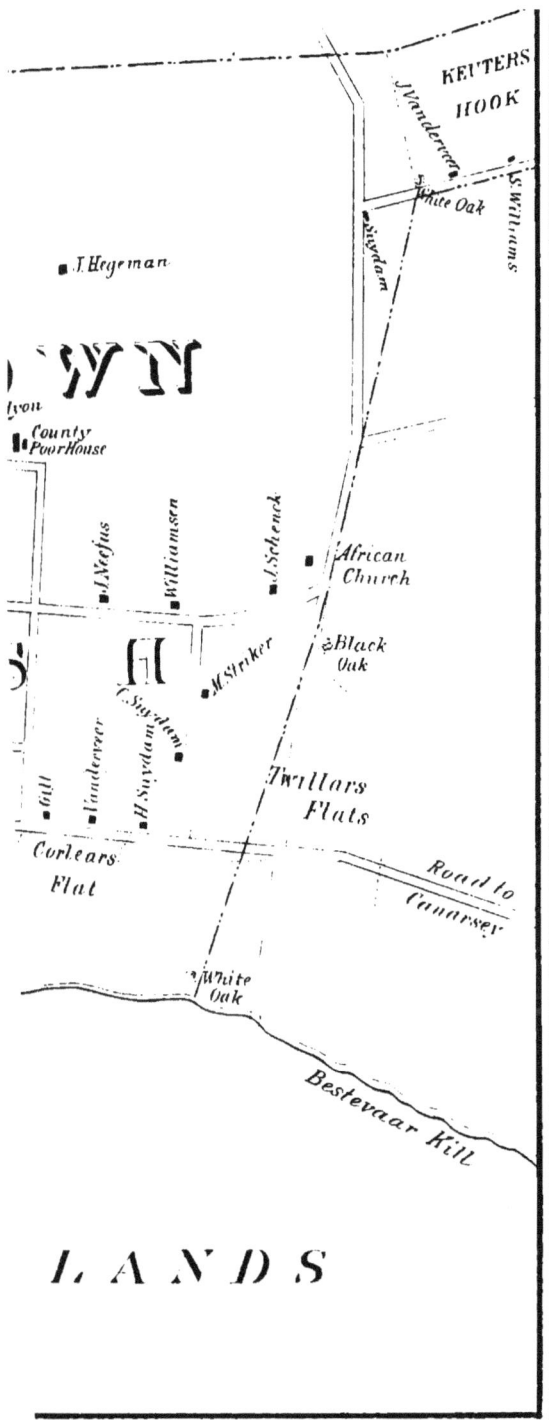

KEUTERS HOOK

J Vanderveen

Js Williams

White Oak

Suydam

J. Hegeman

SII.

O

ton

County
PoorHouse

ast end
e long Hill

J. Nefus

Williamsen

J. Schenck

African
Church

H

M. Striker

Black
Oak

C. Suydam

w l'trecht

A & B

H. Suydam

Gill

Vanderveer

Twillars
Flats

Corlears
Flat

Road to
Canarsey

l'trecht

White
Oak

Bestevaar Kill

LANDS

t bush fence

W

GRA

COPY OF THE MAP OF THE TOWN OF FLATBUSH. IN DR. STRONG'S HISTORY. 1842.

CHAPTER XXI.

DOMESTIC SERVICE.

It is not probable that slavery ever exhibited its worst features on Long Island.

A kindly feeling existed between the owner and the slave. For the protection, the simple fare, and the homespun clothing, which, in accordance with the custom of the age, the master provided, the slave returned generally a cheerful obedience and a reasonable amount of labor.

We do not credit our Dutch ancestors, in this respect, with being more humane or wiser than the age in which they lived ; but there are certain conditions under which slavery assumes its most cruel aspect, and these conditions did not exist in Kings County.

If a slave was dissatisfied with his master, it was very common for the master to give him a paper on which his age, his price, etc., were written, and allow him to go and look for some one with whom he would prefer to live, and who would be willing to pay the price stated. When the slave found a purchaser, the master completed the arrangement by selling his discontented slave to the person whom, for some cause best known to himself, he preferred. It may not have been from ill-treatment or neglect that the negro desired to change masters, but because of greater attractions elsewhere.

Valentine, in his "History of New York," says that slaves had been held in that city from the earliest period of the Dutch settlement.

Riker, in the "Annals of Newtown," tells us that slavery "originated in the scarcity and consequent high price of white labor, and extended not only to the negro, but to the free-born Indian brought hither from the South." He also confirms the statement that they were treated with much humanity.

Judge Benson in 1816, speaking of negro slavery, says : "A milder form of it than among the Dutch of New Netherlands is scarcely to be imagined."

Furman says that they "were much attached to the families in which they were owned, and where they would remain from generation to generation."

O'Callaghan says : "Slaves [in New York] constituted, as far back as 1628, a portion of the population. The introduction of this class was facilitated by the establishments which the Dutch possessed in Brazil and on the coast of Guinea, as well as by the periodical capture of Spanish and Portuguese prizes, and the circumstances attendant on the early settlement of the country. The expense of obtaining labor from Europe was great, and the supply by no means equal to the demand. To add to these embarrassments, the temptations held out by the fur trade were so irresistible that the servants, or 'boere knechts,' who were brought over from Holland were soon seduced from the pursuits of agriculture. Farmers were consequently obliged to employ negroes, and slave labor thus became, by its cheapness and the necessity of the case, one of the staples of the country."

In confirmation of what we have said in regard to the condition of the slave here, compared to what it was later in other parts of the country, he adds : "The lot of the African under the Dutch was not as hopeless as his situation might lead us to expect. He was a chattel, it is true, but he could still look forward to the hour when he too might become a freeman."

Sometimes the slaves were given their choice of a home among the married children of their master. In a will in possession of the writer, dated 1759, the following clause appears : "If any of my slaves shall after my decease have a mind [preference] to live with any of my children, then it is my will, and I do order, that the rest of my children shall consent to it, and that he, or they, shall have him or her for a reasonable price."

This is by no means a solitary instance of provision made for allowing the slave to have his choice as to his home ; it was frequently done. Although this does not seem to us with our present views of slavery to exhibit much generosity, yet it certainly did abate the evils attendant upon his condition, and give him the opportunity of choosing the home he preferred.

Stiles, in his "History of Brooklyn," says : "Slaves were as a general thing kindly treated and well cared for ; but, after all, the institution of slavery was one that commended itself to the Dutch mind rather as a necessity than as a desirable system." Speaking of a public sale of slaves in 1773, he adds : "It was even at that time considered an odious departure from the time-honored and more humane practice which then prevailed of permitting slaves who wished to be sold, or who were offered for sale, to select their own masters."

The slave spoke the language of the family. Dutch became the mother tongue of the Kings County negroes. There are at present a few of the old colored people still living who not only understand Dutch, but who speak that language to each other when they meet.

In the newspapers published previous to 1822, about the period of emancipation, in advertisements offering a slave for sale, it was customary to state as a peculiar advantage that he or she could speak English as well as Dutch.

We find in the "New York Gazette" for February 22, 1773, an advertisement for a runaway slave, which states, after giving a personal description of the man, that he "can speak both English and Dutch, but *sounds mostly on the latter*. He is very strong and nimble, and does not want for wit. He can play well on the violin and is fond of company."

Another advertisement, bearing date May 6, 1776, gives the following curious description of a runaway slave : ". . . he speaks good English and middling good Low Dutch ; is a pretty likely fellow, apt to drink, wears his own hair tied behind. Had on when he went away an old, blue coat, lined with woolen check, the sleeves partly torn off, a new striped flannel jacket, a streaked woolen shirt, and a pair of superfine broadcloth breeches, mixed woolen stockings, half-worn beaver hat with a silver loop and button."

The first slaves in Kings County were sent here by Governor Stuyvesant in February, 1660. They never increased rapidly in numbers on Long Island, as they did in a more congenial southern climate, for the variableness of the weather and the extreme cold by which some of our winters are marked were not favorable to them. They easily succumbed to consumption, and had very little power of resistance when attacked by disease.

The first public record of the number of slaves appears in 1698.

At that time there were 296 in Kings County. They were distributed as follows : In Brooklyn 65, Bushwick 52, New Utrecht 48, Flatlands 40, Gravesend 17, Flatbush 71.

From this it will be seen that the largest number of slaves was owned in Flatbush.

In following the census of the slave population through successive periods, as we gather it from the "Documentary History of New York State," we find the returns in Kings County to be as follows :

1698	296	1749	783
1723	444	1756	845
1731	492	1771	1,162
1737	564		

The names given the slaves were a curious mingling of the nomenclature of the old Latin heroes with queer, twisted nicknames.

The men were known as Cæsar, Nero, Cato, Pompey, and Plato. Flora, Diana, and Juno were the goddesses whose names were most frequently assumed by the women.

With these were mingled names which might have come with them from the far-off native land of their ancestors : Mink, Syne, Bass, Jafta, Roos, Kouba, Yaft, etc.

All these appear upon the census list of 1755.

We find also such nicknames as these : Claes, Judey, Gin, Peg, York, Cuffee, France.

The name Cuffee, which was at one time quite common among the colored people, was probably Indian, for there was an Indian preacher of the Shinnecock tribe, born in 1757, whose name was Paul Cuffee. He labored among the Long Island tribes in the year 1800, and was said to be eloquent and possessed of much intelligence.

There is a name which has been in use among the colored people of Kings County for at least one hundred and twenty-three years. It appears upon the census of 1755, and it is still borne by more than one person now living. This name is Commenic ; it is said to be an Indian name. We have never known of its being used except among the colored people.

O'Callaghan says that in 1646 the price of a negro in New York averaged between one hundred and one hundred and fifty dollars.

It may be curious to know what was once paid for a slave on Long Island. We give some veritable bills of sale, from which we only omit the names of the parties :

FLATBUSH *Aug 16th* 1763

Recv⁴ of Mr. —— —— the sum of one hundred and ten pounds in full for a negro man Cæsar.

Sold him this day. Which negro I oblige myself my heirs Executors and Administrators to warrant and defend against all persons whatsoever.

As witness my hand

——— ———

In a similar bill of a few years later a less sum is given :

April 23, 1773.

Rec'd of Mr. —— —— the sum of sixty three pounds Ten Shillings in full for a negro man named Mink. Sold him this day. Which Negro I oblige myself my heirs Ex' Adm' to warrent and defend against all persons whatsoever.

As witness my hand

From several old bills still preserved we find that it was customary to have the account for the making and mending of shoes for the slaves paid yearly. One of these bills, from August 14, 1817, to June 13, 1818, amounts to £8 17s. 6d. The bill runs through a long sheet of coarse-grained, yellowish paper, peculiar to that age, as follows :

		s.	d.
To mend a pair of shoes for Brom		2	0
" " " " " " Cato		3	6
" " " " " " Flora		3	0
To make a pair of shoes for Nan		5	0
" " " " " " Dick		16	0
etc. etc.			

The physician's bill for professional services rendered for the slaves is also somewhat of a curiosity, not only as being a bill of items, but as showing that the slave and the master had the same medical adviser. As is here shown, the medicine prescribed by the physician is also furnished by him :

—— —— Esq. to Dr. M—— D^r.

1789		£	s.	d.
Aug 14th	To an Emetic for Brom	—	9	—
Oct 6th	To bleeding in the arm Dick	—	2	—
Nov 5th	To an aperient for Flora's child	—	2	—
Nov 24th	To extracting a tooth for Miss Sally	—	2	—
Dec 3^d	To extracting a tooth for Ben	—	2	—
Dec 19th	To an Emetic for Mrs. —— ——	—	9	—
1790				
Feb 1st	To dressing a wound on his lip and			
	ointment & attendance for Brom	—	9	—
etc. etc.				

For sixteen visits, the dates of which are given, and for the medicines needed, the amount of the bill is £10 14s. 0d.

Among other items for the slaves is the bill of a cabinet-maker:

May 7th 1817
To making a coffin for Flora.....................$2 —

In the State of New York manumission of the slaves was effected by the slow enactment of laws which gradually gave them their freedom.

In 1781 a law was passed by which freedom was given to such able-bodied men as served in certain regiments for three years or until regularly discharged.

In 1788 a law was enacted to the effect that when the owner of a slave under fifty years of age, and of sufficient ability to provide for himself or herself, should be disposed to manumit such slave, that previous thereto he, she, or they should procure a certificate signed by the overseers of the poor of the city or town, and of two justices of the peace of the county, certifying that such slave appeared to be under fifty years of age and of sufficient ability to provide for himself or herself; and when such a certificate of manumission was registered, that the slave should be adjudged to be free.

A number of slaves were freed in Flatbush under this law.

To show the form of manumission, we copy some of these from the old records:

I Stephen B. Schoonmaker of the Town of Flatbush, Kings County, State of New York, Do hereby certify that I have manumitted and set free my negro man named Harry aged twenty-eight years. Given under my hand this 16th day of April 1814.

STEPHEN B. SCHOONMAKER
NICH' SCHOONMAKER
WILLIAM W. STOOTHOFF
Overseers of the poor.

Signed in presence of
CORNELIUS DURYEE JR
JACOB DURYEE.

We the subscribers being Overseers of the Poor for the said Town of Flatbush Do hereby Certify that an application to us made by Stephen B. Schoonmaker of Flatbush to approve the manumission of a negro man named Harry and it appears to us that the said Harry is under the age of fifty years and of sufficient ability to provide for himself we do hereby approve of said manumission.

In witness whereof we have hereunto set our hands this 19th day of April 1814.

I, John Vanderbilt have manumitted and set free a certain female slave named Isabella, April 10th 1822.

(Signed)   JOHN VANDERBILT.

Sealed and delivered in presence of
GERRET MARTENSE.

She appears to be under the age of forty-five years and of sufficient ability to provide for herself and her children Cornelius and Thomas.

Witnesses
ADRIAN VANDERVEER
JOHANNES ELDERT.

On the same day, April 10, 1822, John Vanderbilt manumitted his slave Frances Young.

John Lefferts, August 17, 1822, manumitted his slave Susan.

A law was passed to the effect that every child born

of a slave within this State after July 4, 1799, should be free, but remain the servant of the former master until the age, if a male, of twenty-eight years; if a female, until twenty-five years of age.

It will thus be seen that great care was taken lest the slaves should become a public charge. The town authorities were not willing to accept any liabilities by which they might be obliged to support those who ought to be supported upon the private means of their former owners.

In order to secure the rights given them by this law, it was necessary to have the date of birth of every one applying for freedom thoroughly established; this was attended to by the town authorities. Among the town records we find a large number of these notifications of birth. We give a few as samples of the rest :

I Lawrence Voorhees of the town of Flatbush do hereby certify that a female child named Sawr aged three months was born of a slave belonging to me

Witness my hand this
21st day of Feb 1801.

I Abraham Ditmas of the Town of Flatbush, yeoman, do certify that a female child named Sook aged eight months was born the fifth day of July last of a slave belonging to me. Witness my hand March 5, 1803.   ABRAHAM DITMAS.

I, John Van der Bilt of the Town of Flatbush in Kings Co. do hereby declare that on the 15th day of Dec. last a male negro child was born named Will.

In witness my hand this 29th day of May 1802

JOHN VAN DER BILT.

The dawn of greater freedom was, however, rapidly approaching, and even the right to the services of the children was being abandoned :

Sir, I do hereby notify you that I abandon my right of service to a female child named Nancy, born Jan 20ᵗʰ 1803, which said child you have got on record in your office

ELSIE GERRETSEN.

May 6, 1803
To the TOWN CLERK OF FLATBUSH.

Sir I do hereby notify that I abandon my right of servitude to a female child named Bett, which said child you have on record in your office

HENDRICK VANDERVEER.

To JOHN C. VANDERVEER, *Town Clerk.*

FLATBUSH *Aug* 4 1800
Sir This is to certify that I abandon all my right of servitude to a negro child named Will, born Aug 5ᵗʰ 1799.

LEFFERTS MARTENSE.

To Mr JOHN C. VANDERVEER
Town Clerk.

The early settlers on Long Island were not, however, bound to slave labor exclusively; there were also indentured apprentices and laborers. Advertisements for runaway apprentices appeared in the New York papers as well as for runaway slaves.

An indenture paper, bearing date June 8, 1758, by which a young girl from Queens County was bound out to a family in Flatbush, is still extant. The terms are very much like those of an indenture made for a child bound out from an institution or by the county superintendent of the poor at this present time, except as to the remuneration due her for her services at the expiration of her term of indenture. In that respect they differ as widely as do the customs and manners of the centuries in which they were written. "The master shall give unto the said apprentice," says this old document, "a *cow*, a new wrapper, calico, at five shillings per yard, a new bonnet, a new pair of shoes and stockings, two new shifts, two new petticoats, two caps, and two handkerchiefs and her wearing apparel" — this last probably referring to the clothing she had been wearing previous to the limited outfit with which she was supposed to start out in life.

We have also a copy of an indenture made in the early part of the following century, in which no mention is made of a cow, but a more generous provision of clothing is imperative in the terms of the indenture.

The girl at the age of twelve is indentured, voluntarily and with consent of her parents, until she reach the age of eighteen.

During all of which time [thus quaintly reads this old, time-stained paper] the said Lydia her said master faithfully shall serve, his secrets keep, his lawful commands everywhere readily obey: she shall do no damage to her said master nor see it done by others, without letting or giving notice thereof to her said master. She shall not waste her said master's goods, nor lend them unlawfully to any: she must not contract matrimony within the said term : at cards, dice, or any unlawful game she shall not play whereby her said master may have damage : she shall neither traffic with her own goods or the goods of others, nor shall she buy or sell without license from her said master. She shall not absent herself day nor night from her said master's service without his leave, nor haunt ale houses, taverns, or playhouses, but in all things behave herself as a faithful servant ought to do during the term of service aforesaid.

The date of this indenture is "the nineteenth day of February, in the year of our Lord one thousand eight hundred and fourteen, and in the thirty-eighth year of American Independence."

We copy the following as a sample of an indenture of an apprentice to learn a trade :

This Indenture, made the 22d of July, A. D. 1695, is to certify to all and every one whom it may concern that Jonathan Mills, senior, of Jamaica, in Queens Co., and Jacob Hendricksen of Flatbush, in Kings Co., smith, are agreed and have made covenant in manner and form following:

Imprimis, Jonathan Mills, Jr., son of the above-named Jonathan Mills, senior, is bound to serve his master, Jacob Hendricksen, of Zuyt dam, above said, the time and space of three years begun the 5th day of June last, to expire the 5th day of June, 1698, in which time the said Jonathan Mills, Jr., is to serve his said master duly and faithfully, principally in and about the trade and art of a smith, and also sometimes for other occasions.

Secondly, Jacob Hendricksen, of Zuyt dam, abovesaid, is bound to said Jonathan Mills, Jr., to find washing, sleeping, victuals, and drink during said time of three years, and also to endeavor to instruct said Jonathan in said art and trade of a smith during said term of three years, and also that said Jonathan may have the liberty to go in night school in the winter, and at the expiration of said time his master is to give him a good suit of clothes for Sabbath-day, and also two pair of tongs and two hammers, one big and one small one.

In Testimony and performance whereof we have set hereunto our hands and seals the day and year above written.

his
JONATHAN + MILLS
mark.
JACOB HENDRECKSE,
von Zuyt dam.

Witness
JOHANNES VAN EKELEN.

In an indenture made by the overseers of the poor in Kings County at a later period, there seems to be nothing given to the girl when her time of indenture expires except a Bible, which was rather a mockery if she did not receive with it the just wages which the Bible enjoins should be given. This girl, Suzanne, born 1801, is indentured to Jacob Ryerson of the town of Brooklyn as a servant.

He shall [says the indenture] cause her to be instructed in the art of housekeeping and also of spinning and knitting. She shall also be instructed to read and write, and at the expiration of her time of service shall give unto the said Suzanne a new Bible.

In 1812 there appears on record an indenture more liberal as to its terms for the young girl :

Jane White [indentured as before] is to receive one new suit of holiday clothes of the value at least of $5, and two other good suits for everyday wear and one new Bible.

Intelligence offices for procuring domestics were established in New York some time before slavery was abolished.

That they were a more reliable dependence than the establishments of the present day, we should judge from the fact that premiums were offered—not to those servants who were constantly returning to the offices— but to those who remained a long time with the same employer. Perhaps this method would be a relief to the housekeepers of this age. We find the following in a newspaper of May 13, 1809 :

WARNE'S ESTABLISHED AND EQUITABLE OFFICE FOR SERVANTS,

No. 2 Robinson Street, first door from Broadway, where families are supplied with servants of every description, and it being the sincere wish of the proprietor that they would continue a long time in their places, both for the comfort of families and themselves, he offers as an inducement to this laudable end the following Premiums, which extend to such servants only as are registered for that purpose at this office:

$5. Every servant that lives three years with one family obtained at this office, shall, on having a good character from the said family, receive the above Premium.

$7. Every servant living five years with one family, obtained at the said office, shall on producing a good character receive the above Premium.

$10. Servants that live seven years in one place obtained as aforesaid shall, on having a good character from the said family, receive ten dollars.

Also a gift according to merit to sober, industrious, civil, and cleanly boys and girls, who live twelve months in one place.

The children of deserving poor parents shall be provided with places free of expense, and also entitled to a gratuity on the aforesaid conditions.

It being a common practice at many offices to take sums of money from servants, exclusive of their first charge for providing them with places, Mr. Warne assures servants that no more than one shilling first paid (unless for a lucrative situation) will be permitted to be taken at this office.

The proprietor is happy in having it in his power to relieve servants who have a long time labored under great hardships by falling into the hands of unprincipled persons who keep offices in different parts of the metropolis and strip them of their all under false pretenses.

Travelers, Taverns, Coffee-Houses, and Publicans supplied with servants agreeably to their orders.

It is probable that there were few, if any, foreigners employed as domestics in the family or as laborers on the farms in Flatbush previous to 1822, the year in which all traces of slavery ceased to exist.

At that time those who were formerly slaves, and their descendants, still found employment in the families of which they had once formed a part. They felt a certain claim upon the master and mistress under whose roof they were born ; this claim, if not legally recognized after this period, was at least so far acknowledged in the higher realm of duty that a kindly oversight was extended to the families of their former slaves, and they were provided for in cases of sickness and destitution.

As there was no almshouse in Kings County until 1830, when the county supervisors purchased the poorhouse farm at Flatbush, those who needed help, or were upon the town, were boarded and lodged in the private houses of individuals at the public expense.

To show how the poor were provided for, we here insert some bills which were found among some old papers :

The Overseers of the Town of Flatbush
　　　　　　To Nich⁺ Schoonmaker Dr

For medicine & attendance on blk man named
　Wall from Jan 6ᵗʰ until 13, 1813..........£2　5　0
Jan. 19, 1813. ·　　Recᵈ Payᵗ
　　　　　　　Nich⁺ Schoonmaker M. D.
of Mr Lefferts one of the
　overseers of the poor
　of aforesaid Town.

　　　　　　　　　Flatbush *Feb* 10th 1813
Overseers of the Poor of the Town of Flatbush
　　　　　　To Stephen B. Schoonmaker Dr.
For boarding and lodging a Negro man named
　Wall, a pauper to the State, 9 days...........$4.50
　　　Recᵈ Feb 12ᵗʰ 1813 the above in full
　　　　　for Stephen B. Schoonmaker
　　　　　Corn⁺ Duryee Jr.

Overseers of the poor of the Town of Flatbush.

To WILLIAM ALGEO D^r

Jan 12th 1813.

For making a coffin for Wall a state pauper.....$3.25

Received the above in full of John Lefferts
one of the overseers of the poor of the
town of Flatbush.

WILLIAM ALGEO.

In some of the colored families on Long Island there was a mixture of Indian blood with the African. It was very plainly traceable in their straight hair and in their lighter complexion ; but this mixture of the two races was not an improvement upon the character of the negro. The pure-blooded African was more kindly in his nature, more cheerful in disposition, more gentle and teachable. Those marked traits of the Indian character, the brooding over an injury with a view to retaliation, vindictiveness, and vengeful temper, clouded the good-natured hilarity of the African and made him unwilling to work, lazy, shiftless, and morose.

There is a strong tendency to superstitious belief in the African race. Strangely enough, it may be found to coexist with the acceptance of the purest Christian doctrine, and in those who lead an exemplary Christian life. It appears like some weed which is so natural to the soil of a garden that no amount of cultivation will wholly uproot it. They accept most readily not only the little superstitions which are always afloat as to dreams and signs and premonitions of coming events, but they are very credulous as to the power of charms and their antidotes. They believe in spells and poisons, and in the power and control which some persons may obtain over others, even when widely separated from

12

them. They believe in the noxious power of certain charms hidden in the ground which may affect the passer-by, and in the potency of spells exercised upon each other, to help or to harm, as either may be intended.

In times gone by, they were a kind-hearted, quiet people, fond of amusement, always looking upon the bright side of things, never worrying over coming misfortunes, but content to live in abiding faith upon a literal rendering of that Scripture which says : "Take no thought for the morrow. Sufficient unto the day is the evil thereof. Take no thought, saying, What shall we eat ? or, What shall we drink ? or, Wherewithal shall we be clothed ?"

Thus it happened too often that want came, and improvidence brought with it many misfortunes ; and they have begun to dwindle away and disappear before the rugged industries in which neither their taste nor their physical strength enables them to take a share.

In some instances colored families continued after their manumission in the employ of those to whom they had once belonged, and always found employment when well and assistance when sick from their old master and mistress.

Scarcely twenty-five years ago traces of this, the only pleasant phase of that institution, still existed in Flatbush. There were elderly persons who were always called " old Mis'es " or " old Master " in certain colored families, and the allegiance was not that compelled by law, but tendered by affection.

If relief was needed in any one of the old colored families who had been brought up in the town, they knew at once where to find it ; if they applied elsewhere, they were sure to be referred back to those with whom either themselves or their parents had been reared.

Thus it happened that the miscellaneous appeals for assistance which now come from every quarter for the poor were in earlier days unknown. The foreign element in our population which now preys so largely upon our pity and our purse had not then come to our gates. The housekeeper knew just who would apply at her kitchen-door for help, and just how much would be required. She might be willingly blinded, and give more or less than was necessary; but she could not be ignorant of the amount that was needed, for their circumstances and the number in their families were as familiar to her as those of her own household, of which they had once formed a part.

It was considered in times gone by rather a sign of a well-to-do farmer to have a large family of colored people in his kitchen. The elder members of these families had been so thoroughly drilled in the work required of them, that they were almost invaluable to the master and mistress as cooks, coachmen, and farm-hands. There were always small boys of every age to do the running of errands to "the store," bringing home the cows from the field, and calling the reapers to their meals, and such other work as required swift running and young feet. There were little colored girls of every age to help or hinder, as the case might be, in the various household duties. In most of the old Dutch houses there were small kitchens in which these families of colored people lived. They were not so far from the house as the slave-quarters on a Southern plantation, but the building was a separate one, annexed to the main kitchen of the house.

As a race, the colored people have strong religious feelings. They are excitable and demonstrative under the enthusiasm of a thoroughly aroused interest in religious duties ; but these feelings are variable, and apt to fade out when the exciting cause is removed. There have been, however, such noble examples among them of strong and abiding faith, characterizing a long and unspotted life, such steadfast adherence to duty amid temptations and discouragements, that they have proved themselves capable of reaching high Christian attainment and of illustrating the strength and beauty of Christian character.

This race for more than a century and a half formed part of the family of every Dutch inhabitant of Kings County. Speaking the same language, brought up to the same habits and customs, with many cares and interests in common, there existed a sympathy with and an affection between them and the white members of the household such as could scarcely be felt toward the strangers who now perform the same labor under such different circumstances.

We have given so much space to this subject, because a history of the social life of our ancestors would be incomplete if it did not include these people, who were so closely associated with the family, and who formed as to numbers so large a part of the household.

CHAPTER XXII.

AGRICULTURE.

THE head of every family in Flatbush, with few exceptions, was a farmer, until within the last thirty years. They cultivated their land in the most careful manner, and were among the best farmers in the State. It was rarely that one saw old and dilapidated outhouses or broken fences. The barns, wagon-houses, and hay-ricks were kept in good repair, and all the outhouses were covered with a heavy coat of dark-red paint. In the southern section of the town stones were scarce, so that the fences were post and rail. Only along the central ridge, which has been called the "backbone of the island," could stone be procured for walls to divide the farms. It has been asserted that there are no rocks south of that ridge.

There was formerly a stone wall running on the easterly side of the road that led from Bedford southward toward Canarsie, north of where the county buildings now stand. Little red chipmunks might be seen skipping over and through the interstices of this wall, for it was then a quiet nook, and the cultivated fields, shut in from the cold winds by the woods at the northeast, were always rich with the beauty of waving grain in the various stages of growth as the season advanced.

Here the running blackberry vines twined and inter-
laced themselves in arabesque figures across the stone
wall, their prickly stems and the toppling stones serving
to protect the enticing fruit.   High stalks of the golden-
rod in the autumn, and celandine and wild roses hid
their roots in the soil, kept damp by the fallen stones,
under which numerous bugs might be at housekeeping,
or from beneath which a family of ants would scatter if
their homes were unroofed.

Here the children clambered among the nettles for
blackberries in the summer, and under the great nut-tree
which stood midway the field they went nutting in the
autumn.   It was a pleasant, peaceful scene ; the robin and
the thrush, or meadow-lark, as it was called, here made
their nest, and sang their morning song in the apple orchards near ; crows flapped their heavy wings and cawed
from the tree-tops as they watched in the distance the
farmer dropping the corn.   Fresh and green the fields,
with an almost imperceptible slope, rolled southward, and
from this, the dividing line between Flatbush and Brooklyn, the Flatbush farmers had an unbroken and beautifully cultivated expanse of farming land to the limits
southward of the village.   Upon this northern border
of the town, which was once so fair a picture of agricultural prosperity, the change into a city suburb has
begun.   To the northeast fences are thrown down, the
old stone wall is leveled, the sickly-looking cows of the
city milkmen endeavor to graze upon the short and dried
grass ; pigs and dogs and goats, rough men and dirty
women, scold and scream and bark in mingled confusion from the shanties of the squatters that have taken
possession of the open commons.   It is sad for us who
have been so fond of this country life to think that

this may be a precursor of the change which shall slowly creep onward in advance of the city growth.

The cultivation of grain was found by the Long Island farmers to be less remunerative when the canals and railroads opened up the competition of the Western agriculturist; then the increased demand for the produce of the market gardener by degrees changed the whole character of the farm work on this island. Flatbush farmers, being so near to the city, began to raise those vegetables which were to supply the markets of New York and Brooklyn.

Where formerly wheat, rye, buckwheat, oats, corn, flax, and barley were the products of the farm, with only so much of cabbage, peas, potatoes, and turnips as were necessary for the family use, all this is now reversed; only so much hay and grain as the farmer needs are raised, while he depends upon his market produce for remunerative sales.

Under this system of cultivation the farms are not so picturesque as they were when the fields were waving with the graceful growth of grain. The market gardens and the great fields of potatoes and cabbage show signs of industry and thrift, but the farms are not so beautiful as they were before this change took place.

BARNS AND OUTHOUSES.

The barns of the Dutch farmers were broad and capacious. The roof, like that on their houses, was very heavy, and sloped to within eight or ten feet of the ground. There were holes near the roof for the barn swallows that flitted in and out above the rafters, surging to and fro in long, swift circles around the barnyard. Through the chinks of broken shingles the rays of the sun fell across the darkness as if to winnow the dust through the long shafts of light, or, where the crevice was on the shady side, the daylight glittered through like stars, for there were no windows in these barns ; there was light sufficient when the great double doors, large enough to admit a load of hay, were open.

There were beams across the second story, supporting poles on which the hay was piled. What great haymows they were, choice romping places for the children ! Just the spot in which to hunt for hens' nests, or from which to jump to the soft bedding of hay thrown down on the lower floor ! And then what boisterous laughter followed the leap, as the frolicsome little ones were almost buried by the downward plunge into the fragrant clover hay !

The hens were sure to select places for their nests in the farthest corners of the mow or in the mangers, and many a hatful or apronful of fresh, clean eggs the children would find and carry exultingly into the house. If by mistake they frightened a setting hen from her nest, what a noisy cackling was heard, followed by the unnecessary advice from some of the farm-hands to "let that hen alone ! "

The granary was usually boarded off in one corner. Opening the door suddenly, there was apt to be a scampering of mice and rats. If the pet dogs of the family were the companions of the children, chase was given at once. At it they went, scattering the threshed grain upon the floor, tumbling down the wooden grain-shovel and half-bushel measure, leaping over the wheat-bags ready for the mill, and sliding down great heaps of shelled corn, until the mischief was arrested by calling off the dogs and closing the doors, leaving these hunting-grounds to those more careful hunters, the cats.

The stable for the farmer's horses formed part of the barn ; it was entered by a smaller door at the side. There were several pairs of horses and generally a pair of mules owned by every farmer ; if oxen were kept, there was a stable for their use on the opposite side.

In these huge barns the cereal wealth of the farmer was stored. Reaping and threshing machines were not in use at the time that the land in Flatbush lay in cultivated farms, and the process of separating the wheat and chaff was more tedious than it is now.

The grain to be threshed was spread in a circle upon the barn-floor. It was trodden out by the feet of the horses which were driven round and round upon it, the driver standing in the middle, and his assistants keeping with their wooden forks the grain in its position, if it happened to be displaced by the horses. Rye was threshed out by the flail, a sound that one never hears now ; then, on many an autumn or winter day, one might hear from the open barn-door the regular thump, thump ! thump, thump ! of the flail as the farmer and his men threshed out the grain for winter use preparatory to taking it to the mill.

The cobwebs, begrimed with dust, in tattered festoons, ornamented with hayseed, hanging from the beams ; the horses, stretching out their long noses from their stalls ; the rough rope harness ; the detached bits of wagons, board seats, tongue, or shaft ; the farming implements, the bags of grain, and beside them the iron-rimmed half-bushel measure ; the old knife or broken scythe stuck in the shingled sides of the barn ; the black bucket of tar for the wagon-wheels ; the accounts chalked on the doors, and, above all, the sweet smell of hay pervading the place—how these things come back to memory as we recall the old barns in the days when all the village was tilled as farming land !

There are not many of these old barns left ; here and there one may still be found in Flatbush. Even in the outskirts of Brooklyn, where the city has suddenly overgrown an old farm, there are one or two standing. We feel as if they were out of place in the unaccustomed whirl in which they find themselves, for they belong not to the living, busy present, but to a different order of things that can never come back to us from the past.

Near the barn stood the wagon-house of the farmer, in the loft of which were sheltered the wheelbarrow, the grindstone, the plows and harrows, the rakes and hoes. Corn-cribs, filled during the winter with cobs of golden corn, formed the outer compartments of this building. The farm wagons were in the open central space. Even these wagons have changed in form during the last fifty years ; those then in use were wholly without springs and were painted red ; the sides were loose, and could be separated from the rest of the body so as to unload the more easily ; they sloped up both to the front and to the back, but were highest behind. There are none of this style of vehicle in use on the farms at present in Kings County, but the traveler may find them in Holland at the present day.

It may be interesting to know the money value of cattle raised by the old Dutch farmers. An old bill of sale, bearing date 1767, having been preserved among other and more valuable papers, its age has now given it a value which it did not once possess. We give it just as it was written :

Zeven beeste [seven cows]......................£25
Vif jong beeste [five young cows]............... 12
Vier kalveren [four calves]   6

HARVEST-TIME.

Before the invention of labor-saving machines, the time of harvest was one of immense labor to the farmer. The men who were useful with scythe and cradle were all engaged in advance at good wages. The rich golden grain was a beautiful sight, falling before the regular and graceful sweep of the scythe as the mowers advanced in rows, marking their progress by long swathes, while before them, with the slightest ripple of summer breeze, the ripened wheat swayed gently, bending itself like the lengthened undulations of the sea. As the reaper whetted his scythe, and stood resting a moment to wipe the perspiration that stood in beads on his forehead, his red flannel shirt gave the bit of color the artist loves in a picture.

At the bars let down in the lane his coat was thrown ; under a bunch of fresh cut hay to keep it cool stood the pail of drink for the thirsty reapers, and the tin cup. It was watched by the dog that lay beside it, his tongue hanging out of his mouth, panting from the heat, and snapping lazily at the insects that buzzed about his head.

The men turned the hay over with long forks before it was ready for the barn, and after that it was put up in haycocks. If a-heavy black cloud loomed up from the western horizon, threatening a shower, then the utmost haste was necessary to secure shelter lest the hay should be wet, and the wagons were driven rapidly to and fro between the barns and the hayfield. The men, with their long forks beside them, rode high on the top of the load. With the help of one man stationed above and one below, the fragrant hay was pitched rapidly into the mow.

A framework, consisting of four heavy corner posts and a thatched straw roofing, which could be raised or lowered upon these corner posts, was called by the farmers a barrack.

One or more of these barracks was in every farmyard for the straw and hay, and served to relieve the overcrowded barns in seasons of a bountiful harvest. There were also rows of haycocks of salt hay from the meadows, of which every farmer owned a certain share, and which was highly valued. This was harvested in the months of September and October.

In the late autumn long rows of cornstalks were stacked higher than the fences for the use of the cows in the cattle-yard, and the great golden pumpkins which grew between the rows of corn were laid along the sunny sides of the corn-crib to ripen.

Thus on all sides there were signs of peace and plenty. The returning seasons rarely failed to bring the farmer an abundant return for the labor he had bestowed upon his land. The smooth fields, under the careful cultivation of their respective owners, were never unduly taxed so as to exhaust their fertility. They were judiciously planted with a view to changing crops, and they were enriched as the experienced eye of the farmer saw what was needed.

Though the life was quiet and unostentatious, yet the farmer had a peaceful, happy home, undisturbed by the cares which to-day make the life of the citizen so full of turmoil and disquiet.

CHAPTER XXIII.

THE Dutch travelers who visited Long Island at the time of its settlement, and to whom allusion has already been made, say of the peach-trees that they "were so laden that one might doubt whether there were more leaves or fruit on them."

This statement is corroborated by what the old people tell us of the enormous quantity of peaches raised even as late as 1776. At that period, and subsequently, peaches were so abundant in Flatbush that they lay ungathered under the trees. The supply was greater than the demand, and after the animals in the barnyard had been abundantly fed on them, the remainder lay rotting in the sun.

The reverse of this is true at this present time. For some twenty-five years it has been impossible to cultivate successfully this delicious fruit upon the soil of Flatbush. A worm or some disease attacks the tree, and before they are in full bearing they look as if blighted, turn yellow, and die.

The peach-tree continued to grow and bear fruit in some of the adjacent towns long after it had ceased to repay its cultivation in Flatbush.

Plums and cherries were once very abundant; the trees were healthy and the fruit large and fine ; but with these, as with the peach, some disease attacking the tree, they were blighted, and the fruit, if the trees continued in bearing, was poor.

Grapevines were not so generally cultivated as they are at present. The Isabella grape was the variety preferred, as being the most hardy.

Of the small fruits, there were currants, gooseberries, strawberries, and raspberries ; but there were none of the large varieties of these plants, such as are now the result of careful selection and cultivation. Mulberrytrees were once abundant, but this very sweet fruit is now rarely seen.

Pears live to a great age on this soil. There were trees standing in 1855 which are known to have been in full bearing in 1776. Pears were formerly as abundant as were peaches, and the trees being more hardy continued longer in bearing.

The first of this delicious fruit which led the continuous procession of gradually ripening pears from August to November was what was called the " sugar pear." This was a small, yellow, sweet pear which ripened just at the close of harvest. It was very nice when first ripe, but apt to become mealy and decay if kept long after being gathered.

Another variety of this pear was called the "sugartop." These were very nice, being more juicy than the sugar pear and a little larger.

The "bell pear," named from its shape, was a rich, juicy pear, and bore very abundantly.

A pear called " the Engelbert Lott," probably named after the cultivator, was an excellent pear, and bore well.

The last of the crop was gathered in October or November; this late variety was called the "pound pear," from its great size. They ripened in the house after being gathered, but were used chiefly for sweet-meats. The Dutch housewife valued these pears, because she could preserve them at her leisure during the winter, as they were not apt to decay even if kept until almost spring. Flavored with orange, lemon, or ginger, they made very nice preserves.

There was a prolific bearer among the pear-trees called the "Cornelis Scooter" (we do not vouch for the correctness of the spelling). Every farmer had a number of these trees. The fruit ripened in the early autumn; they were juicy, but not highly flavored. The children brought them to school in their dinner-baskets, for as long as they lasted they were very abundant, but they could not be kept late in the season.

There were a number of fine apple and pear orchards in the village. Some of these, set out at an early period, have ceased bearing; but many of the old residents paid great attention to the cultivation of these fruits. and there was not a farm without its choice orchard. Some forty years ago these were in full bearing, and the fruit ripened to greater perfection than it has done for the past thirty years.

Every family had apples enough for winter use and for cider-making. The surplus was sent to the New York market; for at that period the markets were chiefly supplied from the produce of the Middle and Eastern States.

"Bough apples" began to ripen in harvest-time, and they were followed by a regular succession of ripening varieties until, latest of all, the russets were gathered.

What beautiful fruit, and how abundant it was in the orchards upon every farm! Great yellow apples peeped from under the glossy green leaves; bright red apples shone from beneath gnarled boughs of old trees; Newtown pippins fell dead ripe upon the stubble of the wheat-field, and swarms of bumble-bees and wasps and golden-winged flies feasted on the ripened and decaying fruit that had burst the mellow rind in falling. There were "sheep apples," in shape like flattened cheeses, that grew in the pasture-lots on low trees just high enough to entice the boys to climb after them; there were great yellow apples streaked with red, the embroidery of the sun; there were "guelderlengs," beautiful to look upon; and there were many others, like the fruit in the garden of Eden, "good for food and pleasant to the eyes," but without the ban placed upon the apples in Paradise, for as generously as they yielded, so freely all partook of the enticing fruit. The very shape of those old apple-trees was suggestive of a bountiful Nature; for even where the fruit was high up beyond the reach, the tree stretched downward its sloping limbs as if inviting the children to shake the boughs; willingly the response came; plump the fruit fell, sometimes, as if enjoying a practical joke, upon the very heads of the little ones, whose upturned faces were scarcely prepared for the sudden response. The pleasant sound of bees humming among the pink-streaked apple-blossoms in the springtime seemed to find its contrasted quiet under those trees in the autumn, when only the stillness was broken by the fall now and then of the ripened fruit which hid itself under the clover or the nettles, or rolled into the ridges of the plowed ground.

Even when the apple-tree has been blown down, it

will continue to bear if it has any connection with its root for the supply of sap. Was there ever an old apple orchard that did not have one or more trees in a recumbent posture, easy and inviting, for the children to climb? Under such circumstances, it seems almost impossible that they should still blossom and bear fruit, so gnarly and sapless the boughs seem to be; and yet there are well-authenticated instances of these gnarled, recumbent trees in full bearing for many years.

An old apple-tree in an orchard of Mr. John Lefferts blossomed and bore fruit in 1878, two years after it had fallen to the ground, and was only connected with the root by a small portion of the trunk. What made this case remarkable was the fact that this tree was the last of a large orchard which was full grown in 1776.

The holes in the decaying trunks of fruit-trees from which large limbs have been twisted by sudden gusts have always been favorite resorts of owls, from which through the long summer twilight they hoot in reply to each other, from orchard to orchard. Here also the squirrels love to secrete their winter store of nuts, especially if these orchards be close upon the line of forest from which they secure their food.

There was a severe gale in the year 1821, known as the "September gale," which the old people used to think, we can not say with how much of foundation for the belief, was the cause of the destruction of many of the old orchards. "At least," they would say, "the fruit has never been so abundant since," for in that severe and long-remembered storm the salt spray was found upon trees far inland, and the south side of trees turned black. Indirectly it may have had that effect, but, on the whole, we incline to think it a mere coinci-

dence, and that there has been a constant and regular
decadence in the fruit orchards of Flatbush.

After the apples were gathered and assorted, cider-
making was part of the farmer's work. The cider-
presses were usually placed along the farm lanes, near
the orchards, and every farmer made from one to ten
or more barrels of cider. It was in almost daily use on
the dinner-table during the winter season, and in the
following summer was often diluted with water, sweet-
ened, and flavored with nutmeg, as a pleasant drink in
warm weather.

It formed the common beverage of the men in the
harvest field, and, as it was the pure and unadulterated
juice of the apple, without any of the doctoring which
it is to be feared it receives from retail dealers of the
article at the present day, it was doubtless a wholesome
drink.

The vinegar used in the family was this cider in its
later stages of fermentation, so that pure "cider vinegar" was not the doubtful material which often appears
now under that name.

Vegetables grew in abundance on the rich soil of
Long Island. Asparagus, peas, lettuce, beets, radishes,
beans, cabbage, parsnips, sweet-corn, turnips, cucum-
bers, squash, pumpkins, and potatoes were to be found
in the kitchen garden of every farm. Egg-plant and
tomatoes are the only vegetables of comparatively recent introduction. Tomatoes first came into use upon
the table somewhere about 1840.

Spinach was covered with salt hay, to be cut for table
use in the winter. A narrow-leaved variety of dock
was used as "greens" when vegetables were scarce.
Pursley and dandelion were gathered in the spring

from the fields by those who had no vegetable gardens. Melons were easily cultivated in localities where there was sandy soil; they could be purchased at a moderate price through August.

While the revolving seasons brought an abundance of fruit and vegetables to the tables, yet there were times when the farmer was almost without them, for there were then none of the foreign fruits which are now supplied by every incoming steamer to complement the period when the native varieties are out of the market. Oranges and pineapples were rare and expensive; bananas were not to be had; lemons were not as abundant as now. Raisins, dried currants, prunes, and figs were by no means as cheap as they are at present; white grapes were only purchased for the sick or for special entertainments. All the luxuries which steam navigation brings to the householder to-day formed no part of the bill of fare of the farmer, who fifty years ago was confined to the produce of his own farm.

CHAPTER XXIV.

GARDENS, WILD FLOWERS, AND WOODS.

THERE is a fashion even in the cultivation of flowers. The greater or less demand for the propagation of different plants, or the ready sale for particular varieties, brings certain flowers into prominence at one period which a few years after are neglected for some newer favorite.

There was a time when most exorbitant sums were offered in Holland for the single bulb of a favorite tulip. Now tulips hold a comparatively low place in the estimation of the florist.

At one time the beautiful garden lily known as the Annunciation lily was considered a common flower, although it held its place by its hardy growth in our gardens. Now these lilies, forced from their natural July flowering to bloom at Easter, are cultivated by gardeners with the greatest care.

New varieties of roses bring large prices, and premiums are paid for novelties in all kinds of plants, so that, according to the gardener's estimate, plants are valued not so much because they are beautiful as because they are rare or new.

There are many plants now cultivated in every garden which some fifty years ago had not been intro-

duced; some of these were even unknown in our greenhouses.

The dahlia was brought into the United States from
Mexico. At first it was highly prized as a rich and rare
plant; every variety was eagerly sought and propagated with care. Forty years ago our gardens were
planted with dahlia poles almost as soon as the bulbs
had sprouted; these were anything but ornamental,
even when the long stalk stood like a twin growth
at the side; but when the velvety petals began to unfold, and all the varieties of crimson, scarlet, yellow,
and purple unrolled their regal robes, they received unbounded admiration. At every agricultural fair there
was rivalry as to who should exhibit the greatest variety. But the cultivation of this flower no longer claims
attention from the florist, and the neglect is not to be
regretted, for it was a coarse flower, without odor, and
ungraceful in growth upon its straight, stiff stalk.

When the fuchsia was first introduced it was called
lady's eardrop, and the elongated, slender shape justified the name by its likeness to the long, pendent ear-
rings which were fashionable at that time. They were at
first crimson and blue; cultivation has given us many
varieties both as to color and form, but none are as
graceful and pretty as those long crimson ones with
their blue centers from which the first were propagated.

Many plants are now successfully cultivated in this
country which were natives of China or Japan. These,
although at present we can scarcely call them new, were
not common here some thirty years ago; among such
we can name the camellia Japonica, the pyrus Japonica, dielytra, deutzia, wigelia, etc.

All the varieties of beautiful colored leaves—coleus—

were unknown in the horticulture of fifty years ago in Flatbush. Now they form a very large part of the brilliant decoration of every garden spot. Whether variegated, shaded, or the blending of one or more harmonizing tints, they are all so beautiful that they form a rich and valuable addition to our flora.

There are many flowers to which protection is given in the winter in the greenhouse that in the summer give variety to our gardens ; these were wholly wanting years ago, for the reason that there were fewer public hothouses and conservatories, and only solitary specimens of these plants found their way to the lover of flowers. They were not, as now, for sale in the springtime at every street-corner. We never saw growing in our gardens some thirty years ago heliotrope, abutilon, salvias, begonias, bouvardia, verbenas, calceolarias, pelargoniums, etc., flowers which now make their summer home in the beds with our native hardy plants.

The wisteria is also a stranger which has come to feel at home with us ; its rich clusters were not seen once as they are now, climbing from trellis to window.

The madeira-vine was then unknown. The trumpet-creeper, matrimony, woodbine, honeysuckle, and climbing roses were the only vines which clustered over the porticoes and clambered up the trellis.

But the memory of the pretty gardens throughout Flatbush rebukes even the intimation that we were without flowers ; and those which we had were quite as diligently cultivated, perhaps more lovingly, than the abundant beds which bloom in such luxuriance around our houses to-day.

We used to have an abundance of what are now called old-fashioned flowers.

Lilacs, white and purple, bloomed along the hedges. How delicious their perfume, how beautiful their color, how graceful their form ! Theirs was no scant and penurious flowering ! They gave so abundantly of their beautiful treasures that, even in the poor man's cottage, one might find great bunches of them on the mantelpiece in the spring-time ; children gathered them unrestricted ; wayside pedestrians leaned over the paling and broke off great stalks unrebuked, for no one thought it stealing. They have been called common, but they are so generous, so beautiful, so fragrant, that they will ever be associated with sweet memories of pleasant things.

Syringas were also very abundant, and their perfume filled the air with fragrance in the latter part of May and first of June.

Honeysuckles overhung many a trellis. The greenish-white snowball, that finally the sun bleached, as it grew into fitness to its name, recalling the drifts of January, had its place among the shrubbery.

Red peonies, huge and florid, thrust themselves forward in every corner of the garden ; those more delicately tinted did not come to our notice until a later period, when the pink-and-white peony divided the attention which had been given to the earlier and deeply colored specimens of that hardy bulb.

The flower-de-luce, known as the blue flag, and later as the fleur-de-lis, also formed a thicket with its sword-shaped leaves, but the varieties in color which may now be found were then unknown.

Pansies were abundant, but they were very small, and, under the common name of "jump-up Johnnies," crept out from the garden-bed to the grass-plot unno-

ticed and almost uncared for. The huge velvet petals
and exquisite shadings of their successors were develop-
ments unthought of in connection with the simple pansies which hid themselves under the box bordering or
crept under the shadow of taller plants.

There was a species of rose which was very hardy
and bloomed early in the season, called a May rose ; in
the Eastern States it bore the name of cinnamon rose ;
the leaf was small, and the rose itself, crimped and
curly, did not unfold its leaves as fully as did the later
and larger varieties. This opened the season to the succession of beautiful roses which followed.

The pink monthly rose bloomed, as its name indicated, all the season through, although the flowers were
most perfect in June and October. The color was exquisite, the petals being somewhat the tint of the pink
in the sea-shell.

There was a bush of this species of "monthly rose"
which held its place in a well-known garden in Flatbush for fifty years, the young shoots renewing the
bush from the same root as the old stalk was trimmed
out.

June roses of all shades of pink, dark-red, velvet-
leafed roses, great cabbage-roses, little yellow Scotch
roses, and small white roses were very abundant through
the summer.

There was a white climbing rose which was peculiarly fragrant, having somewhat the odor of new-
mown hay ; it only bloomed in June.

All these were so far hardy that they only required
some little protection to live out in the garden all winter ; they were generally thatched with straw or bent
down and covered with earth or compost.

We had tulips, chiefly red and yellow ones; they grew up without much care, often coming up year after year in the same bed, even if it had been sodded and no longer used as a garden. Crocuses and hyacinths came also with the May sunshine, and lilies of the valley strung their pale bells upon their slender stalks and gave notice of their presence by the sweet odor which rose up from their leaf-hidden flowers. Daffodils and jonquils came as harbingers of the long procession of the season, and the little pink roses of the flowering almond held a conspicuous place in the early blooming shrubbery. Pinks were abundant in June, and in that season also the honeysuckle filled the evening air with its luscious perfume.

In July the tall phlox—rocket, as it is sometimes called—sent up its bushy-headed spires of purple or white, favorite hiding-place for great humble-bees.

Ragged-robin made its appearance then, and sweet-william, bachelor's buttons, the red balm of Gilead, spiderwort, and yellow coreopsis made the beds gay with their bright colors.

Tall stalks of white lilies rose up from the bed of leaves at their feet, their stamens balancing the little puff of yellow pollen which was ever ready to play its innocent practical joke upon any unwary nose that ventured to steal the perfume from its chalice.

Morning-glories ran in riotous profusion over any tall object within their reach; here poppies flaunted their red petals, there was the purplish foxglove with its uncanny flowers; ice-plant, valerian, and bright-hued four-o'clocks grew abundantly. There were beds of lady's-slipper of many colors, larkspurs, prince's feather, and perhaps near these a few favorite sweet

13

peas. Cockscombs held up their ugly stiff flowers, and none the less stiff were the tall spikes of Canterbury bells.

Hollyhocks stood in groups, generally near the fence; they were pink, lemon-color, and maroon, tall, coarse flowers, but they had an honest way of trying to do their best to make the garden look gay.

Marigolds of all shades, from the brightest orange to the darkest maroon, stood in great, bushy plants, and mourning-brides, hydrangea, and love-in-the-mist showed the contrast of more quiet colors.

Later in the season the stockgillies bloomed, and the fragrant wallflowers, and in the autumn a great variety of chrysanthemums—artemisias, as they were then called—a plant that not all the spring sunshine nor summer heat could coax into bloom; only when all beautiful things were on the wane, it came as if to throw a garland of flowers upon the graves of its kindred.

There were other plants which were transplanted to the garden after being sheltered during the winter, such as geraniums, the fragrant Cape jessamine, a glossy-leaved plant bearing a bright-red fruit known as " Jerusalem cherry," and wax-plant; but, as we have been recounting the glories of the garden, we have only named the flowers which could stand the climate, and which grew freely in the open air. The addition to the summer glory which the house-plants might offer was quite insignificant then, and was lost in the abundant bloom of the hardy garden flowers.

Every careful matron valued the bed of herbs which she cultivated for medicinal purposes in a secluded corner of her garden. As many a human being possessed of useful homely virtues, but not particularly attractive to the eye, gets pushed aside to make room for gayer creatures, so these plants with their healing and health-giving properties, useful as they might be, were not beautiful to look upon, and therefore were confined within the limits of the beds along the garden fence, or where the huge beds of feathery asparagus marked the boundary between the flower and the vegetable garden.

There were bunches of tansy, rue, motherwort, southernwood, catnip, boneset, wormwood, and penny-royal. These formed the domestic pharmacy which was the reliance of the family, and which was perhaps quite as effective as the contents of the vials which serve to run up the long bills of the apothecary.

In companionship with these medicinal herbs grew others for culinary purposes : thyme, sage, sweet mar-joram, mint, and summer savory. A corner of the gar-den was reserved for the cultivation of mustard. To prepare it for table use, the seed was thrown into a large wooden bowl, within which a cannon-ball was dexter-ously rolled round until the seed was pulverized.

The close-shaven lawns, such as now present a beau-tiful velvety appearance, would have been almost an impossibility for us before the invention of the lawn-mower.

The whetting of the scythe might occasionally have been heard during the season, though the grass was not often cut. Clover, both red and white, grew rich and abundant, as it would not be allowed to grow now. It was intermingled with buttercups and daisies. It swayed under the breeze like the undulations of the sea ; yellow-jackets and humble-bees rocked themselves to and fro upon the clover-heads, and little butterflies raised and lowered their pretty canary - colored wings as they rested themselves upon the flowers in the grass.

At the time of mowing the air was sweet with the perfume of new-mown hay. Often in the second growth white clover came up abundantly, so that the grass looked as if sifted over with drifts of snow. This growth of white clover was even more fragrant than the red. A flower, called by its common name stariches (little stars), or known as star of Bethlehem, grew wild in many of the pasture-fields. Pretty as it was to look at when in bloom in the spring, it was persistently regarded by the gardener as his enemy, for where it once obtained hold upon the soil it was impossible to eradicate it.

The dandelion was abundant in all the fields—beautiful, whether in its tiny mimicry of the golden sun, or in its gossamer state when, like a flower-spirit, it is about to ascend and lose itself in the upper air.

Along the borders of the fields and in the woods there grew abundantly wild flowers of every kind.

Jack-in-the-pulpit preached from every southern slope in May ; the beautiful white bloodroot fluttered its tender leaves in the shivering spring wind ; anemones were plentiful. Hepaticas looked up in little groups from between the mossy roots of old trees, and wild violets, scentless but pretty, held up their heads amid the drifts of the dead leaves in the hollows.

Later in the season the purplish-pink flowers of the wild geranium appeared upon their slender stalks. The fragrant pyrola, called sometimes wild lily of the valley, threw up its single stem from the little green plate of leaves below, and mitchella or partridge-berry matted the ground with dark-green leaves and coral beads.

Specimens of the Indian pipe have been found in the woods, but the plant is very rare with us.

May-apple, or "Pinkster bloomitje," as the Dutch people called it, was abundant early in the season.

The trailing arbutus (mayflower) never grows at this end of Long Island, although it is to be found in the eastern counties.

In the autumn the gentian might be gathered in the woods, and in the swamps the brilliant lobelia cardinalis.

Celandine grew along the fences, and the running blackberry added its tangle of prickly vines to the thicket. These running blackberries were known as dewberries, and were much larger and sweeter than the "bush blackberry," as, for distinction, those were called.

The elder bloomed the first of July; the flowers were beautiful—a close examination could only reveal how perfect the minute petals were—but the odor was not pleasant, and they withered quickly from the warmth of the hand in carrying them. The clusters of purple-stemmed berries ripened in the early autumn, and contrasted with the brilliant yellow of the golden-rod which nodded from the same thicket. Its feather-like plumes were sometimes cultivated in the garden under the name of amaranth.

Sumach, glossy-leaved and tough-stemmed, thrust itself wherever a stone wall or post-and-rail fence offered its protection from the farmer's axe, and held aloft stiffly its maroon fruitage. Bitter-sweet vines also grew in the tangle of unkempt hedges, and in the frosts of October and November opened their bunches of curious berries, which the housewife loved to mix with cedar twigs in her vases on the mantel-piece.

TREES.

There were formerly many locusts planted in the gardens and along the village roadside. But these beautiful trees with their delicate, pale-green foliage in the spring-time contrasting with their furrowed, mossy trunks, have no power to resist the wind, and are unsafe by reason of the broken limbs and the lodgment of dead branches among the foliage. This brittleness of stem and branch is the result of the depredations of a worm which infests the tree, and by its continuous boring weakens the strength of the limbs so that they fall under the slightest pressure of winter snow or summer wind. It is feared that the locust will in time disappear entirely under the ravages of this worm. This is to be regretted, for the odor of the flower is almost equal to that of the orange-blossom.

There were formerly many sycamore (or button-ball) trees in Flatbush, but these have nearly all died, as also have the Lombardy poplars, of which Dr. Strong says there were many along the sidewalks when he first saw the town.

In May the horse-chestnut held up its pyramidal spires of pink and buff flowers ; but there were not many of these trees in the village. They are not among our trees of native growth, although we have no memory of the time when they were introduced.

In midsummer the tulip-tree hides its green and salmon-colored flowers among its abundant leaves.

The large and single althea—we used to call it the " rose of Sharon "—was to be found in every garden. It bloomed in August ; the flowers were large—some pink, others purple or white.

Lindens and maples have always grown rapidly in Flatbush and have attained a great size. Until recently there were few, if any, elms. This beautiful tree, however, grows freely in this soil, and well repays the care in planting.

Our woods were not without a full supply of nuts. Chestnut-blossoms spread their long green tassels upon their outer branches in June, the green balls slowly ripening until the frosts of October gave the watching and waiting children the coveted treasures.

Hickory-nuts might be gathered in the woods in almost every direction. There was a nut-tree which grew on a line with, and directly north of, what is now the Almshouse. It bore nuts which were highly valued; they were thin-shelled, and were a superior species of hickory-nut. They were called heart-nuts from their shape. The tree was on the farm then owned by Mr. J. Lefferts.

Butternut-trees also grew in Flatbush: one was on the property of the Martense family, and stood about where Mr. Wilbur's house now stands. From a nut taken from that tree and planted, another grew in the grounds of Mr. John Lefferts. There were one or two in the south end of the town.

Black-walnut trees were numerous. One, which is very old, still stands upon the property of General Crooke. A grove of them once stood upon the land of the late Mr. Willink, but were cut down when the property was sold.

The roots of this tree are said to poison the ground around them. Other trees die when their roots extend in the same direction, possibly because the walnut exhausts the fertility of the soil.

Hazelnuts were to be gathered in some parts of Flatbush, but there were not many of these bushes. There were a number of persimmon-trees in the outskirts of the village. This fruit was called "messerples" by the old people ; the fruit was ripened by the frost, and was only fit to be eaten when the leaves had fallen from the tree.

The woods which formerly encircled Flatbush consisted chiefly of hickory, gum, chestnut, and oak trees ; hickory-trees predominated as to numbers.

There was a long belt of woodland southward, the last remnant of which now lies just beyond the boundary line between Flatbush and Flatlands. To the west it extended from the line between Flatbush and New Utrecht, and took in the high ground in Greenwood, and the hill in Prospect Park, then known as Vanderbilt's Hill. It bounded the road for the distance between Mr. Willink's house and the hill on the Polhemus farm upon the old road.

On the east side of the old turnpike, the woods, untouched by the woodman's axe, extended from the point opposite Mr. Willink's house both northward and eastward. The road known as the Clove road followed along the southerly side of the woods, parallel to where the Penitentiary now stands, to a point at which it was intersected by a road which led to Canarsie, and then continued in an unbroken line toward the north and east to the limit of the village.

Thus Flatbush was pleasantly and picturesquely encircled with woods ; its little group of houses surrounded by gardens and farms, its chimney-tops and roofs projecting from among the trees, and the spire of its church forming the central object in the view, it presented a beautiful picture of rural life, of peace, quiet, and comfort.

Looking down from the height of Vanderbilt Hill, or farther northward to what used to be Prospect Hill, but a few years ago it might still have been entitled to the first name given it by the old Dutch settlers—Midwood.

There were formerly beautiful walks about the village. The wood at the north had fine, large trees with a brook running through, and was without underbrush. The same might be said of the wood north of Mr. Willink's, now in the Park. There was no underbrush, and the grass was thick and soft. The most attractive walk was that upon the high hill, Vanderbilt's Hill, as it was called. The farm lane led round what is now the Plaza, near the restaurant, and gradually mounted the hill known now as Breeze Hill. From this spot an extent of country could be seen that could scarcely be excelled as a calm picture of pleasant farm-life. To the north extended unbroken woods; eastward, at the foot of the spectator, was a stretch of level and beautifully cultivated farms; here were fields of waving grain; there the red clover wafted its perfume from acres ripening for hay; cattle were grazing in pasture-fields; horses stood under the trees along the fences, switching away the flies, now stooping to eat, now raising their heads and pointing forward their ears as the farmer's dog chased up the birds from the hedges, or the farmer held out to them some oats to decoy them within reach of the bridle.

Perhaps the wagons, laden with hay, slowly wound along the narrow farm lanes; or it might be that the plow was being guided up and down a field, making broad, straight furrows. From the orchards below, the robin's song arose ; the thrush whistled his sweet, wild note ; the oriole, the bobolink, and the wren came out to the field to add their snatch of song. From distant tree-tops the crow flapped his wings, and with a loud caw went to seek his mates.

A succession of highly cultivated fields stretched still farther eastward until the eye reached the faint silver rim of the distant bays which, in irregular curves, bound the shores. Southward, the ocean glimmered under the sunlight, and the white sails of ships outward bound could be distinctly seen. Farther to the southwest the heights of Navesink loomed up faintly, and, after twilight, the twin revolving lights threw out a glimmering beacon from the lighthouse like the faint sparks from the opening and closing of a firefly's light. To the westward the woodland extended in an unbroken background of forest. Such was the view from this hilltop of the village, surrounded by woodlands inclosing with their green circlet the golden grain-fields of the farmers, like a ring of emerald upon embossed gold.

CHAPTER XXV.

SOME thirty years ago there were two or three miles of country road between Flatbush and Brooklyn, with farms, meadows, and woodland upon the roadside. Through all these years, however, Brooklyn has been throwing out vigorous branches in all directions, like the spreading boughs of trees that have rapid growth, and at last it has reached our very borders. Unlike the budding of tree and shrub, however, this mingling of urban and suburban presents an unsightly growth. The sunken city lot, with its encampment of shanties, its hummocks of refuse, its open, treeless commons, the resort of goats and geese, its rocks flaunting placards for advertising quacks and speculators—all these are the ugly pioneers of the advancing city.

On one side of the village these have been held in abeyance by the intervening green slopes and shrubbery of Prospect Park and their protecting barrier of hickory, oak, and elm trees.

The distance between Flatbush and Brooklyn was rendered more noticeable by the limited means of intercourse in public conveyance between the two places.

Most of the village residents kept their own carriages and horses. The old-fashioned gig, the red farm-wagon, the family barouche, and the time-honored stage-coach, each held undisturbed possession of the dusty turnpike. The old stage-coach, pleasantly associated with roads winding between green hills and shady woods, was the only means of public conveyance within the limits of Kings County.

Until the year 1838 or '39 there were two regular stage-coach lines running between Flatbush and Brooklyn. The oldest inhabitant well remembers Smith Birdsall, the proprietor of one line, leaving his house, which stood on what is now the corner of Flatbush and Vernon Avenues, at eight o'clock in the morning, and returning about four in the afternoon.

A loud blast from a horn announced the coming of the coach. We can readily recall the picture, which now we only see in the most secluded country towns, of the stopping of the stage-coach, the door held open by friends to "speed the parting guest." The last words are spoken as the passenger leans over the half door ; the driver shouts " All ready ! " and mounts his high seat ; there is the waving of handkerchiefs, and the journey is begun ; the children are frolicking in the gateway to enjoy the excitement of the prancing horses, the cracking of the long whip-lash, and the prolonged blast of the driver's horn.

Soon after this stage had gone its way toward the distant city, but scarcely before the whirl of dust had altogether subsided, another opportunity was afforded the traveler to reach town that morning.

The mail-stage came in at nine o'clock from Fort Hamilton. This was more pretentious, if not more comfortable, than the first. It was drawn by four horses, and owned by Colonel Church, of New Utrecht. With a still louder blast upon a bugle, its arrival was announced as it turned the corner by the church from the post road to New Utrecht, and drew up before the little inn of the Widow Schoonmaker, opposite Erasmus Hall.

The mail-bag, not a very bulky one in those days, was taken over to the post-office, nearly opposite the Dutch church, and assorted by Mr. Michael Schoonmaker, and then it was flung back to the driver, and deposited under the boot at the foot of the driver's high seat.

There was a prolonged snapping of the long whip-lash over the heads of the leaders, the stage rocked to and fro as the horses pranced hither and thither in the long, loose traces, and finally started off gayly under the inspiring flourish of a fresh blast and a final snap of the driver's whip.

Then the village sunk into quiet, and the lookers-on proceeded to their ordinary work for the day. If any one through drowsiness, or for any other cause, missed this last nine-o'clock stage, the unfortunate individual must wait over until the next day, for there was no other opportunity to reach Brooklyn by public conveyance for the next twenty-four hours.

At four o'clock in the afternoon the first stage returned, and at five the mail-coach. Then the same bustle was repeated ; the friends who were expected from the city to visit in the country were looked for by these returning coaches, and the members of the family who had been to New York or Brooklyn for the day returned home, tired and hungry, and were met at the gate by the children who had been stationed there to await and announce the approach of the stage-coach. Father had brought, perhaps, the weekly paper at least ; he had the latest news ; and mother had been shopping in Maiden Lane or William Street.

Until the year 1842 or '43 these stages were the only modes of public conveyance. They then gave place to an omnibus line.

These omnibuses ran every hour, and as to convenience, in this respect they were certainly an improvement upon the stage-coaches.

Flatbush Avenue was opened from Fulton Avenue, Brooklyn, to the entrance of the village in 1856. At first the cars· ran to the city limits, and were there met by the omnibus, but when the whole line of railroad was completed, the old omnibus line passed into disuse.

It was a strange sight for us to see the cars from the city, associated as they then were with shops and city life, passing to and fro upon the country turnpike, to catch a glimpse of them through the shrubbery, and to hear the unmusical tinkling of the bells upon the car-horses amid suburban sounds.

VILLAGE ROADS.

Before the railway tracks somewhat incumbered the country turnpike, the old road to Flatbush was a favorite summer drive for the citizens of Brooklyn and New York. As there were then no city parks for carriage-driving, and the country had not been so widely opened up for extended travel, the pleasant rural aspect of the village made it an attraction toward which the large majority of the people who lived down town in New

York turned for an excursion on a summer afternoon. The shore road along the Narrows could be included, making a long and pleasant drive in the country suburbs.

The roads and sidewalks in this town have always been kept in order. Dr. Strong speaks of a time when there were low stone fences along the main street "surmounted by primrose hedges." These have all passed out of the memory of even the oldest inhabitant. About 1840 the sidewalks were separated from the carriage road by a slight fence made of posts joined either by chains or by a top rail.

At this time every farmer owned several cows, which were sometimes allowed to graze on the roadside, or loitered there on their way home from their pasture-fields. The cow-bell, tinkling on the neck of the leader, was a rural sound which was always heard at sunset in summer. These railings between the sidewalk and the carriage road served to keep the cows from annoying pedestrians, and were really a safeguard for children. They also gave a finished appearance to the sidewalk, as they were neatly painted and generally kept in good repair.

THE TOLL-GATE.

When the road to Brooklyn was a turnpike, the care of the road was paid for from the money collected at the toll-gate. This, in or about 1842, stood near where Flatbush Avenue forms the terminus of Hanson Place, or between Hanson Place and Lafayette Avenue. Afterward it was removed to what is now called Atlantic Street, somewhat easterly of the present intersection of Atlantic Avenue and Flatbush Avenue. Next it was placed near the Battle Pass, south of the Valley Grove

Hotel, on the old road. After this it was placed opposite the Willink property. Finally, it was removed within the limits of the village, and at present stands on the avenue between Fenimore and Winthrop Streets.

CHAPTER XXVI.

THERE are seven churches in Flatbush. In their order of erection, they are as follows : The Reformed Dutch Church, St. Paul's Protestant Episcopal, the Methodist, the Roman Catholic, the Mission Church, the Baptist, and the German Reformed.

The name of the Dutch Church was first officially given in the memorial which Domine Selyns, of New York, and his consistory offered to Governor Dongan in 1688. It was confirmed by a charter which Governor Fletcher granted to the metropolitan corporation in 1696, under the title of "The Ministers, Elders, and Deacons of the Reformed Protestant Dutch Church in New York." This is the oldest religious corporation in this country.

The first church in Flatbush was built in 1654, by order of Governor Stuyvesant. He directed that it should be sixty or sixty-five feet long, twenty-eight feet broad, and from twelve to fourteen feet under the beams ; that it should be built in the form of a cross, and that the rear should be reserved for the minister's dwelling. The Governor also directed that the morning service for Brooklyn, Flatbush, and Flatlands should be held at Midwout ; the afternoon service alternately at Brooklyn and Flatlands. The first church was erected in Flatlands in 1662, in Brooklyn in 1666. The second church in Flatbush, on the same spot, was erected in 1698. It was of stone, facing the east, with a steep, four-sided roof, in the center of which was a small steeple.

The site of the present Reformed Church was, therefore, that of the first church of any denomination in Kings County; on this spot there has been preaching continuously since 1655, a period of two hundred and twenty-five years.

The salary paid Rev. Johannes Theodorus Polhemus, the first pastor, was a sum equal to about four hundred and sixteen dollars. The Rev. Henricus Selyns was sent over from Amsterdam in 1660, to have charge of matters ecclesiastical in Brooklyn, upon complaint as to "the difficulty of the road from Breucklin to Midwout." Domine Selyns returned to Holland in 1664. After the death of Domine Polhemus in 1676, the Rev. Casparus Van Zuren was sent over by the classis of Amsterdam, and installed in 1677 as pastor of the four churches, i. e., Breucklin, Midwout, Amersfort, and New Utrecht. He returned to Holland in 1685. The Rev. Rudolphus Varick was the next minister over the Kings County churches; he continued in office until 1694, and was succeeded by Domine Lupardus, who died in 1702.

The church at Jamaica was now added to the number, and there seems to have been a little disturbance upon the occasion of calling another minister. Some of the people were anxious to have a call given to Rev. Bernardus Freeman, of Schenectady; others made a formal application to the classis of Amsterdam, and, in response to their request, Rev. Vincentius Antonides was sent out and installed in 1705. Meantime Domine Freeman had also accepted the call, and party spirit ran high as to the claims of the respective ministers. The controversy increased in bitterness until the year 1714, when a more Christian spirit prevailed, and the churches agreed to accept both ministers and to lay aside their differences. The charge of the two ministers consisted of the churches of Breucklin, Bushwick, Flatbush, Flat- lands, New Utrecht, and Jamaica. Breucklin, Bush- wick, and Flatbush communed together, and Flatlands, Gravesend, and New Utrecht ; Jamaica had a separate communion.

The churches were, about this time, greatly agitated upon the question of ordaining ministers. One portion, called the " Cætus party," claimed that, in view of the inconvenience of sending for ministers from Holland, there should be a regular organization into classes and synods in this country. The " Conferentie party " be- lieved that the ministers should be ordained and sent out by the classis of Amsterdam. In 1746 the appro- bation of the classis of Amsterdam was given, and the first meeting of the new Cætus was held in September, 1747, in New York City, this being the first judicial organization, higher than a consistory, established in the Dutch Church in America.

Mr. Freeman died in 1741. Johannes Arondeus was appointed as his successor, but he does not seem to have shown a Christian spirit, and was not held in high esteem. He was deposed from his office, and Domine Curtenius was installed in 1755. Rev. Ulpianus Van Sinderin was called to fill the place of Rev. Vincentius Antonides, who died in 1744 ; his colleague was Johannes Casparus Rubel.

Domine Rubel was a violent Tory during the Revolution, and gave much offense for this cause. He had also faults which were very inconsistent with his Christian profession.

There was nothing charged against the moral character of Mr. Van Sinderin ; but his eccentricity and his advanced age made it desirable that he should withdraw from active duty. He was declared emeritus, and a stated salary was given him until his death, at Flatlands, in 1796. Rubel was deposed from office, and his subsequent career proved that the people had acted wisely in doing so.

Van Sinderin and Rubel were the last ministers sent to America from the classis of Amsterdam.

The Rev. Martinus Schoonmaker and the Rev. Peter Lowe were the colleagues next placed over the six collegiate churches of Kings County. The former preached in the Dutch language until his death, which occurred in 1824. At that time he was nearly ninety years of age. "He was," says Furman, "the last connecting link of the chain which had bound together the churches of Flatbush and Gravesend from 1654." It is said that Domine Schoonmaker never but once (in 1788) preached in English. With his death, in 1824, the regular and public use of the Dutch language in the pulpit ceased. Until 1792, however, all the church service was in Dutch ; at that date it was arranged that Mr. Lowe should preach in English in the afternoon service at Brooklyn, Flatbush, and New Utrecht. The combination of the six congregations composed of the towns of Brooklyn, Bushwick, Flatbush, New Utrecht, Flatlands, and Gravesend continued until 1805. As these towns increased in size they gradually formed separate churches.

After the death of Rev. Peter Lowe, Flatbush and Flatlands, the only remaining united congregations, called
Rev. Walter Monteith. In 1822, the Flatbush church
called Rev. Thomas M. Strong, he being the first pastor
settled over this church alone. The Rev. Dr. Strong
died in 1861, and was succeeded by Rev. C. L. Wells,
who is still the pastor.

The present church is the third upon the same spot ;
it was completed in 1796. The temporalities of the
church were judiciously managed by church masters for
a period of one hundred and seventy years. The last
of these church masters were John Vanderbilt, Isaac
Snediker, and Johannes E. Lott. This church was the
first on Long Island incorporated under the general act
of the Legislature of the State in 1784. It continued
under this act until 1804, when, under a special act
providing for the incorporation of the Reformed Dutch
churches, the title became that of the " Trustees of the
Reformed Protestant Dutch Church of the Town of
Flatbush, in King's County." Dr. Strong says that
much of the labor in building the present church was
done by the congregation. So well did they love the
house of the Lord ! The cost, exclusive of the work
thus given, was £4,873 7s. 7d. The bell in present use
was the gift of Hon. John Vanderbilt, who imported it
from Holland.

In speaking of the interior arrangement of the second church, Dr. Strong says : " The male part of the
congregation were seated in a continuous pew all along
the wall, divided into twenty apartments, with a sufficient number of doors for entrance, each person having
one or more seats in one or the other of these apartments. The residue of the interior of the building was

for the accommodation of the female part of the congregation, who were seated on chairs. These were arranged into seven different rows or blocks, and every family had one or more chairs in some one of these blocks. This arrangement of seats was called 'De Gestoeltens.' Each chair was marked on the back by a number or by the name of the person to whom it belonged. The windows of this church were formed of small panes of glass; those on either side of the pulpit were painted or ornamented and set in lead."

The interior of the present church has been constantly modernized in accordance with the changes of fashion, and to keep pace with the appearance of sister churches in the adjacent city. At first the aisles were not carpeted, but were scrubbed when necessary and sanded. Until 1836 the pew-doors were as high as, and on a line with, the back and front, so that the level pew-tops gave them the appearance of pens. The wood was grained and of a very dark color. The galleries at the north and south were never used; the front of these was so high that a person sitting there could not have been seen from below. There was no gallery across the east side of the church. There were a few pews between the belfry and the side galleries which were given for the use of the colored people. There were no blinds on the windows. The pulpit, which was reached by means of winding stairs on each side, was made of mahogany, and was some five feet above the floor, supported on columns. The church was heated by two cast-iron stoves, but these were not sufficient to make the people comfortable, and foot-stoves were provided by every pew-holder for the use of his family. These foot-stoves were boxes about a foot long, made either of tin or wood perforated. Within this box was placed an iron cup containing hickory coals. The colored servants carried these foot-stoves to church. It was common to see a small colored boy or girl preceding the mistress with her stove and placing it in her pew. They were pushed from one member of the family to the next when needed, and the peculiar scratching noise upon the floor thus made was quite a familiar sound in church. Sometimes a careless child upset the stove, which occasioned some commotion in the pew. In 1836 the gallery front was lowered, as were also the tops of the pews ; a gallery was thrown across the east side of the church, and the woodwork was painted white. Back of the pulpit was a fluting of damask, forming a crimson arch behind the minister. Two bronze lamps stood upon the desk. The next change made in the church was to paper it to represent stone. But this did not meet with general approval. Taking the flimsiest material to represent the most durable was not characteristic of the Dutch. In place of the crimson satin arch, a painting representing a curtain looped back was inserted back of the pulpit. About this time blinds were placed upon the north and south windows. Unfortunately, the exterior of the church, although stone, was painted like the front, which was stuccoed. It was a great mistake, and has since been much regretted. Somewhere about 1864 the church was again renovated, and it still remains as it was at that time decorated. After this renovation a new church-clock was placed in the steeple, which has proved to be an excellent time-keeper. It strikes upon the old bell given in 1796. The organ was purchased about 1860. Instead of the cast-iron stoves, large heaters are now used, which make the temperature very pleasant throughout the building. Furnaces such as require pipes laid below the flooring can never be placed under the foundation, for fear of disturbing the graves of those who were buried under the church.

While the service was in the Dutch language the music was only vocal. Many of the old Psalm-books are still extant ; the music was on every page beside the words. The square notes look very odd compared with the music of this age. The New Testament and Psalms were bound together, and the books were usually mounted and clasped in silver, and had small rings attached, through which chains or ribbons were passed, so as to hang the book, when not in use, on the back of the chair.

The earliest recollection which we personally have of the singing during the church service is that of Mr. John Antonides as precentor or " voorzanger." He was an old man even then (somewhere about 1836) ; he was very tall, with a strong frame, and a voice so powerful that it filled the church without an effort. His place was in the corner of the elders' seat, for then, as now, the elders' bench was at the right side of the minister and the deacons' at the left. When the Psalm was given out he leisurely put on his spectacles, and, beating time with his hand once or twice on the top of the pew, took the proper key from his tuning-fork, and then slowly rose from his seat and led some of those old tunes which are now almost forgotten : Dundee, Lenox, Mear, Duke Street, and St. Martin. When he struck the keynote, the people all sang, not leaving the praise of God to the choir alone.

At that time the metrical version of the Psalms was used ; the old tunes adapted to them have a peculiar power to recall vividly the past. How well are those old hymns remembered ! and how often they come to mind : "Teach me the measure of my days"; "O God, our help in ages past"; "Sweet is the day of sacred rest"; "Lord, in the morning thou shalt hear." They recall the memory of the beloved minister whose lips shall no more speak the words, and of the chorister who has slept for more than a quarter of a century in the old churchyard with the congregation whose hymns of praise he led.

Thus we have rapidly passed over a period of two hundred and twenty-six years. The fact that this venerable church was the first organization in Kings County invests it with peculiar interest. Where now there are so many places of worship that our adjacent city has been called "the City of Churches," this one stands first in the line, and is the oldest in the sisterhood. On the very spot where the present building was erected, the Indian tribes of western Long Island first saw an assemblage for worship in a house dedicated to God.

OTHER CHURCHES.

There were at one time in Flatbush many colored children, the descendants of those who were once slaves on Long Island. The majority of them did not attend Sunday-school, and they were rarely seen at church.

The month of February, 1856, was ushered in by a heavy fall of snow ; so severe was this storm that travel was impeded, and even after the highways were cleared it was almost impossible for those who lived off from the main streets to make their way through the drifts. At this time some of these colored children were gathered into a small building upon a hillside in what is now Prospect Park, but which was then the private

14

property of Judge Vanderbilt. A little whitewashed room, about twelve feet square, in an unoccupied house built for the use of a gardener, was the primitive schoolroom. The school was opened with five scholars; it met the need of the people, and the number rapidly increased.

In order to hold the money legally which was raised to build a schoolroom, a society was organized and duly incorporated under the general law. It was called the "Society for the Amelioration of the Colored Population of Flatbush," and was organized October 27, 1858.

The money raised through subscription by the managers amounted to $939.75. A lot of ground was then purchased, and a building erected at a cost of $1,000.76, leaving a debt of $64.12, which was subsequently liquidated by the managers themselves.

The school-house was neat and comfortable, and the situation, on the old turnpike, was all that could be desired for quiet and seclusion. A Sunday-school was held here regularly, and at times public worship; there were also occasional prayer meetings and temperance meetings, and, when necessary, the room was offered for funeral services.

Another cause for anxiety soon disturbed the friends of this little mission. At the opening of Prospect Park the building was found to be within the park limits. Owing to the increased value of property in the vicinity, it was difficult to purchase desirable lots; but for the strenuous exertions of friends, the work would have been abandoned.

At a meeting of the society held December 14, 1864, Mr. John Lefferts was authorized to transact the business in regard to the sale and purchase of the building and lots. He selected some land in Catharine Street, a small street running through the center of what was then called the " Point lot.".

These two lots were purchased for $1,600. The moving of the building cost $125, and to the Park Commissioners, for the repurchase of the same, was paid $250. A room for the infant department was now added at the cost of $1,600. There were many other items consequent upon the grading, laying gas-pipes, etc., which increased the cost to $3,877.

To meet this, the funds in hand were $1,363, as the award for the land taken by the Park Commissioners; $700, the result of a fair held by the ladies of the Reformed Dutch Church; $500, a legacy from the estate of Mrs. Eliza J. Lefferts, and some donations from friends, the sum total being $3,084. There remained a deficit of $800, which was canceled by Mr. John Lefferts as a gift to the society. A bell was at this time kindly presented to the chapel by Miss Esther J. Martense.

Upon the opening of Washington Avenue and Malbone Street, the successive assessments were paid for with the returns of fairs held for that purpose.

At a meeting of the "Society for the Amelioration of the Colored Population," it was resolved to transfer the property to the Consistory of the Reformed Dutch Church. As it was entirely free from debt, and the building in good repair, it was a valuable gift. After this transfer was made the society was dissolved, having accomplished with a good measure of success the purpose for which, years before, it was organized.

The Consistory of the Dutch Church had upon request established regular church services in the chapel. The ministers who have successively had charge of the mission are : Rev. Mr. Gleason, Rev. R. G. Strong, Rev. V. B. Carroll, Rev. J. A. Gerhard, and Rev. C. S. Wright. On the first communion Sunday a neat service, consisting of two goblets, two plates, a wine-pitcher, and a baptismal bowl, was presented by Mr. J. Lefferts. A beautiful pulpit Bible was also presented " in memoriam " by Mrs. Eliza J. Zabriskie.

In 1878 the chapel was found to be on the proposed line of the Brooklyn, Flatbush, and Coney Island Railway ; it was purchased by the company for $2,500.

The Consistory of the Reformed Church appointed Mr. J. Lefferts to transact the business of moving the house once more. Lots were purchased, and the building was removed to Lefferts Street ; for this and other expenses beyond the money in hand ($2,500) a debt was incurred, which was once more defrayed by Mr. J. Lefferts. The room was now newly furnished, a fine organ was presented by some friends, two pulpit chairs were given by Miss Mary J. Williams, and in July, 1878, the chapel was once more thrown open for the use of the congregation ; it now presented a very neat and cheerful interior, and offered ample accommodation for all in the neighborhood who might desire to assemble there for worship.

St. Paul's Episcopal Church was built in 1836. The Christian courtesy of the Dutch church was shown in the fact that the first service preparatory to the organization of the Episcopal church was held in the lecture-room, which was offered for that purpose by the Consistory of the Reformed Church. Dr. Strong says, alluding to this : " Although it was the first attempt to introduce the services of another denomination of Christians in the town, the kindest feelings were entertained and expressed, and such facilities were afforded to further it as Christian courtesy dictated on behalf of the officers and members of the Reformed Dutch church."

The building first erected by this congregation was taken down some eight years since, and a smaller but picturesque and tasteful edifice was erected upon the same ground.

The Methodist church was at first a wooden building in the English Neighborhood. The congregation afterward selected Diamond Street as the locality upon which to build their new brick church. For want of funds it has not yet been wholly completed, service being held in the lower story. The members of the Dutch church have contributed large sums not only toward the erection, but also toward extinguishing the debt upon this church.

The Roman Catholic is the largest church in Flatbush. It is built of brick with stone coping ; the exterior is varied in outline and presents an imposing appearance. The congregation is large, including those of this faith from an extended area beyond the limits of the village.

The Baptist society have erected a small building to serve temporarily for their worship until their number and their funds render enlargement advisable.

The German church is included in the South Classis of Long Island, as one of the churches in its care. It was built for the Protestant Germans of this vicinity who could not understand the service in the English language.

As we are limited in the general scope of our work to the subject of the Dutch settlers in this village, we are obliged to forego reference to the other churches beyond the mere statement of their order of organization.

CHAPTER XXVII.

RELIGIOUS SOCIETIES.

Sunday-School.

THE first Sunday-school in Flatbush was held December 17, 1816, in a barn, for the benefit of the slaves. It was doubtless the philanthropic work of some Christian heart, but the mere fact of its organization is all that is known of it now. It was probably of short duration.

The Sunday-school of the Reformed Dutch church was organized in 1823, and was first held in the galleries of the church. In 1831 the consistory-room adjoining the church was built, and the Sunday-school was held there. When the new chapel, corner of Grant Street and Flatbush Avenue, was completed in 1871, ample accommodation was afforded to the increased size of the school, which at present numbers about three hundred scholars, with an able and efficient corps of teachers.

Tract Society.

As early as 1815 a society for the distribution of religious reading was organized, called "The Female Religious Tract Society of Flatbush and Flatlands," these villages being united in the work. In 1816 the society enlarged its work, and changed the name to

" The Female Bible and Religious Tract Society of Kings County," and the surplus funds were given to the American Bible Society.

We realize the changes of half a century when we read from the minutes of their meetings that in 1816 they distributed 1,493 tracts in the following places : New Brunswick, Bergen, Allentown, Raritan, Millstone, Middlebush, Monmouth, the garrison at Fort Lewis, Hempstead Harbor, city of Hudson, N. Y.; Cedar Swamp, Long Island ; Staten Island ; Johnstown, N. Y.

This society is still in existence, but its work is at present confined to the distribution of tracts and religious newspapers within the limits of the village of Flatbush.

Weekly Prayer-Meetings.

During the pastorate of Dr. Strong, the prayer-meetings of the Reformed Dutch church were held in the homes of the members of the congregation.

Each house in turn was thrown open on Friday evening for this purpose. A year was necessary to go through the village, and no family, rich or poor, refused their rooms for this meeting, and none were omitted in their regular order of succession. At present all prayer-meetings are held in the chapel, the congregation being too large to have it otherwise.

For twenty years, dating from 1832, a Sunday-school teachers' prayer-meeting was held weekly at the house of Mrs. Maria L. Lefferts.

Catechetical Lessons.

Until the conclusion of Dr. Strong's pastorate, it was customary to collect the children of the congregation together once a week during the summer for catechetical exercises. On these occasions they were obliged to repeat the lessons they had committed to memory from the Westminster and Heidelberg Catechisms. This was probably the last remnant of the custom, established as early as 1682, of having the children instructed "on every Wednesday and Saturday, in the common prayers, and the questions and answers in the catechism, to enable them to repeat them the better on Sunday before the afternoon service."

CHAPTER XXVIII.

DURING the War of the Revolution Long Island was held by the British under military rule. After the disastrous Battle of Flatbush, Kings County was in a most lawless condition. It is almost impossible to realize the picture of devastation this village presented at that period. The cattle belonging to the farmers had been driven by command of the American officers into Queens and Suffolk counties, to prevent their falling into the possession of the invaders, and the grain, the produce of the year, was stacked in the fields and burned for the same reason. The houses of those in the northern section of the town were burned. In the line of march of the British, and over the district of hills and woods which embraced or bounded the area of the battle-ground, were strewn the bodies of the dead who had fallen either in battle or in irregular fighting in the hills and hollows, for there was no quarter given by the Hessians. It is probable that some of these were never buried, for bones were frequently found long after the engagement, and the superstitious avoided a locality said to be haunted. During that dreadful August many of the inhabitants fled from their homes, which were taken possession of by lawless adventurers. The sick

and wounded were placed in the church, and the want
of attention to their suffering condition caused the
whole air to be infected. In the autumn a camp fever
became epidemic, and proved very fatal. The grass
grew in the streets ; all business was at an end ; the wet
autumn which succeeded a hot summer added to the
filth of the encampment, and the want of many of the
common comforts of life caused almost constant illness, even among those who escaped the fever. Amid
all their sickness and poverty they were constantly har-
assed by petty exactions from which there was no appeal ;
their fences and even their farming utensils were used
for firewood ; their horses were taken from before the
plow; their cattle were driven away or butchered ;
their fowls were stolen ; and frequently small parties of
soldiers on the march took temporary possession of their
houses, driving out the owners if the room was needed.
As a sort of practical joke, the feather-beds were sometimes emptied into the wells. The dark cherry-wood
cupboards were dismantled, and from the shelves the
horses of the cavalry officers were fed. It was useless
to seek redress ; none could be had.

To make the scanty supply still more inadequate, the
whole town was filled with soldiers. Some of these were
of the roughest class. These were billeted upon the people without their consent, and often in opposition to
their express wishes. For a regiment of Waldeckers
no compensation was ever given. Even where Congress
promised two dollars per week, there was very little
prospect at that time that it would be paid ; and the
Continental money, which was a legal tender, was much
depreciated.

There was no safety from thieves either day or night,

but the loss of property was small compared to the danger to life and the constant feeling of personal insecurity. A band of men of notoriously bad character constituted a company under the name of the "Nassau Blues," and were in possession of the Court-house. They not only helped themselves freely to the property of the inhabitants, of whom they were called the "Guard," but they were the terror of respectable people.

Is it to be wondered at that under these circumstances the people became disheartened, and that in their dispirited condition they considered further resistance as useless ?

The inhabitants of Suffolk and Queens counties were comparatively safe in their resistance, but there was not a county in the State that suffered more than Kings, and there was not a town in Kings County that was more exposed than Flatbush. The people here, equally with the other colonists, resisted the encroachments and taxation of their foreign rulers ; they also at first had their meetings and expressed their sympathy with the general uprising. On April 5, 1775, a meeting was held at Flatbush, at which deputies were appointed for choosing delegates to the Continental Congress to be held at Philadelphia in May. From Flatbush, David Clarkson, Adrian Voorhees, Jacobus Vandeventer, and John Vanderbilt were appointed, and May 20 the magistrates and freeholders met in Brooklyn to co-operate with the freeholders of the city and county of New York, and other meetings for a similar purpose were afterward held.

There was a great change in the surroundings of the people after the Battle of Flatbush. The withdrawal of Washington's army left the inhabitants so entirely at the mercy of the enemy that there is no doubt that the majority of them considered the cause hopeless and further resistance useless.

We differ from Mr. Stiles with regard to an assertion he makes respecting the county towns at this period. He says that "a greater degree of peace and order prevailed in the country towns than in Brooklyn"; also that the farmers had " the twofold advantage of receiving a high price for their produce and pay for boarding the prisoners," and that, " the inhabitants returning to their desolated and long-deserted homes, their first efforts were directed to the cultivation of their lands." As to the pay for boarding the prisoners, only 7s. per week for a room for officers, and 1s. 4d. for privates, or $2 per week for board, was all that Congress promised. Food was very scarce, fuel still more so ; the negro servants were in a state of insubordination ; no regard was paid to the disinclination of the people to accept these boarders, and no notice was taken of the protests of such as felt themselves unable to provide for them. " Boarding the prisoners" under such circumstances was neither desirable nor profitable.

As to the cultivation of the land in Flatbush, it was conducted under great disadvantages. The horses had nearly all been stolen ; those that escaped detection on the part of officers or men were liable at any moment to be taken from the plow. The tools had been stolen or burned by foraging parties for kindling camp-fires. The farm laborer was scarcely to be had for hire, and the negro slave preferred the lighter work of grooming the cavalry horses, or following the brilliant red troops of his Majesty.

Before the close of hostilities some of the inhabitants of Kings County were enabled to furnish the pecuniary aid which was so much needed to carry on the war. This was done at the risk not only of property but of life.

Dr. Strong says that the amount of money lent to the State by the Whig inhabitants of Flatbush can not be fully ascertained, but it is supposed that, before the termination of the war, not far from $200,000 in specie had been furnished by the Whigs of Kings County.

CHAPTER XXIX.

DURING the late rebellion the ladies of Flatbush were active in preparing relief for the sick and wounded in camp and hospital. The following are some of the articles made by them and forwarded for use in the army : Havelocks, 1,100 ; haversacks, 312 ; night-shirts, 105 ; flannel shirts, 97 ; cotton shirts, 500 ; dressing-gowns (double), 26 ; knit socks (woolen), 60 pairs ; drawers, 161 pairs ; handkerchiefs, 772. Towels, " housewives," clothing (not new), lint, old linen, bandages.

The amount handed in from the Kings County table at the time of the Sanitary Fair in Brooklyn has been estimated as follows :

Kings County (country towns) amount of sale at table. $3,974 00
Contributions in cash.................... 2,988 03
_____
$6,962 03

From newspaper accounts published during the war we find Flatbush credited with the sum of $2,543.99, and also, at a later period, with that of $2,188.05, as contributions in cash.

Additional to the work of the ladies at their sewing society, there were also forwarded from Flatbush large quantities of stores and delicacies for the wounded in the hospitals.

CHAPTER XXX.

THE Flatbush town-hall was erected in 1874–'75, under the supervision and according to the direction of the Board of Improvement. This Board consisted of the following gentlemen, residents of Flatbush : Judge John A. Lott, John J. Vanderbilt, Philip S. Crook, Jacob V. B. Martense, Abraham J. Ditmas, John Lefferts, and Dr. John L. Zabriskie.

The town allowed the Board of Improvement forty thousand dollars for the purchase of land and for the erection of a building suitable for the purpose. This money was put out at interest, and for this sum and the interest upon it the town-hall was built.

The Building Committee consisted of John Lefferts, John J. Vanderbilt, and Dr. John L. Zabriskie. The architect was John Y. Culyer, the builder William Vause.

The land on Grant Street was considered a suitable site, and a handsome brick building was completed there in the autumn of 1875. It gave general satisfaction, and received much praise for its tasteful exterior and the convenience of its interior arrangements.

The Board not only completed the building for the sum specified, but also, in addition, put in the gas-fixtures and all the furniture which would be needed for use in the building. These extra expenses overran the amount allowed for this purpose. The town would have been willing to indemnify the Board for the extra sum expended, and the Board would have been perfectly justified in asking for it, as this furniture was a matter of necessity in the use of the hall ; yet these gentlemen were so disinclined to have any business committed to them cost more than the sum for which they had stipulated to have it done, that they refused to have this money refunded from the public treasury, and paid the extra expense incurred from their own private funds.

Upon the occasion of transferring the completed building to the town authorities, the gentlemen on this Board of Improvement took an honest pride in knowing that this hall had cost the town no more than the forty thousand dollars (principal and interest) which had been given them to spend ; that it was well and substantially built ; and that the work had in no way been slighted, but had been done in the best manner, and the completed structure was in every way suitable for the purpose required.

APPENDIX.

[To give the younger readers of this volume some idea of home life in the village during the War of the Revolution, we append a fireside account of that period as it was told us by an aged lady who was in her sixteenth year when the incidents occurred which she related. She was a woman of great personal courage and of remarkable intelligence, and we can vouch for this as being an unembellished account of what she herself saw and did; and therefore it has the merit of being strictly true. She died some forty years ago, being at that time in full possession of all her faculties, although more than eighty years of age.]

HOME LIFE DURING THE WAR OF THE REVOLUTION.

The morning on which the British troops landed was one of the loveliest we had had that summer. The sky was so clear and bright that you could scarcely think of it as a day which was to bring so much sorrow. I was then just sixteen years old, and my sister was a little older. Father was very feeble—he died of consumption after the close of the war—and, as we had no brothers to protect us, when the news reached us that the army was advancing in the direction of our village, Mother concluded to leave the house and go to a cousin of hers who had a large farm some miles eastward. Accordingly, the great farm-wagon was brought to the door, and such articles of furniture as could be easily removed were placed on it. Our faithful old negro man, Cæsar, received instructions from Father to take his little grandson, Cato, with him, and to drive the cattle through the farm lane to the woods beyond, while Mink, his son, who was a tall, strong, young fellow, was set to watch the premises, and, if possible, to protect the house. Before these arrangements were completed, the rumor reached us that the soldiers were rapidly approaching. The whole village was in commotion. Nothing, as yet, was to be seen of our troops. Women and children were running hither and thither. Men on horseback were riding about in all directions. Farmers might be seen cleaning up their rifles, and half-grown boys practicing shooting at a mark. As I stood near our wagon, which was being loaded, I could see the old Dutch school-master open the door of the little red school-house. The boys rushed out with a shout; it proved to be a longer holiday than they then dreamed of. The advancing army was just beyond the hills. There was an almost incessant firing in that direction. The whole care of the farm, and the management of everything, came upon Mother on account of Father's illness; she was fully equal to any emergency, as many of the women in those days were, but her manners were very quiet and gentle, so that when we all became very much excited over the approach of the British troops she alone remained calm, and proceeded to make the necessary arrangements. General Washington had placed General Greene in command of this part of Long Island, and fortifications had been thrown up in Brooklyn and Flatbush to guard the approach to New York. An intrenchment was thrown up in Flatbush a little to the south of us, and a small redoubt, on which a few pieces of artillery were mounted, was put up at the north of us, on a spot which is now in Prospect Park, Brooklyn, and is called the Battle Pass. From these arrangements we knew that the enemy was expected in the line of our house. As my father was ill, and my sister and self were two young girls more full of life and spirit than of discretion, Mother had resolved to seek our safety in flight. Not very brave, you say? Well, perhaps it was not. But I think if any of you young girls were in the line of an approaching army of English and Hessian soldiers, your mother would do the same.

I can bring before me as if it were but yesterday the scenes of our preparations for flight. Diana, the old cook, Cæsar's wife, stood with her hand on the crane, which she had turned on its hinge outward from the great open fireplace, ready to hang the iron pot upon the trammel when the mistress should give the order. But the mistress, in neat homespun short gown and petticoat, after the fashion of the Dutch farmers' wives, stood with her finger on her lip, silently planning before she spoke. Father, in his high-backed chair, sat leaning his hand on the cane he held before him, while my sister and I were endeavoring to extract a promise from Cæsar that his care should be extended to our pets which we were holding up before him. We had killed a calf that morning. There were no butchers' shops in those days among the Long Island farmers. "You need not cook dinner to-day, Dian," said Mother. "Put all that is left of the calf on the wagon; we must not be a burden upon our friends. Cæsar has harnessed up the farm-horses to the large wagon, and we will put in it such things as we can save. We shall go and stay for a while with Cousin Jacobus."

Cousin Jacobus lived about two miles eastward. Just then old Betty came in; she had brought some herbs for my father's cough. Betty was the wife of the last chief of the Canarsie Indians, a tribe who had once owned land in the west end of Long Island. I am sorry to say that both the chief and his wife were often the worse for liquor. Betty was very fond of my mother. The attachment had sprung up under the following circumstances. In the course of a violent storm years before, Mother, looking from the window, saw a woman, without any protection from the rain, seated on a rough stone wall that fenced off our wheat-field from the public road. Touched with pity, Mother sent Cæsar to bring the forlorn creature in the house and to give her a place at the kitchen fire.

"Why, Betty, is it you? Why didn't you come in?" asked my mother, as the object of her pity proved to be the old chief's wife.

"Because," replied Betty, "I wanted to know if I had any friends; so I waited to see who of the neighbors would call me in."

"Why, Betty, you knew I was your friend," said Mother.

"I thought so once—I know it now," said the old woman; and from that day she was true to my mother's interest upon every occasion. Knowing that we should leave, she came with a supply of herbs for father and the news that the British army was approaching. She told us that the American troops stationed along the western shore were retreating over the hills toward Flatbush; that Lord Cornwallis with the English soldiers was on the march, and that the Hessian troops had landed. This last piece of information was incorrect; the Hessians under General de Heister were daily expected, but they did not come to Flatbush until some days later. The constant although irregular firing in that direction gave weight to Betty's news, and, when the wagon was brought to the door, my sister and I were all excitement, rushing wildly about the house and bringing the most useless things to Cæsar to put in the wagon. Mother coolly took out whatever did not seem to her necessary, reserving space only for such household articles as were in her judgment best to save. The very first thing placed on the wagon was the great Dutch Bible with its huge brass clasps and brass corners. Then the little stand was brought on which this heavy Bible always rested. The old Dutch clock was carefully lifted in, and some one or two articles of furniture, and our clothing. The horses were getting very restive under the firing, which could now be heard distinctly from beyond the western woods.

"Come, Femmetia." Mother called to me again, "you must drive. Where is Gertia?"

"Come, girls, come," exclaimed my father, somewhat impatiently; but, even after we were all seated in the wagon, and I held the long whip over the heads of the horses, ready to give them the signal to go, he himself delayed us with the many parting admonitions he gave to Mink, who was to be left in charge of the barnyard.

"Go as far as Yost Williamse's lane," said my father. "I will leave word there as we pass how much farther you must drive them."

I, almost unconsciously, had given the horses a tap on their cars with the point of my whip; it only needed this in connection with the constant sound of firearms to start them.

"Hold on, Femmetia. How can you be so impatient? Scytie," turning to my mother, "do keep that child quiet."

"But, Father, it was you who hurried us just a moment ago."

Mother shook her head at me. By this time the horses had stopped, and old Cæsar had come up to us again, and now stood listening to my father, with one hand upon the wagon side.

"You know all our year's grain is stacked in the east lot, Cæsar; if you can get them to spare it, it would be well. But I'm afraid it will be burned to save it from falling into the hands of the British. Oh, dear! We never had a more plentiful harvest."

"Never mind," said Mother hopefully, "we are not any worse off than our neighbors. You will bring on another coughing spell if you stay here in this dusty road. Let us go on. Whip up, Femmetia."

"No, no!" said my father, laying his hands on the reins, "hadn't we better stop at Axtell's and see if he can do anything about saving that grain?"

"We may have to seek greater favors than that of Colonel Axtell," said Mother. "Let us not begin already to ask for help. If it is best to burn the grain crop, let it go. Our people will not destroy it sooner than is necessary."

Cæsar turned toward the house, and we drove on. Father and Mother looked back at the old homestead with heavy hearts. There were tears in Mother's eyes, although she tried to speak cheerfully for Father's sake.

It was late in the afternoon before we reached the farmhouse of Cousin Jacobus. They welcomed us very kindly, and were anxious to hear all we could tell them about the landing of the British. I had a great deal to say about the patriotic things I was going to do, which made Mother anxious about me, and quite reconciled to having me out of the way in this quiet place.

That evening a bright light, as of a large fire, shone westward against the sky, and the next morning a heavy smoke brooded over our village. Father took a stout cane to lean on, and my sister and I helped him climb a little eminence which commanded a view in that direction. He looked very pale, and sighed ; his step seemed more feeble than ever.

"I think the fire is directly in the line of our house," he said.

Youth is very hopeful; so we girls said many encouraging things, and would not believe in disaster. We were young and happy, the sky was bright, the birds were singing all around us, and we could not bear to think of anything gloomy. We did not know then that to the westward, just in the woods beyond where as children we had played, there were heaps of dead and dying.

Father was probably thinking of what might be even then happening in the village, for he seemed unusually sad, and we noticed that he trembled, as if he felt weak and feeble. I think that our merry tones jarred upon him. He could not bear to see us so light-hearted, knowing the perils of our people, and the desolation even then threatening our dear village. We were sure that the British had already been driven back to their ships. He shook his head sadly and said: "I am afraid the old homestead is burned down, children! "

Father was right. When, after the Battle of Long Island, we returned home, before we reached the village we could see the tall old trees that had stretched their arms so protectingly over our roof; they were all charred and blackened by the flames. Yes, Father was right ; the old homestead was burned down.

Two of our neighbors' houses, as well as our own, were burned to the ground. This was done by order of Lord Cornwallis, because they offered a defense behind which the American riflemen could reload, and from which they could discharge their firearms.

When we returned to the village we were obliged to live in the house of friends who left when we did, but remained longer from home. What a scene of desolation met us on our return!

There had been a most reckless destruction and waste of property. What could not be used was broken and destroyed.

Our church was used for the accommodation of prisoners and the sick, and the wounded soldiers were placed in the old school-house. Three of our neighbors who had left the village had their houses turned into hospitals for the American officers as the sickness increased. There had been very heavy rains all through the autumn of 1776, and an epidemic had broken out, arising from the effluvia connected with the British and Hessian encampment. Many of our neighbors and friends were taken ill with this fever, and very few of those who were seized survived. Food was scanty; even the little to be obtained by hard work we were likely to be robbed of at any moment by the lawless plunderers who had followed in the train of the army.

Some of the houses seem to have been used indiscriminately as stables for horses and as barracks for soldiers. The fences were torn down, the gardens trampled on, the crops destroyed. The roads were so cut up by the passage of artillery wagons that, as it proved to be a very rainy season, they were almost impassable. There was scarcely a family in the whole town which was not visited by the camp fever. I was very ill, and poor Mother had the care of me during all that dreary autumn, as well as of Father, who seemed to be very much prostrated, and to cough more than ever. We were all depressed in consequence of the discouraging rumors which were circulated as to the general state of the country. The newspapers reached us rarely. "The New York Journal and General Advertiser," printed by John Holt, near the Coffee House, was a very warm advocate of the American cause. It was sometimes brought to us by the prisoner officers who were billeted on the inhabitants after the capture of Fort Washington. This hopeful little sheet was handed from neighbor to neighbor, and it helped to cheer us up in those dull November days. There were two other newspapers of which we often obtained copies from the British officers: "The New York Gazette and Weekly Mercury," printed by Hugh Gaine, and "Rivington's New York Gazetteer, or the Connecticut, Hudson's River, New Jersey and Quebec Weekly

Advertiser "—such was its ambitious name. The last mentioned of these papers left us in doubt about everything, except the loyalty due to the King of England.

You may imagine how difficult it was for us to get the papers when I tell you that the Fulton Ferry, that great thoroughfare of to-day, was then only crossed by occasional row-boats.

My mother was very active and energetic; she was naturally of a cheerful disposition, and disposed to look upon the bright side of things. She would not allow us girls to sit down and mope over our discomforts, but insisted upon our sharing with her the support of the family. Old Cæsar had managed to keep some of our cows hidden in the woods at the end of the farm lane. Mother set aside every morning as much milk as Father needed, but she would not reserve any for herself nor for us girls. She sold milk and butter to the British officers; they paid a good price for it, and this was our main dependence that winter. We used to spin and knit a great deal, for Mother would not allow us an idle moment. I was very fond of reading, and I would hide away ends of candle to read by when the rest of the family were asleep. All my education was in the Dutch language; I never went to an English school in my life, but I taught myself to read English, so that I would take up an English newspaper and read it aloud to my sister in Dutch, or, reading a Dutch book, I could translate it into English for the prisoner officers as rapidly as if it was written in English.

It was useless to try and raise grain that year, for the fences were all destroyed, and our beautiful farm was laid waste. Our faithful Cæsar managed, however, to pasture some of the horses of the cavalry officers in the wood-lots at the back of the farm, out of sight of the road, and that was very profitable. I must tell you of something in this connection which afforded us much amusement.

We had a wood-lot at the north end of the farm, known familiarly as Nova Scotia. There was no undergrowth, and, as the grass was luxuriant, here the horses were pastured. One morning an English officer came in great haste to Cæsar, asking

15

for his horse. Cæsar, who had had no great opinion of British troops, seeing the trouble their coming had given, replied, without looking up from his work, that the horse was in Nova Scotia. "How dared you send my horse to Nova Scotia?" demanded the Englishman, getting very red in the face. The old colored man looked up in surprise, but he merely said that "Master had ordered it to be sent there." The officer stamped his foot in rage. "I tell you I want my horse; I meant to use him this very day. What right had he to send him away?" Cæsar thought his conduct was certainly remarkable, inasmuch as there was no better pasture than Nova Scotia lot for miles around. In great rage the Englishman advanced toward the house. He was too much of a gentleman to be rude to a young girl who received him with politeness, and when I met him at the door the struggle between his anger and the desire to appear calm kept him silent. I invited him in, and, knowing him to be the owner of one of the finest horses in the pasture-lot, I sent Mink to bring down "the Financier." The struggle to repress his pent-up indignation was ineffectual. You may imagine his embarrassment when, in the midst of his reproaches, he looked up and saw his spirited horse come gayly cantering down the farm lane. He was a kind-hearted man, and very much of a gentleman. He could scarcely forgive himself for being so rude, and he tried in every way to make reparation for his conduct. He was a fast friend of ours after that, and was enabled by his position to do us many an act of kindness, which in our defenseless state we certainly needed. Cæsar was not as reticent as we wished him to be, and when the officers got hold of the story, they joked him for months after about the disposition which the rebels had made of his horse.

All Mother's energies were now directed to gaining a home, so that she might make Father more comfortable. It was almost impossible to get building materials. With the money she had saved she purchased some lumber from a neighbor, but it was not sufficient to complete the house. The room intended for my sister and myself was not floored all the way across. This was fun for me, but my sister did not view it in that light.

It is strange what different dispositions may be in the same family. I looked on the bright side of everything, Sister on the dark side. I thought of our unfloored room as a good joke, she as a great misfortune. On the first night that we went up to our room, I skipped over the beams to the flooring as nimbly as a squirrel. While she stood trembling at the other side, in the doorway, insisting that she could not get over, I stood coolly combing out my long hair and teasing her.

"I can never get over," she said dolefully.

"Oh, yes, you can; it is very easy. I like it. Mother wants to get a board laid from the door to the bed, but I sha'n't let her. It's better so. It's such fun. Besides, we have only to go to the edge, and we can look right down to the room below. I like it better than our room in the old house. If you don't come soon I shall put out the light and go to bed." She knew this was what I would be quite likely to do, for I was, I confess, fond of teasing her.

"Oh! now don't; I shall break my neck, and then Mother will have the care of me as well as Father."

"Oh, no, she wouldn't. That would be the end of you and all your troubles. Still, if you're going to be so serious, I suppose I must come."

Then I skipped across to her, and, leading her just half way over, let go her hand. Of course she screamed, and Mother opened the door below. "Hush-sh-sh, girls! You'll waken your father."

My sister appealed to Mother for help, but the door had already closed below. Before I had time to relieve my "prisoner," as I called her, we heard the heavy bare foot of Diana approaching. She came to the room beneath and called up to us:

"Dere's a hull lot of sogers jes come inter de barn. Spec dey'll kill all what's lef of de chickens."

It was no new thing. We were constantly being plundered. There was no redress for the depredations daily committed. One pair of our farm-horses had been taken from the harrow, even while Cæsar was using them. I remarked to my sister that this was a "harrowing case." She wouldn't laugh. I can't say whether she felt so disheartened at our loss that she did not appreciate my poor attempt at wit, or whether she understood so little English that she did not see it. We always spoke Dutch in the family. We only used English in speaking with the prisoners who were billeted upon us, and to the British officers. To return to Dian, who was standing below, her arms akimbo, looking up at us:

"You jes come down," she said.

The hint was enough. I helped my sister to cross the room to the safe flooring, and rushed down stairs to Diana. Good, faithful soul, I was her favorite and her accomplice in all her attacks upon the enemy. Mother never knew how many scouting parties of two she and I formed that winter to watch our premises. She had concealed weapons at the kitchen-door—an old rifle and a broomstick; with these we proceeded to the barn, dodging from the great walnut-tree to the corn-crib, and from there flitting behind the wagon-house, until we reached the shadow of the great barn. It was moonlight. I often wonder now that I could ever have been so fearless, but I was young and knew no danger or cause for alarm. Besides, I had perfect faith in my leader. Dian and I were fast friends, and she had never failed in any of our expeditions against the invaders of the poultry-yard. She had confided to me the plan she would have pursued had she been in Cæsar's place when they stole the horses, and I had accredited her with the victory she might have gained.

In this instance it was by stratagem that we were to conquer. She had privately surveyed the field of action before calling me, and the moonlight had enabled her to recognize in the thieves some of the members of the company who were appointed to protect (?) the town. Concealed between a corn-crib and the barn, she thrust her rifle through a hole in the side door, I at the same time flinging a stone against the barn to attract the notice of the parties within to the fact of their close proximity to the rifle. The moonlight fell upon the weapon pointed at them by unseen hands. It was enough; we were left in possession of the field. Mother knew nothing about the raid until the next day, when Dian told her that we were to have roast fowls for dinner.

We could not buy any nails for building, so that we were obliged to use those taken from the ruins of the burned houses. The prisoner officers used to meet with us and other young girls of our age, and help us straighten the nails there gathered. Thus the ruins got to be a place of fashionable resort. The young people collected there for an afternoon's chat, but Mother, who did not look with friendly eyes on the attentions of all these young officers, insisted that there was quite as much talking and flirting as there was work. The young girls of our age, of course, could not but sympathize with the prisoners, and as the officers had little to beguile their time, both parties had an excellent excuse for meeting there, and boasted very much of their industry, as people are apt to do when work and pleasure are united.

I have heard that four hundred prisoners were billeted in the southern towns of Kings County. The only regiment left in Flatbush after the Battle of Long Island was the Forty-second Regiment of Highlanders.

There was little protection for property at this time; appeal to law was impossible; indeed, people acted as if there was no law. Everything in the shape of personal property was kept at the risk of the owner. The cattle were not safe unless watched vigilantly. Mother went on one occasion to our neighbor, Colonel Axtell, and submitted to him the fact that all our cows had been driven off in spite of her remonstrance. She was a great favorite among her neighbors, and the Colonel listened to her story. After conferring with his English friends, he sent us word that Cæsar might go on a certain day to a place which he named, and from among the herd of cattle which he would find there he might point out those which belonged to us. It was a great relief to see Cæsar let down the bars, and turn the herd once more into their accustomed pasture. From this you may see how insecure property was, and with what audacity we were plundered. Our household arti-

cles of value we were obliged to conceal. Many persons hid
boxes containing valuables in their fields and gardens. It has
been asserted that some of this hidden treasure was never taken
up, but this is very doubtful.

Our spoons, tankard, and such pieces of silver tea-service as
every Dutch housekeeper at that time possessed were placed
in a box and hidden under the hearthstone. The insecurity of
the hiding-place was made evident to us by Mink, who was not
in the secret. He remarked in Dutch to his father, old Cæsar,
that some evil spirit must have taken lodging under the hearth,
for it seemed loose and uneven. The negroes were so superstitious that the supposed presence of an evil spirit would have
insured it from their examination, but we felt that it was insecure if it attracted any observation whatever, and with the assistance of Cæsar, who was fully to be trusted, we found for it
another hiding-place.

A neighbor of ours related to us her experience in this matter. She had secreted a number of gold coins in one of those
round, ball-shaped pincushions which the Dutch matrons sometimes wore suspended by a ribbon at their side. A party of
English soldiers, on entering the room, noticed this novelty (as
it was to them) in the good lady's dress. One of them playfully,
although not very politely, cut the ribbon with his sword, and
the whole party had a boisterous game of ball with the pincushion. Once or twice it bounced in the ashes of the broad,
open fireplace, from which it was snatched up and tossed again
from hand to hand. To show any anxiety would have betrayed
the value of the property, so that the owner was obliged to continue her work unmoved, although, had they torn the cushion
in their rough play, she would have lost all the money she had
saved when the war broke out.

Not only was our property insecure, but our homes were
liable at any time to be invaded, and seclusion was almost impossible; there were at various times soldiers billeted upon us
arbitrarily without our consent, and often without compensation. A Waldeck regiment, commanded by Colonel De Horn,
was quartered upon our village in this manner, as were also

some soldiers who had fought in Canada through the French war, and afterward a Saxon regiment. In addition to this, the quiet of our homes was invaded by companies of soldiers marching from place to place. I remember one evening that we were all, even sick Father, turned out of the house by a small company of soldiers who took possession. . Fortunately, they soon received marching orders, and they left as suddenly as they came.

The American prisoners had our warmest sympathy. They were on parole, and were not guarded strictly; they could go about where they chose. When the French fleet under Count D'Estaing was expected, these prisoners went daily to see the vessels from the hill.

I took no pains to disguise my sympathy for the American prisoners and my warm interest in the cause of freedom. My sister sometimes begged me not to express my opinions so openly in the presence of the British, and Mother checked me often, telling me that I was acting unwisely. On one occasion a line of artillery wagons was passing. The foremost driver, to avoid a muddy portion of road, turned his horses upon the sidewalk in front of our house. I was determined that the second should not do the same; I rushed out to frighten the horses, and succeeded so well that they overturned the wagon. I was obliged to retreat precipitately, and Mother had to meet the storm I had raised. An old German doctor, who was a frequent visitor at our house, laughed immoderately at my heroic attack upon the artillery and my subsequent discomfiture. I can see him now as he stood giving a description of the whole scene to a tall Hessian officer. He turned to me, exclaiming between the paroxysms of laughter :

"Oh, vat a heroine vas our leetle Femmetia! She attack dese big artillery-mon! She attack him wis a gun? Oh, no! wis a broomsteek! eh, Fem? a broomsteek!"

Then he broke out afresh, and the contagion extended to the tall Hessian, whose name was so impressed upon me by the very vividness of the whole scene that I can recall it to this day, unpronounceable as it is. When the old doctor saw me blushing deeply, mortified as I was at his description, his kind heart misgave him, for I was a great pet of his, and, patting me affectionately on the head, he said :

" Navair mind; she's our brave leetle lady, Captain Bumbbochk, and een moije vrouw, eh ? "

The old doctor was very fond of a joke, and I knew that he was telling Father the story over again soon after, for I heard his voice in Father's room, and he was laughing as loudly as before.

We were, as I have said, subjected to constant exactions, from which we had no means of redress. On one occasion, as old Cæsar was plowing, in the almost hopeless endeavor to cultivate our vegetable garden, a soldier came up and demanded the horses for the British service. Cæsar, always true to us, promptly and indignantly refused to take them from the plow. Little Cato, who was an interested spectator, ran to the house to inform Mother of the predatory design of the redcoat. Father overheard the child's account. He had a high fever, and had been ill in bed for some time. Under the excitement of anger and fever united, he rose and dressed himself. Taking his heavy cane, he went to the field, and with the aid of Cæsar he administered such correction to the soldier that he sought safety in flight. Strange to say, the exertion cured Father of the fever. He broke out in a profuse perspiration, and, although he was much exhausted, he had no fever afterward, and was able to sit up in his arm-chair for the rest of the day.

Large sums of money were loaned by the inhabitants of Kings County for the advancement of the American cause. The agent for collecting this money was intrusted by Governor Clinton with blank notes signed by himself. These blanks the agent filled out with the sum given. The greatest secrecy was necessary in collecting this money, as it was attended with imminent danger to all concerned. Through her thrift, economy, and industry, Mother was enabled to appropriate five hundred pounds to this object. This she gave in small sums at a time, and on one occasion, as she was counting out the money into the hands of the agent, she saw, on looking up, a British officer enter the door-yard. For the Major to escape from the house was impossible, and had he been seen his life would have been forfeited.

"Femmetia," said my mother, "hurry out to meet that officer. Don't let him come in this room as you value your life."

"Talk as fast as you can, Fem, and be as entertaining as possible," said the Major, looking anxiously toward the approaching figure.

"Let my sister come with me," said I, rather timid at accepting so great responsibility.

"No! no!" said my mother imperatively. "Too much depends on it. Don't fail us now, child!"

She looked sternly at me, and I felt she was right, for the consciousness of danger had already brought the color to my sister's face; it must depend upon me alone to divert any suspicion, should such be aroused, on the part of the Englishman.

I hurried out of the room as they rapidly gathered up the coin they had been counting, and Mother went to look for a hiding-place for the Major, who was an old friend of ours. I could hear the doors opened and closed; I could hear a word in Dutch now and then; happily, our visitor could not understand it; but I did my best to look unconscious, and I believe I succeeded. I had been in the habit of expressing my opinions pretty freely, and, if I chatted on this occasion more rapidly than usual, the officer probably thought that I was in good spirits, and would be rather more entertaining company than if he went in the next room to look for my father and mother. He staid what appeared to me an unreasonably long time, and left without a suspicion of who was under the same roof with himself, and of the treason being enacted almost within his reach.

Never before nor since have I had such weighty reasons for striving to attract attention to myself, and this was the only time during the war that Mother ever expressed gratification that I had succeeded in entertaining an English officer.

LEGENDS.

[The Dutch word for legend is "Een verzierde vertelling," or "gebloemd vertelling." As told to children, in contradistinction to the real or probable, such legendary lore and ghost stories were called " sprookjes." Flatbush, like every old town, has its legends. They grow as do the mosses on old houses or the lichens on tombstones, the gradual and undisturbed accumulations of time. We regret that more of these were not preserved; of some we have only the tattered fragments, too scanty and too much frayed to piece together. There are two legends which have been preserved, fortunately for us, as they were caught in the meshes of the. printer before they escaped the memories of those who held them, and those we here offer.]

THE LEGEND OF POPE'S LANE.

Once upon a time—the true legendary date—there lived among us a sable son of Africa, who possessed, like most of his race, an intense love of music and wondrous skill upon the violin. He was familiarly known as Pope's Joe, from his employer, who also gave his name to the narrow lane in which he lived, which led from Flatbush to the ancient settlement of Gowanus.

It was on a sultry summer night that our modern Orpheus went forth to win his Ethiopian Eurydice from the Cerberus of daily toil; but, owing to the oppressive heat, he seated himself by the wayside, not far from his master's gate, to rest, and drawing forth his violin began to beguile his time with his beloved instrument. Southward a great bank of cloud piled up in masses had gathered to itself with miserly avidity all the gold of sunset; then, as the twilight had stolen its treasure, it grew black and glowered darkly on the panting earth below. Flashes of heat-lightning shimmered along the horizon ; more and more oppressive seemed the heated air. All was silent save our musician ; he, all unconscious of cloud or heat, was spellbound by his own music, as if his instrument had been the very masterpiece of Stradivarius.

Suddenly, with thunderous sound and vivid flash, there stood before him a wild demon form. Before, he played from love of the melody he evoked ; now he dared not pause, for his Satanic Majesty imperiously motioned him to play, and then began to dance in the wildest measure to which a musician was ever called to furnish music. The witches who lured Macbeth to destruction, the weird creatures who meet in conclave on the Harz Mountains, were tame in movement compared with the wondrous agility of this specter. Its motions were as if the heat-lightning played and flashed, and then, instead of going out into sudden darkness, continued to entwine and braid itself and twist its vivid length into fiery contortions; now gliding in vivid convolutions, like wheels in a pyrotechnic display, and anon dropping its lithe limbs into kaleidoscopic variety of attitude and position. The wearied arm of the musician dared not falter; longer and longer he played, more and more rapid grew the movements of the dance, until a false note produced a sudden discord that jarred upon the temper of the fiend. In angry passion, he stamped his foot upon a stone and disappeared in a blinding flash.

The clear sun was shining upon the multitudinous raindrops on every bush and blade when the musician opened his eyes. The birds were singing their morning songs, and the sky was as blue as if no cloud had ever dimmed its serene height.

There were those who had vainly striven to compete with the skill of this performer on the violin, and, when he related to his wondering listeners the story of his marvelous adventure, they attempted to impugn his veracity. In sheer envy they suggested that his ability needed the endorsement of such Satanic approval. They even meanly hinted that he might have imbibed something from old Master's cellar—perhaps it was apple-jack, or it may have been metheglin, a strong and heady drink much thought of in those times, and apt to produce diabolic appearances to the infatuated mortal who had contracted a love for the insidious beverage.

Vain endeavor to rob the hero of that one laurel with which he sought to crown himself! Idle attempt to explain away the supernatural! Nature had made herself his ally; the very stone upon the highway has testified to his story and perpetuated the record!

The imprint of the cloven foot of the evil one was stamped upon the stone before he vanished out of sight. There it remained long after the old musician had passed away, and he and his violin had become mute together.

Is it not well that the haunted spot has become part of Greenwood, and the stone—the foundation-stone of the legend—has been lost amid the somber, ghostly shadows of that city of the dead?

We should not have ventured to point out the imprint of that cloven foot to the incredulity of this age. The hammer of science might have rapped too heavily upon our legend, and broken into the secret that for so many years it held up to the undoubting faith of a past generation.

THE DOMINE'S RIDE—A LEGEND OF THE OLD ROAD.

In the year 1746 the distance between Flatbush and Brooklyn seemed greater than at present. The one town was not any more thickly settled than the other, and they were divided by long intervals of forest, broad farms, and a stony ridge of hills. Where now the cars roll by every few minutes, offering easy access from the shady village road to the busy streets of the city, then only from time to time a solitary wagon lumbered on along the sandy highway, or a horseman, with perhaps some Dutch vrouw on the pillion behind him, plodded wearily over the intervening hill. The house in which Mr. John Lefferts now resides was the last in the village, and marked the limits of Steenraap, as this portion of Flatbush was called in distinction from Dorp, which was more central. From this spot to what is now the very heart of Brooklyn, only here and there a lonely farmhouse, separated by tracts of woodland, cheered the solitude.

The Domine, accustomed to city life in Amsterdam, was in the habit of beguiling his spare time by friendly visits among the settlers at Brooklyn. Upon one of these occasions he became deeply involved in a discussion on the newly organized Cœtus, an assembly of ministers and elders subordinate to the Classis of Holland, then just established, being the first judicatory higher than a consistory in the Dutch Church in America. He had himself been appointed by the Classis of Amsterdam as bearer of dispatches on this subject; "the appointment indicating," as Carlyle says of Sterling, "a man expected to do the best on the occasion." It was, therefore, natural that he should enter into the subject with a zeal which made him forgetful of the flight of time, and the solemn Dutch clock in the corner raised both astonished hands to warn him that midnight approached ere he was recalled to the fact of the long, lonely ride before him. Hastily lighting his pipe, and bidding Mynheer his host good night, he rode out through the wide barnyard gate, which old Cato swung open for him, into the darkness beyond.

It was a moonless, cloudy night. The road was darkened by the over-reaching trees that seemed to nod to each other mysteriously overhead, and to whisper some secret across his path at the suggestion of the evening breeze. Through the narrow opening cut by the road he could see the faint line of sky, but it gave no light down through this rift of the forest. As he approached the clearing of a settler, he could see the farmhouse outlined in the shadow, with, perhaps, a solitary candle lighted in an upper chamber by an anxious mother for a restless child. Then the fireflies seemed to beckon him off again into the uncertain darkness, and as he passed on the woods closed around him, and the night seemed darker than before. The hill crossed, he must descend where the road led through a low and marshy district. An uncanny spot was this which now lay before him! Old legends place evil spirits and ghosts in such shadowy corners. Even to this day a damper air strikes the traveler as he turns down to this hollow; a darker shadow rests upon the road here, and a mistiness and dampness from the ponds beyond make the place miasmatic and unhealthy.

As he approached this spot the Domine tightened the reins and strove to encourage his steed into some gait quicker than the usual pace of a ministerial horse. He thrust his pipe in his pocket, and, patting the neck of the animal, in grateful acknowledgment it started off into a brisk trot. A pleasant breeze springing up at the same time, induced the traveler to hope that this haunted region might prove even an agreeable change from the stony hilltop. Suddenly he was startled by a faint light which seemed to follow him at close and equal rate. Vainly he looked around; no object was perceptible. A vigorous application of the whip roused the horse to increase his speed, but no diminution of the light proved that he had gone beyond its source.

Away went the horse under application of whip and spur, but with increased rapidity the noiseless pursuer seemed to follow. The puzzled Domine looked over his shoulder, but the darkness of the road revealed no cause for the strange phenomenon. The trees glided swiftly by; the little round-topped hill, like an inverted bowl, was soon passed; the limits of this haunted region seemed near, and yet brighter and brighter grew the light, and warmer and warmer its breath. The woods that until now had almost closed above his head began to disappear; familiar trees here and there stood out in bold relief, and the distant crowing of a cock announced close proximity to the village. Presently he had left the swampy hollow behind, but still in pursuit as swift, with its hot breath close behind him, the phantom followed. Vainly the Domine applied the whip: the swiftest pace of the tired animal could not increase the distance between the pursuer and the pursued.

The saints and monks of early date who record with evident gusto their battlings with supernatural visitors, and even with the foul fiend himself, were not taken at the same disadvantage as our hero. What cause for boasting had St. Jerome, St. Francis, or St. Simon, who met the adversary in fair field and had only to say an Ave Maria, a Paternoster, or to make the sign of the cross, and their grim opponent was utterly annihilated? Such a stock of spiritual weapons was utterly unavailable to one of the good Domine's faith. He would have refused to equip himself thus from the armory of Rome; carnal weapons he had none, and he had professed utter disbelief in the whole battalion of ghosts, spirits, phantoms, and fiends which were marshaled in fearful array in the superstitious credulity of the age. It was therefore a malicious as well as an ungenerous onslaught upon him, this pursuit in the darkness. It was not a chivalrous phantom that, instead of a bold face-to-face attack, would come upon him unawares and follow him unseen. The culpable neglect of all ghostly etiquette, moreover, was inexcusable in his indefatigable pursuer. Had not the ghost-haunted hollow been left behind, and yet the phantom not been exorcised? Had not the cock crowed, but the ghost had turned deaf ear to the warning?

Now he reaches the village; house after house flies by him unnoticed, for he knows that home is near. Utterly exhausted, he no longer urges on his weary steed; he is unequal to any further effort, and the horse, by his own instinct, turns in at the open gate and stops at the back stoop of the low-eaved house, where the negro boy Tom, finding his excuse in the lateness of the hour, has lost, in the oblivion of sleep, all consciousness that he was stationed there to await his master's return.

The candle of the Juffrouw reveals the fact that the voluminous garments then so generally worn had suffered severely from contact with fire. The half-extinguished pipe thrust hastily in his pocket *might* account for the result; but let us scorn such a subterfuge from incredulity. It is well known that ghosts are opposed to knowledge as deadly to their very existence; and as the old Domine was a very learned man, we see good reason why they should be particularly exasperated against him. We therefore take a bold stand, and agree with those who at the time did not hesitate to assert as their belief that the Domine was pursued with vindictive zeal by a fiery phantom from the Clove in the Hollow.

THE END.

www.ingramcontent.com/pod-product-compliance
Lightning Source LLC
Chambersburg PA
CBHW021111270326

41929CB00009B/820